Contents

Workshops Index

London Print Studio 66
www.londonprintstudio.org.uk
London Printworks 65
www.londonprintworks.com
Lorg Printmakers, Galway 69
www.lorgprintmakers.com
Lovers' Knot, London 71
no website
Maplebeck Press, Notts. 72
no website
Milton Keynes Printmakers 73
www.mkprintmakers.co.uk
Morley College Print Room, London 74
www.morleycollege.ac.uk
North Notts. Non-toxic Print Studio 76
www.nontoxicprintmaking.co.uk
Northern Print Studio, Tyne & Wear 77
www.northernprint.org.uk
North Star Studios Ltd, Brighton 79
www.northstarprintmakers.co.uk
Oaks Fine Art, London 80
www.oaksfineart.co.uk
Ochre Print Studio, Farnham 81
www.juliehoyle.com/ochreprint.html
Oxford Printmakers' Cooperative 82
www.oxfordprintmakers.co.uk
Peacock Visual Arts, Aberdeen 83
www.peacockvisualarts.co.uk
Poole Printmakers 85
no website
Porthmeor Printmakers' Workshop 86
www.kantaris.com/rachael/index
Print Club, London 87
www.printclub.com
Print Market Workshop, Cardiff 88
www.printmarket.co.uk
Prospect Studios, Rossendale,
Lancs. 89
no website
Red Hot Press, Southampton 90
www.redhotpress.org.uk
Ropewalk, Lincolnshire 91
www.the-ropewalk.com
Seacourt Print Workshop, Bangor 92
www.seacourt-ni.org.uk
Sheffield Print Workshop 93
www.peterpainterprintmaker.co.uk
Sidney Nolan Trust, Presteigne 94
www.sidneynolantrust.org
SNAP Studio, Bristol 95
www.snapstudio.org.uk
Soulisquoy Printmakers, Orkney 96
no website

South Hill Park, Bracknell 97
www.southhillpark.org.uk
Spike Island Printmakers, Bristol 98
www.spikeisland-printmakers.com
St Barnabas Press 100
www.stbarnabaspress.co.uk
Swansea Print Workshop 102
www.swanseaprintworkshop.org.uk
Taigh Chearsabhagh, North Uist 104
www.taigh-chearsabhagh.org
Tamar Print Workshop, Devon 105
www.marygillett.co.uk
The Art House, Wakefield 106
www.the-arthouse.org.uk
The Print Shed, Hereford 107
website planned
West Yorkshire Print Workshop 108
www.westyorkshireprintmakers.co.uk
Wrexham Regional Print Centre 110
www.yale-wrexham.co.uk/facilities
Wyards, Faversham, Kent 112
www.wyards.com
York Print Workshop 113
no website

Introduction

Print workshops have evolved. In the UK, artists now have the next generation of print resources at their disposal, and overall there are more open-access print facilities than ever before. Printmaking is also going through a relatively rapid period of change, with the emergence of acrylic-resist etching, solar plate, not to mention digital media and much more. Whilst some print workshops embrace the acrylic-resist etching approaches championed by Keith Howard, and some keep 'traditional' print techniques such as resin aquatint and nitric etching alive, others adopt a hybrid approach, offering a broad spectrum of techniques and approaches.

To paraphrase Richard Hamilton, 'Just what is it that makes print workshops so different, so appealing?' From the smallest to the largest, the oldest to the newest, there are workshops catering for all aspects of printmaking across the UK and Ireland. On offer are everything from trial memberships through to 24-hour keyholder access, from beginners' courses through to masterclasses. Editioning and publishing facilities sit comfortably alongside the provision of printmaking to schools and colleges. Specialist printmaking galleries are now run by the print workshops themselves; and why not - we are the experts, after all. Some workshops have also developed artist residency schemes, international exchange programmes and graduate research schemes.

Where some university printmaking departments in England are cutting back or even going to the wall, print workshops are thriving and even filling the gaps left behind by institutions, offering a 'broader experience of art'. Workshops are now running accredited courses and even postgraduate degrees. Of course, the whole picture is a little more complicated than this generalisation makes it seem, but the truth remains that print workshops play a very large part in keeping printmaking as strong as it is today.

A large number of people discovering printmaking do so every year in workshops the length and breadth of the country. Short weekend or evening courses are the ideal tasters and open-access workshops have the advantage of being able to offer course participants the opportunity to join as members and to become part of a growing community. Some people even choose to book themselves on a number of specialist courses through print workshops instead of paying for a degree. Print workshops allow the experienced professional earning a living from being an artist to rub shoulders with recent art graduates or vocational artists practising printmaking in their spare time. Those fresh from art degrees also find themselves either looking for somewhere to print or in some cases setting up print workshops or printmaking groups themselves.

Printmaking is a social affair, unlike painting and drawing, video and digital media. The need for expensive equipment causes printmakers to come together, and it's while mixing with other like-minded artists that we can beg, borrow or steal new techniques or individual approaches, engaging with other printmakers in the knowledge that there is always something else to learn or another way of doing things.

It seems that at this point in the evolution of printmaking it is a good time to take stock.

In the course of compiling this directory, I have visited over 60 print workshops in the UK and Ireland, each one with its own character but all sharing similar goals, with of course the common binding factor of the promotion and support of printmaking itself. When via Mike Simms of Printmaking

Today I was able to approach A&C Black to propose the need for this book I did not know the journey I would be embarking upon, or the sheer number of work hours it would take to complete, but I feel stronger than ever that it was the right thing to do. I have now succumbed to the notion that I will always be travelling to workshops, always looking for the next one that I did not know about; a lifetime of commitment to the cause lies before me. When Linda Lambert, Commissioning Editor for A&C Black, put to me the question, 'Is this not better left on the internet?', my response was a resounding 'No'. I challenged her to see how many print workshops she could find online. It did not take too long before Linda got back to me, agreeing that such a search was no easy task, and that therefore a book of this kind could be a success.

Please don't misunderstand me. There are some great websites out there listing a lot of workshops, but one of the problems with the internet (and one which I have found frustrating at many turns during this process) is that these sites are not always checked or updated, and thus you might be looking at something that is three years out of date. Of course, this book will also date, and I hope that you scribble as many notes on yours as I have on my dog-eared copy of the Survey of British Printmaking Studios, published in 1992 by Sylvie Turner (to whom I doff my hat).

Inevitably there will be changes, even in the time it takes to get this book to the bookshelves, and of course I cannot profess to know everything or everyone in the printmaking world. However, I hope that in years to come this book stands up as a comprehensive record of what is out there for the printmaker in 2009. Moreover, I hope that it leads the way for another edition in which all the remaining gaps – and I am sure there are still some – can be filled in. If it can also encourage people, no matter how few, to visit or to join a print workshop, to signing up for courses, etc., then it will have helped printmaking to continue to thrive as it does today.

Sean Rorke

Printmaking Associations in the UK

Greenwich Printmakers
1A Greenwich Market
London
SE10 9HZ

+44 (0)20 8858 1569
etch1a@greenwich-printmakers.co.uk
www.greenwich-printmakers.org.uk

Founded in 1979 with the primary aim of providing a permanent display of members' work, the association runs as a co-operative and staffs their own gallery in the old covered fruit market in the heart of Greenwich. Selection for membership of printmakers living in London is by portfolio of six images to the gallery (see website for details).

Harborne Bookbinders
Harborne Hill School
Edgbaston
Birmingham
B15 3JI

+44 (0)1214 542172
(Contact: Sybil Jones)
+44 (0)1384 379475
(Contact: Don Dunbar)
donsbooks@pedmore16.freeserve.co.uk

A group of amateur bookbinders who meet, under the guidance of an experienced bookbinder, on Wednesday evenings at Harborne Hill School, from 7 to 9 pm during term time. All levels are catered for as we all work on our own individual projects.

Inkers
Membership contact:
juliamclegg@onetel.com
www.inkers.org.uk

Set up in 2000 by a group of members working at West Yorkshire Print Workshop. 'The intention was to establish a caucus of printmakers who through collective activity and interaction would develop their skill base, improve their professional standing, raise the profile of printmaking regionally, offer support to each other and increase their business skills. It is our intention to expand our membership, and so we do not regard ourselves as "resident" to WYP.' Membership is by submission of print portfolio to the membership committee, and the payment of an annual fee. A programme of annual shows of new works ensures an emphasis on development by each member.

Newark Printmakers' Group
Contact via
Maplebeck Farmhouse
Maplebeck, nr. Newark
Nottinghamshire
NG22 0BS

+44 (0)1636 636825
pf@maplepress.co.uk

Organised through Maplebeck Press, the group meet at Millgate Museum, Newark, where there is a printers' shop complete with two working Albion presses.

Penwith Printmakers
enquiries@penwithprintmakers.co.uk
www.penwithprintmake rs.co.uk

A group of printmakers based in West Cornwall who exhibit regularly and promote printmaking.

The Printmakers' Council

Ground-floor unit
23 Blue Anchor Lane
London
SE16 3UL

+44 (0)20 7237 6789
www.printmaker.co.uk/pmc

The Printmakers' Council was founded in 1965 to promote the art of printmaking and the work of contemporary printmakers. It continues to pursue this aim by organising a programme of exhibitions in London, throughout the UK and worldwide. These exhibitions show both traditional skills and innovatory printmaking techniques. The PMC has a slide index and plan chest of PMC members' work, which is regularly consulted by galleries, exhibition organisers and potential buyers. Membership is open to all printmakers, students, interested groups and individuals.

The Royal Society Of Painter-Printmakers

C/o Bankside Gallery
48 Hopton Street
London

+44 (0)20 7928 7521
(President: Hilary Paynter)
www.banksidegallery.com

Founded in 1880 by Seymour Haden and five colleagues to seek recognition for artists working in etching, engraving and mezzotint. In 1888 the Society was granted its Royal Charter.

Artists wishing to put themselves forward for election are asked to submit eight unframed works and six drawings for consideration, accompanied by a current CV and an entry fee. Elections take place once or twice a year. The Society's major exhibition is held at Bankside Gallery each year, and members participate in group exhibitions and mixed watercolour and print shows throughout the year. 'The Society remains committed to raising awareness of the versatility and variety of printmaking as an art through education and a series of demonstrations and gallery talks held during the annual exhibition.'

The Society of Graphic Fine Art
(The Drawing Society)

The Menier Gallery
51 Southwark Street
London
SE1 1RU

enquiries@sgfa.org.uk
www.sgfa.org.uk

Established in 1919, the Society exists to promote good drawing and draughtsmanship in pencil, pen, brush, charcoal, conte or any forms of original printmaking. The Society generally holds two exhibitions a year: an open exhibition for members and non-members, and a 'members only' exhibition with no selection. Artists are elected to the Society on the strength of a portfolio of work submitted to a committee (see website for more details).

The Society of Wood Engravers

Geri Waddington (General Secretary)
The Old Governor's House
Norman Cross
Peterborough
PE7 3TB

+44 (0)1733 242833
g.waddington@dial.pipex.com
www.woodengravers.co.uk

Founded in 1920 by a group of artists that included Lucien Pissaro and Eric Gill among others. 'The Society exists to promote wood engraving. It is the principal organisation and rallying point for those interested in the subject and maintains a lively interest in other forms of relief printing.' There are about 70 members, who are elected or have been invited to membership. Subscriptions are also welcome from anyone wanting to support the Society and receive Multiples, a bi-monthly newsletter (contact: jmfrank@uwclub.net).

Southbank Printmakers
Unit 12
Gabriel's Wharf
56 Upper Ground
London SE1 9PP

+44 (0)20 7928 8184
info@southbank-printmakers.com
www.southbank-printmakers.com

A co-operative of 37 printmakers with a gallery run by the artists at Gabriel's Wharf on the bank of the Thames. The display is re-hung every nine weeks.

OTHER PRINT RELATED SOCIETIES

The British Printers Society
www.bpsnet.org.uk

The Society caters for the small-business or hobby printer rather than the professional printmaker. It was founded in 1944 to 'enable printers to exchange views and experiences, pass on hints and tips, and generally promote a spirit of craftsmanship and friendliness'. Membership is open to all. Members include those who print for pleasure or profit, typographers, teachers, clubs and private publishers. There are nine branches across the UK. The Publishing Group consists of Society members who delight in printing and publishing short runs, purely for the pleasure of it, to an audience of similarly minded members. The group circulates its own monthly bundle to each group member. Printed items will vary from a single sheet or a small card to small booklets and, occasionally, limited-edition books. The website has useful links to suppliers of letterpress and equipment for sale.

The Fine Press Book Association
C/o The Whittington Press
Whittington Court
Whittington
Cheltenham
GL54 4HF

margaretjudithwalker@btinternet.com

The Fine Press Book Association is an organisation of individuals interested in the art of fine printing, formed with the goal of promoting the appreciation of beautiful books and printing skills. Now established for more than ten years, it has a worldwide membership of those interested in the fine book and contemporary fine printing: collectors, printers, artists, illustrators, museums and dealers.

The Association, which publishes Parenthesis, a journal devoted to fine printing and book-making, also issues an occasional e-newsletter, organises events for members and non-members, and has run competitions in book design. Every two years, the UK Provincial Booksellers' Fairs Association works with the Fine Press Book Association to organise the Oxford Fine Press Book Fair in Oxford, UK. This is the largest international show of fine presses and their work outside North America.

The Printing Historical Society
St Bride Library
St Bride Institute
Bride Lane
Fleet Street
London
EC4Y 8EE

secretary@printinghistoricalsociety.org.uk
www.printinghistoricalsociety.org.uk

Founded in London in 1964, the Printing Historical Society now has individual and institutional members worldwide. Still fully committed to its original aims, the Society fosters interest in the history of printing and encourages both the study and the preservation of printing machinery, records and equipment of historical value.

The Society of Bookbinders
www.societyofbookbinders.com

'Dedicated to traditional bookbinding and to the preservation and conservation of the printed and written word.' The Society runs education demonstrations, workshops and competitions. The website has a comprehensive links page to bookbinders, presses/publishers, organisations and suppliers. The Society's individual regions each organise local meetings at which lectures and/or demonstrations are given. Visits to libraries, binderies and suppliers are also arranged. At the national level a conference is held every other year. In non-conference years, a two-day training seminar is held, incorporating the national AGM.

UK & Ireland Print Workshops

Aberystwyth Printmakers (est. 2004)

Lanlwyd
Pennant
Llanon
Ceredigion
SY23 5JH

email
contact@aberystwythprintmakers.org.uk
web   www.aberytwythprintamkers.org.uk

contact
Rob Carpenter,   *Secretary*

Aberystwyth Printmakers was set up by a group of artists who employ a range of printing techniques in their work, including etching, lithography, screenprinting, wood engraving, woodcut and linocut. The principle aim of the group is the promotion of printmaking through a series of talks, lectures, demonstrations and exhibitions of their work and, mostly importantly, through the provision of printmaking workshop facilities. Membership has been growing at a rapid pace. Run on a voluntary basis, printmakers are supported in their work by Judy Carpenter, a printmaking graduate of the Royal College of Art. This active group has big ambitions to be a 'world-class open-access print studio'.

MEMBERSHIP/ACCESS
60 members.
Open Monday, Tuesday and Thursday, 10am-5pm.
Regular membership open to all.

COURSES/EDUCATION
One-to-one tuition arranged on an ad-hoc basis. Courses are planned for the future. The workshop also offers lectures and demonstrations by members, a 'forum for discussing printmaking issues, and arranges visits to print-related events for members'.

EQUIPMENT
Tofko etching press
100 x 180 cm | 39 x 71 in.

Etching press (make unknown)
30 x 80 cm | 12 x 31 in.

Albion relief press
50 x 80 cm | (20 x 31 in.)

Ferric-chloride etching (vertical tank)
60 x 46 cm | 24 x 18 in. deep

Acrylic spray aquatint

Wax grounds and specially formulated acrylic grounds developed at Aberystwyth College.

Screens available, but no vacuum bed.

EXHIBITIONS
Members' exhibitions are organised around the year at regional and national venues.

Airfield (est. 2008)

Upper Kilmacud Road
Dundrum
Dublin 14
Ireland

tel   +353 (0)1 298 4301
email frances@airfield.ie
web   www.airfield.ie

Airfield is the former home, farm and gardens of sisters Letitia and Naomi Overend, gifted ⟵to whom?⟶ as an educational and recreation centre, with a particular emphasis on nature. In the courtyard there are two fully equipped art studios with the capacity for between 12 and 16 students, a print studio which provides artists/printmakers with a facility to develop their work in a professional manner, and a large photographic darkroom which can accommodate eight students/photographers.

The studio is a small etching-specific studio using ferric chloride, providing for daily access and a small membership base.

MEMBERSHIP
Currently 20 members.
Daily access.

COURSES/EDUCATION
We run regular one-day workshops and occasional weekend workshops in etching. There are plans to run some non-acid-based workshops for older children.

EQUIPMENT
Hunter Penrose etching press
71 x 122 cm | 28 x 48 in.

Polymetaal etching press
90 x 180 cm | 36 x 71 in.

Resin aquatint box
(approx.) 66 x 96 cm | 26 x 38 in.

Art Hub (est. 2006)

2B, Building 28
34 Bowater Road
Westminster Industrial Estate
Warspite Road
London
SE18 5TF

tel +44 (0)20 8316 7232
email enquiries@frameworkgallery.co.uk
web www.arthub.org.uk

Art Hub is primarily an artists' studio organisation with 36 studios across two sites in Deptford and Woolwich in London. In the centre of the Woolwich site is a well-equipped and naturally lit print workshop that offers free access to studio members, but has no public access or membership.

COURSES/EDUCATION

Courses in printmaking are run throughout the year by in-house artists and guest tutors, and are open to all. Courses cover screenprinting, etching, relief printing and other print media. They also run courses in life drawing and painting.

EQUIPMENT

Intaglio printmaking press
61 x 92 cm | 24 x 36 in.

Rochat etching press
61 x 92 cm | 24 x 36 in.

Rochat etching press
61 x 92 cm | 24 x 36 in.

hot plates x 2
(largest) 61 x 76 cm | 24 x 30 in.

Albion relief press
46 x 72 cm | 18 x 28 in.

relief nipping press
31 x 46 cm | 12 x 18 in.

Sinks x 2 + fume cupboard for nitric etching

One-arm squeegee tables (flat bed) x 2

Fox Graphics screenprint bed
113 x 168 cm | 44 x 66 in.

Sericol screenprint bed
124 x 192 cm | 47 x 68 in.

Adelco screenbed (small) x 2

Sericol UV exposure unit with vacuum
Photographic darkroom with five enlargers and one colour processing unit

Artichoke Print Workshop (est. 1992)

Unit S1
Bizspace
245A Coldharbour Lane
London
SW9 8RR

tel   +44 (0)207 924 0600
email artichoketrading@btconnect.com
web   www.artichokeprintmaking.com

contact
Colin Gale, Melvyn Patterson or Megan Fishpool

WORKSHOP

Located in a Victorian granary warehouse in the thriving area of Brixton in south-east London, the workshop has a strong reputation as a dedicated printmaking provider and as a promoter of printmaking as a whole. It attracts students and artists from all over the UK and from as far afield as Russia, Hawaii, Japan, New Zealand, America and Korea.

MEMBERSHIP/ACCESS
60 Members
Member and non-member access:
Wednesday, Thursday and Friday,10am-5 pm.
24-hour keyholder access available.

COURSES/EDUCATION
One and two-day courses run throughout the year in many print processes including stone lithography, plate lithography and solar-plate intaglio. Individual tuition also available by appointment. Workshops (held at Artichoke) also run annually in conjunction with Originals at the Mall Galleries.

Printmaking workshops arranged for groups aged 11+, designed to support teachers' own syllabuses. 'Our commitment to teaching printmaking and art to students of all ages and abilities has helped our schools' programme grow from strength to strength over the years.'

EQUIPMENT
Haddon etching press
38 x 91 cm | 15 x 36 in.

Kasten Berglin etching press
66 x 120 cm | 26 x 47 in.

Rochat etching press
91 x 228 cm | 36 x 90 in.

Rochat etching press
81 x 137 cm | 32 x 54 in.

Bewick & Wilson etching press
81 x 137 cm | 32 x 54 in.

Resin aquatint box

Nitric and ferric acids for zinc, copper and steel

Exposure unit
102 x 127 cm | 40 x 50 in.

Mann direct lithography press
91 x 114 cm | 36 x 45 in.

Mann direct lithography press
71 x 91 cm | 28 x 36 in.

Penrose offset lithography press
71 x 96 cm | 28 x 38 in.

Albion relief press
61 x 76 cm | 24 x 30 in.)

Kasten Berglin relief press
66 x 120 cm | 26 x 47 in.

Solar-plate etching also available

EXHIBITIONS
Members are able to participate in exhibition programmes, to be included in the slide library and website, and to have work on display in the browser.

EDITIONING

Artichoke has a professional editioning and plate-making service in which artists work with a team of knowledgeable, technically innovative printmakers to create plates and editioned prints for themselves or through the commissioned support of their galleries.

MISCELLANEOUS

Artichoke also supply top-quality etching blankets (frontings and swanskins) to order, and are distributors for the Kasten Berglin etching press.

Art/Lab Printmaking (est. 2006)

University of Central Lancashire
37 St Peter Street
Preston
PR1 2HE

tel   +44 (0)1772 893193
email MStawarska-beavan@uclan.ac.uk or THill@uclan.ac.uk
web   www.uclan.ac.uk/facs/class /finearts/artlab.html

contact
Tracy or Magda   *Print Technicians*

Art/Lab is part of the University of Central Lancashire, an extension of the facilities to incorporate an open-access print workshop. 'We provide guidance and technical advice on all aspects of printmaking. We offer a wide range of facilities for etching, relief, lithography, silkscreen and digital.'

MEMBERSHIP/ACCESS
Full and associate membership. Timetable of access times posted to work alongside academic timetable, plus members can book extra time in the printmaking studios during the week.

COURSES/EDUCATION
Demonstrations and tutorials arranged plus special workshops in all techniques.

EQUIPMENT
Large etching press
(bed size) 93 x 130 cm ┃ 37 x 52 in.

Small etching press
(bed size) 38 x 80 cm ┃ 15 x 31 in.

Acid room for ferric-chloride and nitric-acid etching on steel, zinc and copper

Photo-etching also available

Columbian press
(bed size) 60 x 90 cm ┃ 24 x 36 in.

Screenprinting tables x 6
(maximum print size) 90 x 140 cm ┃ 36 x 55 in.)

Offset plate and stone lithography with three offset presses and a stone lithography press
Digital printing suite

EXHIBITIONS
Members' exhibitions are also organised.

Artsmix* (est. 2002)

Unit 11
Sheepscar House
15 Sheepscar Street South
Sheepscar
Leeds
LS7 1AD

email joy@artsmix.co.uk
web www.artsmix.co.uk

contact
Joy Hart

A screenprint workshop alongside a wood and jewellery/metal studio. The workshop is available for hire on a pay-as-you-go basis.

'We offer creative and business support to encourage development, and can act as a springboard for ideas, alongside state-of-the-art equipment, training and technical support. The workshop provides an ideal environment for artists to explore, grow and realise their creative potential.'

MEMBERSHIP/ACCESS
Annual membership allows access to the workshop, but the other services Artsmix provides including access to regular exhibitions and specialist craft markets, business-to-business support with selling your work, enterprise support in setting up your business. The workshop also holds networking events and hands out annual awards for emerging artists. Opening hours are from 10am – 10pm on weekdays, and 10am-7pm on weekends.

COURSES/EDUCATION
A series of introductory courses are currently being planned.

EQUIPMENT
Kippax screen bed
193 x 208 cm ⎮ 75 x 81 in.

Kippax screen bed
167 x 182 cm ⎮ 65 x 71 in.

Kippax stencil exposure system
(to suit max. frame size)
148 x 112 cm ⎮ 58 x 44 in.

Kippax stencil removal and

cleaning unit with extraction

Drying cabinet
167 x 182 cm ⎮ 65 x 71 in.

Badger Press (est. 1982)

Unit 4
Clayland Road Industrial Estate
Bishop's Waltham
Hampshire
SO32 1BH

tel   +44 (0)1489 892127
email info@badgerpress.org
web   www.badgerpress.org

contact
Angela, Jo, Marcia and Nicola

The studio is spacious and well equipped, with easy access and parking. It is located a few minutes' walk from the centre of the historic market town of Bishop's Waltham and is a few hundred yards from a nature reserve and open countryside. It has facilities for artists to produce prints in all media, including etchings, relief prints and screenprints.

MEMBERSHIP/ACCESS
40 members.
There is no membership scheme. Users pay a daily rate for access, based on a sliding scale depending on the number of people sharing. Open-access days are timetabled throughout the year, with supervision and technical support on hand.

COURSES/EDUCATION
A diverse programme of weekend and week-long practical courses are run throughout the year in a variety of printmaking methods including etching, solar-plate, relief printing and screenprinting. Staff development for educational institutions arranged.

EQUIPMENT
Hunter Penrose etching press
71 x 122 cm | 28 x 48 in.

Resin aquatint box
66 x 96 cm | 26 x 38 in.)

Ferric (Edinburgh etch) and nitric etching

Solar-plate intaglio/relief printing

Screenprinting vacuum table
84 x 142 cm | 33 x 46 in.

Non-vacuumed hinged screens x 8
71 x 81 cm | 28 x 32 in.

Galley press for relief printing
33 x 61 cm | 13 x 24 in.

Galley press for relief printing
63 x 101 cm | 25 x 40 in.

UV exposure unit
111 x 141 cm | 44 x 56 in.

EXHIBITIONS
Exhibitions are held once or twice a year, showing work by artists connected to the studio, as part of Hampshire Arts Open.

Bath Artist Printmakers (est. 1984)

3b Upper Lambridge Street
Larkhall
Bath
BA1 6RY

tel   +44 (0)1225 446136
email   enquiries@bathartistprintmakers.com
web   www.bathartistprintmakers.com

WORKSHOP

Well-established workshop with small but flexible accommodation in converted shop. Its membership 'has continually sought to develop its aims of bringing about public awareness of printmaking as an important art form' through an active exhibitions profile.

MEMBERSHIP/ACCESS
36 members.
'Membership is open to printmakers with experience who find the exchange of ideas and techniques stimulating.' Full members are entitled to use the facilities any time and to have their own keys; there is no supported open access. Exhibiting membership scheme also available.

COURSES/EDUCATION
One-day and longer courses in various printmaking methods (and book-making).

EXHIBITIONS
Several shows every year, both locally and nationally. Group shows have also been held in Bath's twin towns in Holland, Germany and France.

EQUIPMENT
Rochat etching press
63 x 119 cm | 25 x 47 in.

Bewick & Wilson etching press
76 x 126 cm | 30 x 50 in.

Ferric and nitric etching

Resin aquatint

Hotplates x 3

Screenprinting available
Bookbinding press

MISCELLANEOUS
There is an affiliated workshop in Frome, specialising in lithography (see Frome Printmakers).

Belfast Print Workshop (est. 1977)

Cotton Court
30-42 Waring Street
Belfast
BT1 2ED

tel   +44 (0)289 0231323
email info@belfastprintworkshop.org.uk
web   www.belfastprintworkshop.org.uk

contact
Paula McLernon   *Director*
Struan Hamilton   *Manager*

WORKSHOP

The longest established printmaking resource in Northern Ireland. The workshop provides facilities for professional artists in intaglio, relief, screenprinting and stone lithography. It is housed in a former bonded warehouse in the developing Cathedral Quarter of Belfast, with its own printmaking gallery on the ground floor and a well-established international residency scheme.

MEMBERSHIP/ACCESS
86 members.
Membership is available on an annual, associate and visiting basis, and is open to artists with printmaking experience. Full members have access by keypad codes outside the general opening hours. Open Monday to Friday 10 am-5.30pm. Gallery opening hours are Monday to Friday, 10am-5.30pm, and Saturday, 12-4pm.

COURSES/EDUCATION
A range of intensive day, weekend and evening courses taught by practising printmakers and open to all. BPW works in various educational settings and has two portable presses for demonstrations and outreach workshops.

EQUIPMENT
Modbury etching press
76 x 183 cm ⎮ 30 x 72 in.

Rochat etching press
66 x 122 cm ⎮ 26 x 49 in.

Rochat etching press
53 x 91 cm ⎮ 21 x 36 in.

Polymetaal portable press
50 x 100 cm ⎮ 19 x 39 in.

Resin aquatint box
Motorised Harrild direct lithography
76 x 102 cm ⎮ 30 x 40 in.

Selection of litho stones
(max. size) 61 x 91 cm ⎮ 24 x 36 in.

Screenprinting press
102 x 152 cm ⎮ 40 x 60 in.

Screenprinting press
137 x 210 cm ⎮ 54 x 83 in.

Print down frame
122 x 127 cm ⎮ 48 x 50 in.

Albion press
61 x 81 cm ⎮ 24 x 32 in.

Albion press
61 x 92 cm ⎮ 24 x 36 in.

EXHIBITIONS

The gallery on the ground floor represents all members, with prints also available by mail order via the website. The workshop has an extensive exhibitions programme, with many important shows overseas, including Canada, Germany and the USA. BPW holds an archive of prints by members and visiting artists.

ARTISTS IN RESIDENCE

Residency programmes have become a vital and successful part of the workshop's activities. Past artists involved have included Barbara Rae, David Mach and Mark Balakjian.

EDITIONING

Editioning in all print media is offered to non-members.

Birmingham Printmakers (est. 1982)

Unit 3C
90 Floodgate Street
Digbeth
Birmingham
B5 5SR

tel   +44 (0)121 7668545
email info@birminghamprintmakers.org
web www.birminghamprintmakers.org

WORKSHOP

Birmingham Printmakers have recently moved to new premises in a well-lit workshop in Digbeth. The new workshop has facilities for collagraph, drypoint, etching, acrylic resist, photo-etching, relief printing, silkscreen, solar-plate and waterless lithography.

MEMBERSHIP/ACCESS
34 members.
Full membership with 24-hour access to the studio. Exhibiting membership also available.

COURSES/EDUCATION
Regular workshops in all types of printmaking. Workshops with schools also available.

EQUIPMENT
Tofko intaglio/relief press
79 x 139 cm | 31 x 55 in.

Bewick & Wilson etching press
79 x 139 cm | 31 x 55 in.

Intaglio star-wheel press
51 x 106 cm | 20 x 42 in.

Small portable etching press
Albion relief press
53 x 66 cm | 21 x 26 in.)

Stone lithography press
41 x 56 cm | 16 x 22 in.

Screenprint bed
79 x 139 cm | 31 x 55 in.

Light box
83 x 115 cm | 33 x 45 in.

Darkroom and aquatint room

EXHIBITIONS
'We take part in exhibitions throughout the country and abroad.'

Black Church Print Studio (est. 1982)

4 Temple Bar
Dublin 2
Ireland

tel   +353 (0)1 677 3629
email info@print.ie
web   www.print.ie

contact
Hazel Burke   *Administrator*

'The Black Church Print Studio provides a managed and fully equipped workspace...in a collaborative atmosphere that celebrates the traditions and innovations of printmaking'. It is set in the lively Temple Bar area and with strong connections to the Original Print Gallery, and a successful exhibitions exchange programme. Artists have access to etching, lithography, screenprint and relief presses, and to multi-media equipment. 'Black Church embraces new technology and encourages artists wishing to use print as an ancillary activity as part of other work such as sculpture and painting.'

MEMBERSHIP/ACCESS
65 members.
Full-time/24 Hour Access (by application only). Two portfolio assessments take place each year in March & September.
Temporary Access (Mon-Fri 9-5) by application only. Work will be viewed by the Print-Coordinator & the Studio Manager and decisions are made on a project-by-project basis. Extended Access; applicants must have already reached a particular level of competence and ability in printmaking.

COURSES/EDUCATION
Classes for artists are scheduled every Spring and Autumn. Talks and workshops are also organised on an ongoing basis, and demonstrations organised for educational & corporate groups on request.

EQUIPMENT
Rochat etching press x 2
(largest) 81 x 166 cm | 32 x 65 in.
Hunter Penrose etching press
(largest) 71 x 121 cm | 28 x 48 in.

Hotplates x 3
(max. size) 81 x 101 cm | 32 x 40 in.

Metal guillotine
101 cm | 40 in.

Resin aquatint box
(max. plate size) 81 x 101 cm | 32 x 40 in.

Nitric and ferric (acid room with 2 canopies)
81 x 128 cm | 32 x 51 cm

Takach lithography press
83 x 143 cm | 33 x 57 in.

30 stones (various sizes)
(largest) 61 x 81 cm | 24 x 32 in.

Hydraulic stone lift

Hopkinson & Cope relief press
59 x 74 cm | 23 x 29 in.

Vacuum presses x 2
81 x 116 cm | 32 x 46 in.

Exposure units x 2
146 x 163 cm | 58 x 65 in.

Washout room
(max. screen size)
81 x 151 cm | 32 x 60 in.)

Apple Mac G4 & Apple Mac G3 computers

A4 flatbed scanner & 35 mm scanner (Nikon Coolscan)
A2 & A4 colour printers

Colour and black & white photographic darkroom

EXHIBITIONS

The Studio holds bi-annual exhibitions at the Original Print Gallery, Temple Bar and organises exhibitions of members work at other local and national galleries and arts centres. International exhibitions have included exchange shows with Danske Grafikeres Hus, and the New York Society of Etchers, Grafiska Sallskapet Galleri, Stockholm and Le Trait, Paris in a major exchange of French and Irish contemporary prints

EDITIONING

The studio provides a limited-edition printing service to artists and corporate clients.

MISCELLANEOUS

The studio also runs an international lithography artist-in-residence scheme for emerging, mid-career and established professional artists inspiring new works of art and creative collaborations.

Bluecoat Print Studio (est. pre-1965)

The Bluecoat
School Lane
Liverpool
L1 3BX

tel +44 (0)151 7095297
email print@thebluecoat.org.uk
web www.thebluecoat.org.uk

contact
Emma Gregory   *Print Studio Manager*

Based in the renowned Bluecoat right in the heart of Liverpool, which has recently undergone a massive refurbishment programme, the print studio has reopened with a new room/layout. It is equipped for etching and relief printing, incorporating acrylic resist methods. There are links to the Printmaking Department at Liverpool John Moores University Editions Ltd and the arts centre's own programme of debates and talks.

MEMBERSHIP/ACCESS
Any printmaker over 18 can hire the studio alone or working as part of a group, following receipt of a health and safety induction (free). Three-hour bookable sessions run in the morning, afternoon and evening. There is no membership scheme.

COURSES/EDUCATION
The Bluecoat's print courses and workshops target local artists. There are regular short courses in 'safe' intaglio techniques; approximately eight specialist one/two-day workshops or masterclasses a year; a weekly drop-in session focussing on experimentation; residencies; artists' talks and a schools' programme. In addition, Emma Gregory, the Print Studio Manager, plans to create an online discussion group focussing on 'safer' printmaking, accessible through Bluecoat's web pages. Other one-off collaborations occur from time to time.

EQUIPMENT
Kimber and Hughes etching press
66 x 135 cm ┃ 26 x 53 in.

Small tabletop press
28 x 55 cm ┃ 11 x 21 in.

Spray booth for aquatint
60 x 74 cm ┃ 23 x 29 in.

UV exposure unit
50 x 60 cm ┃ 20 x 23 in.

Brighton Independent Printmakers (est. 2000)

Module B1
Enterprise Point
Melbourne Street
Brighton
BN2 3LH

tel   +44 (0)1273 691496
email bip@brightonprintmaking.co.uk
web   www.brightonprintmaking.co.uk

contact
Jane Sampson/Ann D'Arcy-Hughes

WORKSHOP

An artist-led voluntary organisation dedicated to the production and promotion of original prints as a fine-art medium, 'set up with the aim of securing the future of printmaking in Brighton combined with the development of new technology within the medium'. Open Tuesday to Friday and some weekends and evenings. Situated on the ground floor of an industrial building with free parking, within reach of Brighton city centre.

MEMBERSHIP/ACCESS
80 members.
Gold and Silver membership available. These categories have different rates and annual subscriptions. Users must have sufficient experience to work on their own.

COURSES/EDUCATION
A varied and changing course programme – including one-day tasters, evenings, mornings and week-long courses – runs throughout the year in all print media, including traditional and innovative processes, taught by a pool of experienced teachers.

EQUIPMENT
Rochat etching press
66 x 101 cm | 26 x 40 in.

Polymetaal electric etching press
58 x 101 cm | 23 x 40 in.

Nitric and ferric etching

Resin aquatint

Columbian relief press
46 x 76 cm | 18 x 30 in.

Albion relief press
28 x 41 cm | 11 x 16 in.

Screen beds x 5
(largest) 101 x 151 cm | 40 x 60 in.

Globe offset-litho presses x 3
(up to) 36 x 51 cm | 14 x 20 in.

Letterbed press and type

EXHIBITIONS
BIP runs a lively exhibition programme which includes local and regional galleries, and they regularly have a stand at the Affordable Art Fair in Battersea.

Clo Ceardlann na gCnoc (est. 1998)

Visual Technology Workshop
Aonad S, T & M
Eastat Tionscail
Na Douiri Beaga
Co Dhun na nGall (County Donegal)
Ireland

tel   +353 (0)74 953 1271
email cloceardlann@eircom.net or
       oona@utvinternet.com
web www.clo.ie

contact
Ian Joyce   Artistic Director
Oona Hyland   Workshop Manager

WORKSHOP

Cló is a resource facility for the creation and production of art. Cló is a visual workshop combining traditional forms of image-making with contemporary media. Cló is an artist-led initiative providing a platform for creative exchange between artists worldwide and the Gaeltacht community. Cló fosters the emergence of artists in the Gaeltacht through providing access to professional development services. It is a publisher of original prints, artist's books, art posters, art catalogues, videos, artist's films, CDs and DVDs. Cló is interested in working with artists to create new work by identifying a project that can be realised within a defined timeframe using the workshop facility.

COURSES/EDUCATION

Classes and intensive courses in etching, relief printing and lithography. Projects with schools, other organisations and artists are an integral part of Cló's ethos. Cló also works on a one-to-one basis with artists to create artist's books.

EDITIONING

Editioning, proofing and preparation of lithographic stones, etching plates and other print media available.

EQUIPMENT

American-French tool press
121 x 198 cm │ 48 x 78 in.

Rochat etching press
66 x 121 cm │ 26 x 48 in.

Relief presses x 2
(largest) 61 x 109 cm │ 24 x 43 in.

American Charles Brand lithography press
81 x 106 cm │ 32 x 42 in.

30 lithography stones
up to 76 x 101 cm │ 30 x 40 in.

Large nipping presses for bookbinding x 2

A 'sizeable' aquatint box, plus etching facilities, for copper, zinc and steel

Multimedia lab (including 2 x Apple Mac G4s and sound/video recording suite)

Photographic darkroom

RESIDENCIES / PROJECTS

As well as artist-initiated projects the Tearmann programme invites applications from artists and arts administrators from both sides of the border for artists' professional development, for a visual art and technology training course, and for arts-administration training and work experience.

The Mhadgie Hughie Eoin Scholarship scheme also gives opportunities for Gaelic-speaking artists to enjoy a period of residency at the workshop.

MISCELLANEOUS

The Living Archive (An Fearann Feasa) proposes the creation of a cultural archive, incorporating a multimedia library of books, CDs, DVDs, video and minidisc sound recordings. This archive of contemporary visual culture focuses on the Gaeltacht as inspiration for a unique community resource, which will be made available to the local community in the context of a cross-border programme of training and cultural events, and a visiting-artist programme. The Living Archive will be permanently housed at Teach an tSleibhe at Mín a'Leá, a renovated traditional cottage with a purpose-built extension, and will become a key resource of the local community in an ongoing programme of events and projects.

Cork Printmakers (est. 1991)

Wandesford Quay
Clarke's Bridge
Cork
Ireland

tel +353 (0)21 4322422
email info@corkprintmakers.ie
web www.corkprintmakers.ie

contact
Clare Hennerssey   *Director*
Frances O'Connor   *Assistant Director*

Based in the historic centre of Cork City, Cork Printmakers is located in refurbished 19th-century warehouses at Wandesford Quay, between Sharman Crawford Street and Clarke's Bridge. It is part of a complex comprising 21 artists' studios, 6 sculpture units and a commercial gallery, with a communal courtyard facing the River Lee. 'Cork Printmakers is an artist resource, committed to promoting print as a public art form, and provides a professional, open-access, fine-art print workshop so as to facilitate printmakers and visual artists working through the medium of print.'

MEMBERSHIP/ACCESS
85 members
Full membership: 24-hour access to the workshop; short-term membership: 24-hour access for less than six months of the year; associate membership: access to the workshop under a technician's supervision, from 9am-5pm Monday-Friday. Potential applicants must be capable of demonstrating excellent knowledge of a minimum of one print process. A third-level qualification in fine-art printmaking is preferable, but other qualifications and experience are also considered. The workshop is open from 9.30am-1pm and from 2-5pm, Monday to Friday (closed on public holidays).

COURSES/EDUCATION
Cork Printmakers organises a year-round programme of printmaking workshops, for both beginners and experienced printmakers, in weekend and 10-week-long evening classes. Their artists-in-schools programme won an AIB Better Ireland award. The programme has developed since 1995 to bring workshops to schools, community-arts projects, colleges and youth outreach projects.

EQUIPMENT
Rochat etching press
81 x 163 cm | 32 x 65 in.

Polymetaal JW100 etching press
100 x 200 cm | 40 x 80 in.

Polymetaal JSV etching press
80 x 130 cm | 31 x 51 in.

Starwheel etching press
33 x 76 cm | 13 x 30 in.

Nitric plus vertical ferric dip tanks

Resin aquatint room

Rochat hotplate
64 x 77 cm | 25 x 31 in.

Block printing press
38 x 66 cm | 15 x 26 in.)

Trumax exposure unit
101 x 151 cm | 40 x 60 in.

Trumax printing bed
101 x 151 cm | 40 x 60 in.

Darkroom and washout room

Takach lithography press
83 x 151 cm | 33 x 60 in.

(plus stones and plates of various sizes)
Hydraulic lift

Digital suite with IMac G5 & G4, A3 B&W
laser printer, A2 colour inkjet printer, A4
scanner, digital camera, slide & data
projectors

EXHIBITIONS
'Public engagement is important and so the
workshop is very active in the exhibition of
printmaking in public and private spaces
and embraces critical response.' Fine-art

prints can be purchased from the workshop
sales office, where a large selection of
artist-members' work is on display. Cork
Printmakers also hold an annual art market
in June and a Christmas sale in December.

MISCELLANEOUS
Commissions undertaken. 'We will match
your company with a specific artist, liaise
with you and the artist in drafting the
creative brief, and identify and recommend
the best options.'

Cuckoo Farm Studios (est. 1992)

The Print Workshop
Cuckoo Farm Studios
Boxted Road
Colchester
Essex
CO4 5HH

tel   +44 (0)1206 843530 – Reception
email atwoods100@aol.com
web   www.cuckoofarmstudios.org.uk

contact
Heather Selwood, Secretary, on +44
(0)1206 273928

Cuckoo Farm Print Workshop is situated on the outskirts of Colchester, set in agricultural buildings and houses converted into 18 artists' studios. It 'exists to provide printing facilities for creative printmakers and beginners alike'. The workshop is run as a small cooperative, and membership is available as a Full or Associate member.

MEMBERSHIP/ACCESS
19 members.
Full or associate membership. Associate membership is cheaper, but an additional charge per session is required.

COURSES/EDUCATION
Courses are run on an occasional basis according to demand, usually as a result of open days. Members are encouraged to attend members' days to foster exchanges of ideas and technical information.

EQUIPMENT
Rochat etching press
91 x 126 cm | 36 x 50 in.

Star-wheel etching press
33 x 86 cm | 13 x 34 in.

Colombian relief press
41 x 56 cm | 16 x 22 in.

Pinch press
51 x 61 cm | 20 x 24 in.

Letterpress proofing press
35 x 66 cm | 14 x 26 in.

Silkscreen table
99 x 141 cm | 39 x 56 in.

EXHIBITIONS
The workshop has representation on the Cuckoo Farm Executive Committee and participates in most group-sponsored activities. In general, group exhibitions are arranged two to three times a year.

Curwen Print Study Centre (est. 2000)

Chilford Hall
Linton
Cambridge
CB21 4LE

tel +44 (0)1223 892380
email enquiries@curwenprintstudy.co.uk
web www.curwenprintstudy.co.uk

contact
Lorraine Chitson: *Manager*

WORKSHOP

Established by Stanley Jones - Master Printmaker with Sam Alper OBE of The Curwen Studio as an educational printmaking charity. It is situated in a converted Dutch barn adjacent to The Curwen Studio and operates as a completely separate organisation, whilst having the obvious advantage of the connection with a highly regarded printer/publisher. The rationale and emphasis of the centre is to provide a 'classic' printmaking environment for artists of all ages and all abilities, aiming to preserve and develop the experience and skills which form a background to the concept of the original print.

MEMBERSHIP/ACCESS
No membership as it is primarily based on running courses, outreach activity and raising the profile of printmaking. Professional or amateur artists can arrange to develop their work outside of pre-arranged courses, and technical / artistic support can be organised if required. Previous experience of printmaking is not essential.

EXHIBITIONS
The study centre takes part in Cambridge Art Fair and Open Studios annually.

EDUCATION/COURSES
Education is at the core of the Curwen Print Study Centre. It runs an extensive schools programme for students and Teachers. Tutors deliver Artist in Residence experiences in school. Outreach workshops are taken into schools, museums, galleries and community groups. As well as ready-made workshops for adults Curwen specialises in tailor-made workshops for individuals or groups.

EQUIPMENT
Stone lithography press x 2
55cm x 82cm | 21 x 33in
55cm x 90cm | 21 x 35in

Offset lithography press
65cm x 90cm | 25 x 35in

Colortone Lithography Press
63cm x 53cm | 24 x 20in

Etching press x 2
65cm x 105cm | 25 x 41in
80cm x 100cm | 31 x 40in

Portable presses x 2
Relief press x 2
45cm x 60cm | 18 x 23in
60cm x 85cm | 23 x 33in

1 x vacuum screen bed
90cm x 135cm | 35 x 53in
plus screen boards
resin aquatint booth

Apple Mac digital suite

Exposure facilities for photo techniques

Dartington Print Workshop (est. 1975)

The Craft Education Centre
Dartington Hall
Totnes
Devon
TQ9 6EA

tel   44 (0)1803 847000
web   www.dartington.org

contact
Michael Honor   *printmaking*
Mary Bartlett   *book-making*

WORKSHOP

Set in the fine surroundings of the Dartington Hall Estate, this spacious open-plan workshop has facilities for all forms of etching and intaglio printing, block printing and lithography, together with a range of experimental approaches. There is an emphasis on the use of non-toxic methods and materials. There is also a bookbinding department in the same building.

MEMBERSHIP/ACCESS
Experienced printmakers may apply to use the workshop on non-teaching days.

COURSES/EDUCATION
Classes are run throughout the year and are open to all-comers. All levels of experience, from beginners to experienced printmakers, can be accommodated. Enrolment is for day and evening classes over a ten-week term. Occasional workshop days are provided for schools, teachers, and recently for people with learning difficulties. The Workshop also offers printmaking residencies in both primary and secondary schools. It has a long experience of working with children.

EQUIPMENT
Rochat etching press
66 x 122 cm | 26 x 48 in.

Rochat etching press
46 x 91 cm | 18 x 36 in.

Hunter Penrose etching press
53 x 91 cm | 21 x 36 in.

Greig etching press
56 x 91 cm | 22 x 36 in.

Albion platen press
51 x 71 cm | 20 x 28 in.

Albion platen press
46 x 61 cm | 18 x 24 in.

Furnivall stone-litho press
46 x 91 cm | 18 x 36 in.

Ratcliff flatbed offset-litho press
61 x 91 cm | 24 x 36 in.

Harrild poster-proofing press
76 x 76 cm | 30 x 30 in.

Vicobold electric platen
30 x 46 cm | 12 x 18 in.

Portable presses for use in schools

EXHIBITIONS
Annual 'Off The Peg' exhibition at the Workshop. Regular local exhibitions at, for example, Dartington Gallery, Cider Press Centre, Ariel Centre and Devon Guild of Craftsmen.

MISCELLANEOUS
The bookbinding department offers a programme of classes, provides the opportunity to make artist's books, and has the capacity to enable students to gain knowledge of typography using lead and brass type as well as brass hand letters and decorative tools. Students can choose to work on their own projects in restoration, artist's books, boxes, portfolios or related subjects. There is a comprehensive library of reference books and numerous examples from non-Western traditions of book-making.

Double Elephant Print Workshop (est. 1998)

Exeter Phoenix
Bradninch Place
Gandy Street
Exeter
EX4 3LS

tel   +44 (0)7855 512753 (mob.): Emma
       Moloney, outreach and projects
       +44 (0)7855 206659 (mob.)
email info@doubleelephant.org.uk
web   www.doubleelephant.org.uk

contact
Lynn Bailey   *courses & membership*

WORKSHOP

Recently moved to new premises in Exeter Phoenix Arts Centre. 'Our aim is to encourage and support people to discover their creativity, and we believe that anyone can make prints. A wide variety of people use the workshop. We support professional and semi-professional artists as well as those new to printmaking. In addition, we work with groups of people normally excluded from mainstream arts activity.'

MEMBERSHIP/ACCESS
Full membership is for competent printmakers who feel able to pursue individual projects under their own steam. One day a week technical advice and support provided. A friends scheme is also available for those interested in occasional use of the workshop, exhibiting with the group, having work represented on the website and receiving newsletters and opportunities. Visiting printmakers welcome.

COURSES/EDUCATION
Courses are run in 10-week blocks or on weekends throughout the year, and cover a varied range of printmaking methods. One-to-one tuition is available by arrangement. 'Double Elephant runs an active outreach programme using our mobile print workshop, which enables us to take lots of printing processes to different community groups ranging from primary and secondary schools, museums, galleries, community groups, festivals, prisons and hospitals. This reaches over 2000 people each year. We also run projects for socially excluded groups, such as weekly print-on-prescription sessions for adults dealing with mental-health issues.'

EQUIPMENT
Bewick & Wilson etching press
76 x 150 cm | 30 x 59 in.

Portable Tofko proofing press
41 x 61 cm | 16 x 24 in.

Rochat etching press
30 x 61 cm | 12 x 24 in.

Albion relief press
63 x 79 cm | 25 x 31 in.

Hallmark screen bed
76 x 110 cm | 30 x 43 in.

UV light source
81 x 66 cm | 32 x 26 in.

Equipment for photo-etching and photographic screens

Acrylic resist facilities

EXHIBITIONS
Double Elephant exhibits work regularly throughout the South-west region. Members are encouraged to initiate exhibitions, and the workshop takes part in local open-studios events annually. Members' work is also entered on Double Elephant's website.

EDITIONING

Service offered to edition etchings, collagraphs, relief prints and screenprints. The workshop is also very keen to work in collaboration with artists of all disciplines to create a print project from scratch, and can advise on the appropriate process and work jointly on plates, printing and editioning.

Dundee Print Studio (est. 1977)

Dundee Contemporary Arts
152 Nethergate
Dundee
Scotland
DD1 4DY

tel   +44 (0)1382 909242
email annis.fitzhugh@dundeecity.gov.uk
web   www.dca.org.uk/print

contact
Annis Fitzhugh

WORKSHOP

An extremely well-equipped studio, where size is not an issue. In spite of this, the studio has not lost its friendly and supportive approach. 'DCA Print Studio is uniquely situated in the extensive Dundee Contemporary Arts complex and offers an exciting range of classes and tuition sessions for professional artists, amateur artists and beginners, as well as general facilities for the production of print-based art works. The workshop space provides equipment of diversity, range and scale unparalleled in the UK, for users of all ages and levels of expertise.'

MEMBERSHIP/ACCESS
180 members.
Individuals who wish to have hands-on access to the print area must be able to demonstrate competency in their relevant processes to the studio staff. 'New registered artists' must take part in a brief studio induction, and there is also a six-month probationary period. Opening hours are Tuesday-Thursday, 11am-9pm, and Friday-Saturday, 11am-6pm.

EDUCATION/COURSES
Extensive rolling programme of courses and 'drop-in sessions' in printmaking, photography and digital imaging. In-house 'assisted' and 'non-assisted' courses are available to schools, colleges and community groups, as well as outreach programmes taking printmaking out of the workshop. Inset teacher training is also available.

EQUIPMENT
Praga multipurpose motorised printing press
151 x 226 cm | 60 x 90 in.

Rochat etching press
66 x 121 cm | 26 x 48 in.

Polymetaal etching press x 2
(largest) 81 x 161 cm | 32 x 64 in.

Compressor for spray aquatint

McCrone Engineering hydraulic press
59 x 79 cm | 23 x 31 in.

Electrically driven metal guillotine (cutting length)
126 cm | 50 in.

Ratcliffe direct motorised lithographic press
66 x 100 cm | 26 x 39 in.

McCrone Engineering hydraulic lifting table
Kippax screenprinting table x 2
76 x 101 cm | 30 x 40 in.

Kippax screenprinting table x 1
121 x 181 cm | 48 x 72 in.

Kippax precision hinge learner screens x 10
(max.) 91cm x 91cm | 36 x 36 in.

Portable screenprinting system

EQUIPMENT FOR OUTREACH PROJECTS
AND BEGINNERS
Natgraph vertical printing down frame
169 x 270 cm ┃ 67 x 107 in.

Natgraph enclosed exposure system
101 x 126 cm ┃ 40 x 50 in.

Fully equipped photography darkroom

Fully equipped digital suite

EXHIBITIONS
The Print Gallery features approximately six
exhibitions a year showing work of
internationally renowned printmakers as
well as work produced at DCA Print Studio.
Registered artists may display prints in the
print studio and DCA shop print browsers.

MISCELLANEOUS
The DCA arts centre also has a
contemporary gallery, cinema, shop and
café/bar. In addition, the visual research
centre is one of the world's leading
research centres for art and artists, hosting
a number of large-scale projects. This bit of
the centre is part of Duncan of Jordanstone
College of Art & Design, and aims to be
publicly visible and accessible. It
incorporates a centre for artist's books, an
extensive digital facility and a very large
automated screenprint 'machine'.

Working with other print studios across
Scotland, DCA has now set up the CEL
Scotland website, which features original
artworks by artists working in Dundee,
Edinburgh, Glasgow and Aberdeen. The
website can be accessed at http://www.cel-
scotland.com

East London Printmakers (est. 1998)

The Triangle
129 Mare Street
Hackney
London
E8 3RH

tel   +44 (0)20 8525 4344
email info@eastlondonprintmakers.co.uk
web   www.eastlondonprintmakers.co.uk

An independent group of contemporary artist-printmakers established to develop a resource for artists and the public in East London. It aims to provide an open-access print studio for members and as an educational centre, to act as a forum for debate amongst artist-printmakers, and to promote printmaking as an art form.

MEMBERSHIP/ACCESS
80 members.
ELP Printmaking Studio is used by rent-paying members who have 24-hour access. Experienced printmakers can become open-access users who pay per session, bookable in advance. Open access is limited to Thursdays (10.30am-1.30pm, 2.30-5.30pm and 7-10pm) and Saturdays (10am-2pm).

COURSES/EDUCATION
ELP runs courses and workshops for both experienced and beginner printmakers, and aims to provide affordable training to amateur printmakers within the community. Courses include six-week beginners' workshops, fast-track workshops, professional development and specialist workshops. All workshops take place on Wednesdays. Bi-monthly artist talks are held which alternate between peer critiques and guest speakers.

EQUIPMENT
Tofko etching press
81 x 156 cm ┃ 38 x 62 in.

Large etching/relief press (make unknown)
71 x 156 cm ┃ 28 x 60 in.

Small book/relief press

Nitric and ferric etching facilities plus resin aquatint box

Parker exposure unit for photo-etching
60 x 70 cm ┃ 23 x 27 in.

Potter screenprinting beds x 5
(largest) 121 x 170 cm ┃ 48 x 77 in.

Large exposure unit for photo silkscreens
130 x 180 cm ┃ 51 x 71 in.

Large rubber topped fabric printing table
121 x 242 cm ┃ 48 x 96 in.

Metal guillotine
150 cm ┃ 60 in.

EXHIBITIONS
The studio has a display area/gallery for members' work, and a permanent display of work at thebookartbookshop in nearby Hoxton. Members' work is represented on the website and approximately two exhibitions are held outside the workshop every year, usually within London. Individual members are active in exhibiting their work, and ELP helps promote members' exhibitions.

MISCELLANEOUS
The ELP website is one of the most extensive and easy-to-trawl websites among all print workshops, with excellent links to everything printmaking-related, including workshops, organisations, print events and suppliers, as well as a comprehensive gallery of members' work. It's a great place to start on the internet if you are looking for printmaking information.

Edinburgh Printmakers (est. 1967)

23 Union Street
Edinburgh
EH1 3LR

tel   +44 (0)131 5572479
email info@edinburgh-printmakers.co.uk
web   www.edinburgh-printmakers.co.uk

contact
Sarah Price   *Director*

WORKSHOP

The first truly open-access print workshop in Britain, Edinburgh Printmakers is dedicated to the promotion of contemporary printmaking practice. It aims to promote the understanding of printmaking and pursue excellence in its practice by providing, maintaining and staffing an inexpensive open-access studio and free-admission gallery.

Set in a beautiful warehouse near the centre of Edinburgh, the workshop has an open feel with an in-house gallery that has a viewing window onto the workshop itself. It is undoubtedly a leader in the field of printmaking, having established itself as a 'pioneer' of innovative contemporary printmaking practices, such as acrylic-resist etching and photopolymer films, in the mid-1990s. Through its professional courses it has disseminated these practices to printmakers from all over the world.

MEMBERSHIP/ACCESS
140 members.
Annual (full) membership, associate membership and visiting-artist rates available. Session fees can be paid annually, quarterly, monthly or per session. It is worth noting that EP recently reduced its fees to allow greater access and to provide affordable facilities to printmakers.

COURSES/EDUCATION
A diverse range of courses include taster classes, in-depth weekends, evening classes and summer schools. EP are specialists in the field of innovative printmaking, including acrylic-resist etching, polyester lithography and photopolymer gravure, and are

constantly updating and exploring the processes they have to offer. Their staff and tutors are specialists in their fields, with unparalleled experience and knowledge.

EQUIPMENT
Motorised press x 1
70 x 90 cm | 27 x 35 in.

Rochat etching presses x 2
60 x 76 cm | 23 x 30 in.

Stone, zinc-plate and photolithography – over 100 stones available for use:
(largest stone size) 66 x 92 cm | 26 x 36 in.)
(plates can be printed up to) 66 x 94 cm | 26 x 37 in.

Motorised direct presses
81 x 108 cm | 32 x 42 in.

Motorised direct press
70 x 96 cm | 27 x 38 in.

Direct hand press
53 x 73 cm | 21 x 29 in.

Vacuum-bed presses x 3
(up to) 110 x 150 cm | 44 x 60 in.

Integrated UV exposure unit

Columbian relief press
68 x 102 cm | 27 x 40 in.

Enlarger and safe light areas for photoplate processes

Power Mac G4 and Emac
Flat-bed scanner, A3 laser and inkjet printer

EXHIBITIONS

With three dedicated gallery areas, EP has 'one of Scotland's foremost gallery spaces devoted to contemporary fine-art prints'. It shows internationally recognised printmakers, as well as showcasing new talent, in a rolling programme of exhibitions representing the whole spectrum of contemporary graphic art. EP also attends major art fairs.

EDITIONING

Edinburgh Printmakers is one of the leading publishers of prints by contemporary artists in the UK and abroad collaborating with other galleries and dealers as well as individual artists.

MISCELLANEOUS

EP has a great website. Take a look at the panoramic view of the workshop if you can. It also has good links to technical websites.

Editions 1920 (est. 2005)

19-20 St George's Avenue
Northampton
NN2 6JA

tel   +44 (0)1604 711826
email editions1920@hotmail.com

Set up in the home of artists Sarah Uldall and Adrian Barron, with two sizeable workshops (lithography in the basement and etching in a large shed behind the house), this print studio offers editioning services and short courses for artists in stone lithography and etching. One to one tuition can also be arranged. It is well set out and comfortable to work in, and is ideal for someone needing bespoke printmaking.

MEMBERSHIP/ACCESS

No membership. Short courses and tuition by arrangement. The etching workshop can be hired out on a daily basis. Sarah and Adrian collaborate and guide individuals in printmaking, giving a more intimate and individual print experience to one or two regular users at a time.

COURSES/EDUCATION

Short courses for beginners and weekly drop-in classes for those who have been on a course.

EQUIPMENT

Furnival stone lithography press
61 x 91 cm | 24 x 36 in.

Variety of stones
(up to max.) 51 x 71 cm | 20 x 28 in.

Art Equipment etching press
(bespoke) 90 x 125 cm | 35 x 50 in.

Rochat etching press
60 x 85 cm | 24 x 34 in.

Nitric etching (no aquatint box)

Fife Dunfermline Print Workshop (est. 1982)

The Basement
Del Farquharson Centre
Netherton Broad Street
Dunfermline
KY12 7DS

tel   +44 (0)1383 860306
email sheila.carnduff@fsmail.net
web   www.fifedunfermlineprintmakers.org

contact
Steve Ratomski   *Chair*
Sheila Carnduff   *Treasurer*

WORKSHOP

Fife Dunfermline has been supporting printmakers for over 25 years. Set up from the model of Edinburgh Printmakers, the workshop looks to support experienced printmakers as well as beginners to printmaking.

MEMBERSHIP/ACCESS
20-30 members.
Membership provides access to all equipment, materials at discount rates and the opportunity to exhibit in membership shows. Volunteer technical support is regularly provided on Tuesdays. Key access is granted once a member can demonstrate responsible and safe usage of the equipment. There is one set fee for a year, but no session charges.

COURSES/EDUCATION
Introductory and specialised courses are run throughout the year for members and non-members. These courses usually last one or two days and take place over a weekend. More advanced courses may be longer than this and will either take place over several weekends or be run on one full day per week. Short courses or day events are offered outside of the workshop with a mobile etching press and mobile screen beds.

EQUIPMENT
Rochat etching press
66 x 120 cm ┃ 26 x 47.5 in.

Art Equipment etching press
30.5 x 61 cm ┃ 12 x 24 in.

Winstone direct litho press
57 x 84.5 cm ┃ 22.5 x 33.5 in.

J. Cope Imperial relief press
42.5 x 63 cm ┃ 17 x 25 in.

Book press
61 x 46.5 cm ┃ 24 x 18 in.

Natgraph – screen bed
167.5 x 111.5 cm ┃ 66 x 44 in.

Marler Elite – screen bed
167.5 x 111.5 cm ┃ 66 x 44 in.

Rochat hotplate
61 x 51 cm ┃ 24 x 20 in.

Keetona metal cutter
97 cm ┃ 38 in.

Light box
129.5 x 85 cm ┃ 51 x 33.5 in.

Drying racks (2)
108 x 82 cm ┃ 42.5 x 32 in.

UV light box
81 x 122 cm ┃ 32 x 48 in.

EXHIBITIONS
We hold and participate in exhibitions throughout Scotland. Individual members contribute to galleries and exhibitions, both national and international, many receiving recognition and awards for their work.

Frome Printmakers (est. 2000)

Eagle Lane
Frome
BA11 1DR

tel +44 (0)1373 461664)
No website, email or direct phone line

contact
Russell Milne

Tucked away in a small studio set in a basement in the market town of Frome, until recently this studio was an offshoot of Bath Artist Printmakers, now a separate entity. It was established when an old printing firm was closed due to its owner's retirement. It is mainly set up for lithography, but other print processes, such as collagraphs, drypoint, monoprint, relief printing and letterpress, can also be practised here.

MEMBERSHIP/ACCESS
12 members.

COURSES/EDUCATION
Occasional courses.

EQUIPMENT
Furnival stone lithography press
41 x 71 cm | 16 x 28 in.

Greig stone lithography press
41 x 61 cm | 16 x 24 in.

Hunter Penrose offset lithography press
71 x 103 cm | 28 x 41 in.

Parker exposure unit

20 small litho stones
(up to max.) 38 x 61 cm | 15 x 24 in.

Letterpress and small T.N. Lawrence etching press also available.

Gainsborough's House Print Workshop (est.1978)

Gainsborough's House
46 Gainsborough Street
Sudbury
Suffolk
CO10 6EU

tel   +44 (0)1787 372958
email   mail@gainsborough.org
web   www.gainsborough.org

contact
Sue Molyneux   *Technician*

WORKSHOP

The Print Workshop at Gainsborough's House is 'a well-equipped and welcoming studio for print enthusiasts, artists and students. Recognised as one of the best facilities of its kind in the country, it enjoys a unique setting, sharing the museum's charming garden in the heart of Sudbury.' Membership is open to all, whether newcomers to printmaking or established artists. Beginners can book introductory sessions with the workshop technician before working independently.

Facilities include, on the ground floor, litho, relief and etching presses with work spaces, fume extraction and a screen-wash area. Upstairs, screenprinting equipment, including UV exposure unit and drying cabinet, is available.

MEMBERSHIP/ACCESS
143 members
Open Monday to Saturday, 10am-5pm.

COURSES/EDUCATION
An annual programme of summer courses is held and, in term time, regular morning and evening classes are run. Weekend masterclasses and one day taster sessions are also offered. Summer courses usually run over five days, and all classes are led by professional printmakers. Sessions for different age and ability levels can be arranged for schools and community groups. A popular Saturday art club for children also uses the Print Workshop as part of its exciting creative work.

EQUIPMENT
Albion relief press
43 x 56 cm │ 17 x 22 in.

Britannia relief press
54 x 71 cm │ 21 x 28 in.

Littlejohn etching press
71 x 121 cm │ 28 x 48 in.

Resin aquatint

Takach direct lithography press
81 x 146 cm │ 32 x 58 in.
(plates and stones available)

EMUS screenprint table
91 x 121 cm │ 36 x 48 in.

UV exposure unit (to take screens up to)
91 x 91 cm │ 36 x 36 in.

Screen-wash unit with backlit panel and pressure cleaner

Darkroom with De Vere 54 Jualite black and white photographic enlarger

EXHIBITIONS
Members are invited to offer work for sale in the museum shop and to participate in a regular and varied programme of exhibitions.

Glasgow Print Studio (est.1972)

Trongate 103
Glasgow
G1 5HD

tel +44 (0)141 552 0704
email email: workshop@gpsart.co.uk
web www.gpsart.co.uk

contact
John Mackechnie   *Director*
Claire Forsyth   *Workshop Manager*

Based in the heart of Glasgow, GPS has expanded so that there are now many aspects to its business, not least the publishing arm and three galleries. It is one of the largest publishers of original prints in the UK. Leading artists are invited to work with master printers to create and edition new work. An exchange programme and visiting artists' programme enables 'out-of-town users' to make use of the facilities and expertise.

MEMBERSHIP/ACCESS
162 members.
Access is open to anyone who has printmaking experience. Anyone without print experience can go on one of the regular courses before becoming a member. GPS operates a system of session fees, paid daily, quarterly or yearly. Open 10am-5.30pm, Tuesday to Saturday, or until 9pm Tuesday to Thursday for members. The visiting artists' programme welcomes experienced printmakers from around the world who wish to visit Scotland and work for a period of time in the Print Studio.

COURSES/EDUCATION
There is a rolling programme of seven-week-long evening courses in etching, relief printing, screenprinting lithography and digital imaging, as well as weekend courses in the same disciplines. Glasgow Print Studio's outreach education programme includes activities for schools, teachers, families and children of all ages and abilities, as well as courses for adult learners and artists. A varied programme

of artists' talks and events run alongside the exhibition programme.

EQUIPMENT
Takach motorised etching press
106 cm | 42 in wide

Bewick and Wilson 'Clydesdale' motorised etching press
106cm | 42 in. wide

Rochat etching presses x 2
66cm | 26 in. wide

Nitric and ferric etching

Resin aquatint

Facilities for stone, plate and photo lithography

Hunter Penrose offset press
61 x 91 cm | 24 x 36 in.

Mann motorised direct stone press
61 x 91 cm | 24 x 36 in.

Selection of Bavarian lithographic stones (up to max.) 61 x 91 cm | 24 x 36 in.

Columbian relief press
61 x 91 cm | 24 x 36 in.

Albion proofing press
35 x 66 cm | 14 x 26 in.

Kippax screenprint vacuum table
111 x 141 cm | 44 x 56 in.

McCormack vacuum table
146 x 208 cm | 58 x 83 in.

Print-down frame with 3kW metal halide light source
152 x 203 cm | 60 x 80 in.

Digital imaging suite, including large-format inkjet printer

EXHIBITIONS
A programme of exhibitions runs throughout the year in the two galleries within the workshop building, showing national and international printmakers. Across the road, Gallery III stocks and displays a range of original prints, offers a print-hire scheme and has a framing service.

PUBLICATIONS
Original etchings, lithographs, relief prints and screenprints by internationally renowned artists, including Elizabeth Blackadder, Christine Borland, John Byrne, Ashley Cook, Ken Currie, Peter Howson, Abigail McLellan, Ray Richardson, Carol Rhodes, Ross Sinclair, Adrian Wiszniewski and many others.

EDITIONING
Editioning available in all print media.

Gloucesterhire Printmakers Cooperative (est. 2005)

Unit 16C
Griffin Mill
London Road
Thrupp
Stroud
GL5 2AZ

tel   +44 (0)1453 765281
email info@gpchq.org
web   www.gpchq.org

contact
Sue Drennen   *Coordinator*

Set in a lovely mill on the outskirts of Stroud, this workshop has been growing rapidly, is set out clearly and professionally and is well equipped. Currently across two sites with screenprinting in another building, it is going from strength to strength.

MEMBERSHIP/ACCESS
64 members.
Membership available in keyholder member, standard member (16 hours a week access), occasional user, associate or friend. Office open Monday-Friday, 9am – 1pm. Studios open 24 hours a day for keyholders.

COURSES/EDUCATION
One-day, weekend and evening classes, ranging from tasters to masterclasses. Courses are usually limited to just six people, and range from basic screenprinting, drypoint, letterpress, stone lithography and photo-etching.

EQUIPMENT
Rochat etching press
81 x 136 cm | 32 x 54 in.

Littlejohn etching press
71 x 151 cm | 28 x 60 in.

Lawrence etching press (portable)
41 x 81 cm | 16 x 32 in.

Relief/letterpress
56 x 63 cm | 22 x 25 in.

Screenprint vacuum bed
61 x 86 cm | 24 x 34 in.

Screenprint vacuum bed
86 x 121 cm | 34 x 48 in.

Kippax exposure unit
150 x 175 cm | 60 x 69 in.

Exposure unit
76 x 96 cm | 30 x 38 in.

Offset stone litho press
48 x 58cm | 19 x 23 in.

Direct stone litho press
48 x 58cm | 19 x 23 in.

Ferric chloride dip tanks and tray
69 x 71cm | 27 x 28 in.

Resin aquatint box
69 x 71cm | 27 x 28 in.

EXHIBITIONS
Three exhibitions a year including Stroud Subscription Rooms, Open Studios at Griffin Mill plus a regional exhibition. In March 2009 Gloucestershire Printmakers are organising Impress '09 National Printmaking Festival Stroud, 'a celebration of contemporary printmaking from across Britain, across various venues. This will become a biennial event.'

Graphic Studio Dublin (est.1961)

Distillery House
Distillery Court
537 North Circular Road
Dublin 1
Ireland

tel   +353 (0)1 817 0942
email info@graphicstudiodublin.com
web   www.graphicstudiodublin.com

contact
Robert Russell   *Studio Director*
Osgar O'Neill   *Studio Administrator*
Catherine O'Riordan   *Gallery Manager*

The largest and oldest fine-art print studio in Ireland. Set in the thriving Temple Bar area of Dublin it benefits from, and contributes to, the lively arts scene. Graphic Studio provides professional working facilities on three floors, and studio space, at an affordable cost to Ireland's leading printmakers. The workshop operates a visiting artists' scheme, whereby prominent artists are invited to make prints in the studio.

MEMBERSHIP/ACCESS

65 members/visiting artists.
The Graphic Studio works with upwards of 50 members every year. An additional 15 to 20 visiting artists are invited to the studio each year to make a series of prints with the assistance of a skilled technician.

COURSES/EDUCATION

In addition to offering regular courses in etching, carborundum, lithography and woodblock, the Graphic Studio also fosters creative project ideas and actively supports artist-led projects from the studio. Past successes have involved the Graphic Studio's collaboration with national cultural institutions, in exhibitions such as Art into Art at the National Gallery of Ireland in 1998, Holy Show at the Chester Beatty Library in 2002, and The Garden of Earthly Delights programmed at the Chester Beatty Library in 2005.

EQUIPMENT

Five etching presses made by Graphic Studio
(largest) 240 x 115 cm │ 96 x 46 in.

Rochat etching press x 2
92 x 46 cm │ 36 x 18 in.

Etching trays
(to fit) 180 x 95 cm │ 72 x 38 in.

Aquatint box
(to fit plates) 110 x 70 cm │ 44 x 28 in.

Lithography press
100 x 60 cm │ 40 x 24 in.

Takach lithography press
180 x 100 cm │ 72 x 38 in.

Large selection of stones (140 stones up to)
120cm x 90cm │ 47 x 35 in.)

Litho graining sink
136 x 105 cm │ 54 x 42 in.

Columbian relief press
86 x 66 cm │ 34 x 26 in.

Offset lithography press
96 x 60 cm │ 38 x 24 in.

Digital print area, newly fitted out with computers, printers and internet

Print room including meeting/education room, plus activities such as life drawing, plus display area and print archive

EXHIBITIONS

The impressive gallery space has been based in Temple Bar since 1988. The gallery promotes an understanding of printmaking in a friendly and open environment, with over 3000 works to choose from on the walls, in browsers and available in stock.

Green Door Open Access Printmaking Studio CIC (est. 2007)

St James Centre
Malcolm Street
Derby
DE23 8LU

tel   +44 (0)1332 291 996
        +44 (0)7919 823 097 (mob.)
email   mail@greendoor-printmaking.co.uk
web   www.greendoor-printmaking.co.uk

contact
Anna Johnson

WORKSHOP

Green Door is a small open-access printmaking studio with an environmentally friendly stance. It is based on the second floor of the St James Centre, in the Normanton area of the Derby, close to the city centre. 'Green Door is based on the pioneering work of Edinburgh Printmakers, and draws upon new international printmaking developments. In line with our ethos we also avoid using highly toxic or harmful chemicals and solvents where a safer alternative may be found.'

MEMBERSHIP/ACCESS
32 members.
Members are entitled to non-assisted access to the studio and darkroom facilities on a booked sessional basis.

COURSES/EDUCATION
Courses on photopolymer etching, acrylic relief etching, monoprinting, collagraph, waterless lithography, serigraphy and bookbinding. Group courses are restricted to four or five people. All the above can be tailored to individual tuition.

EQUIPMENT
Etching flat bed
46 x 84 cm | 18 x 33 in.

Adapted mangle
44 x 86 cm | 17 x 34 in.
suitable for relief and intaglio

Nipping press suitable for making artist's books
48 x 64 cm | 19 x 25 in.

Silkscreen Elite vacuum press

Acrylic-spray aquatint booth UV exposure unit
65 x 80 cm | 26 x 31 in.

Photographic darkroom

Facilities for mounting and framing prints

Digital suite

EXHIBITIONS
The Studio also offers a chance to exhibit and sell work upon invitation, and will introduce members to others of like mind who are setting up a community to share ideas about new printmaking techniques.

MISCELLANEOUS
Access to the Centre and the Studio facilities is fully adapted for the disabled, including a loop system for the hearing impaired in the studio. There are free off-road parking facilities just beside the Centre.

Handprint Studio (est. 2005)

Trewidden Studios
Trewidden Gardens
Buryas Bridge
Penzance
TR20 8TT

email handprintstudio@aol.com
web www.handprintstudio.co.uk

contact
Peter Wray (RE) & Judy Collins

Having recently moved from York to Cornwall, Handprint are 'committed to the research and development of innovative practice', including saline sulphate etching on aluminium. The Studio is run by Peter Wray RE, who has 30 years' experience of teaching printmaking and 'enjoys an international reputation as an artist-printmaker' specialising in collagraph/carborundum.

MEMBERSHIP/ACCESS
The Studio is allows open access on selected days throughout the year on a daily rate, but only to students who have already followed one or more of their courses, and are sufficiently competent to work reasonably independently. Open-access dates, listed on their website, are some three to four days a month.

COURSES/EDUCATION
An extensive course programme with one-day, two-day and five-day courses covering drypoint, collagraph/carborundum, non-toxic saline sulphate etching (not ferric, as we regard this as toxic), silkscreen monotype, viscosity monotype, relief printing and book/journal-making. Bed and breakfast is also available for course participants. Groups number no more than six people.

EQUIPMENT
Bewick & Wilson etching press
61 x 121 cm | 24 x 48 in.

Hawthorne etching press
405 x 920 mm | 16 x 36 in.)

Ferric and saline-sulphate etching ('The workshop does not use aquatint, as the main metal used is aluminium, which produces its own aquatint.') Small nipping/bookbinding press Illuminated etching baths/heated drying cupboard

Heatherley's

Heatherley School of Art
80 Upcerne Road
Chelsea
London
SW10 0SH

tel   +44 (0)20 7351 4190
email   info@heatherleys.org
web   www.heatherleys.org

contact
Philip Gibbs

WORKSHOP

Founded in 1845, Heatherley's is the oldest independent art school in London and is among the few art colleges in Britain that focus purely on portraiture, figurative painting and sculpture (numbering Millais, Rossetti and Sickert among its past students).

MEMBERSHIP/ACCESS
18 regular users.
Although essentially an academic print department, Heatherley's has opened its doors outside of term dates, and offers the use of printmaking facilities to students who have some printmaking experience. With a printmaking tutor available to offer guidance and assistance, it is aimed primarily at people who initiate their own ideas and who need time to develop a project, experiment with a new process or who perhaps want to edition a print. A flexible pay-as-you-go scheme runs from 10am to 4pm on Wednesdays (except on vocational student project weeks). Open-print classes run from 10am to 4pm every Saturday.

COURSES/EDUCATION
During the academic year, the full range of print techniques is covered in day and evening classes. These structured classes are appropriate both for beginners requiring a thorough introduction to printmaking and for those who wish to recap and practise printmaking techniques. Students have the opportunity to work from a life model, to visit the Victoria & Albert Museum Print Room, and to take part in producing a print-exchange portfolio at the end of the year.

EQUIPMENT
Etching press
49 x 91cm | 19 x 36 in.

Etching press
66 x 122 cm | 26 x 48 in.

Screenprinting bed

Stone lithography press

Darkroom

Highland Print Studio (est. 1986)

14A Seafield Road
Inverness
IV1 1SG

tel   +44 (0)1463 718999
email info@highlandprintstudio.co.uk
web   www.highlandprintstudio.co.uk

contact
Alison McMenemy   *Studio Manager*

Highland Print Studio is an open-access artist's studio with facilities for intaglio, relief printing, screenprinting and digital media. It is moving back to its original premises in 2009.

MEMBERSHIP/ACCESS
Currently 60 members.
Three-, six- and twelve-month session packages. Daily rates also available.
Opening Hours, Tuesday-Friday, 12-4pm, and Saturday, 10am-4pm.

COURSES/EDUCATION
Classes for all ages and abilities, including acrylic resist and photo-etching, digital imaging, fabric printing and bookbinding.

EQUIPMENT
Rochat etching press
81 x 163 cm | 32 x 65 in.

Facilities for copper and zinc (acrylic resist)
Acrylic spray aquatint

Kippax Printascreen exposure unit
139 x 165 cm | 55 x 65 in.

Kippax parallel-lift vacuum table
76 x 101 cm | 30 x 40 in.

Kippax hinged-lift vacuum table
76 x 101 cm | 30 x 40 in.

Albion Press
Takach combi-etch/litho (motorised)
64 x 121 cm | 25 x 48 in.

Digital suite includes a large-format printer, digital imaging and video-editing software

Horsley Printmakers (est. 2005)

The Hearth@Horsley
Main Road
Horsley
Northumberland
NE15 0NT

tel   07989 955108 (mob.) Carol Nunan, ;
       07717 256169 (mob.) Rebecca Vincent
email info@horsleyprintmakers.co.uk
web   www.horsleyprintmakers.co.uk

WORKSHOP

Horsley Printmakers is one of eight artists' studios at The Hearth, which is based in a converted 17th-century manse and 19th-century schoolrooms. The Hearth is situated in Horsley just one mile south of Hadrian's Wall, ten minutes west of Newcastle and Gateshead. It is a professional working studio run by Carol Nunan and Rebecca Vincent, where the two artists make and sell their own work. Printmaking workshops are run independently and by special arrangement.

MEMBERSHIP/ACCESS
Supported sessions and one-to-one tuition available.

COURSES/EDUCATION
There is a rolling programme of evening, weekend and four-day courses at the Hearth@Horsley, plus tailor-made workshops for schools and community groups, both in-house and 'outreach'.

EQUIPMENT
Bewick & Wilson etching press
60 x 120 cm | 23 x 47 in.

Norup etching press
40 x 60cm | 16 x 23 in.

Acrylic-resist copper with ferric chloride and zinc with saline sulphate

Spray booth for acrylic aquatint with airbrush and compressor

EXHIBITIONS
The studio takes part in the Northumberland Art Tour every year, and has a Christmas open studio. Occasional external exhibitions also organised.

MISCELLANEOUS
Workshops include collagraph, monotype, acrylic-resist etching, linocuts, drypoint, wood engraving, woodcuts, photo-etching, simple artist's books, and printmaking on textiles as a starting point for painting or creative textile/embroidery projects.

Hot Bed Press (est. 1994)

1st Floor
The Casket Works
Cow Lane
Salford
M5 4NB

tel   +44 (0)161 743 3111
email info@hotbedpress.org
web   www.hotbedpress.org

contact
Sean Rorke   *Artistic Director*

Set in a spacious Victorian warehouse which houses 2 other artists' studio groups. The workshop is large and plan workshop, catering for etching, screenprinting, relief printing, book arts and other print related media. The studio is expanding to take on another floor of the building in 2009. Hot Bed Press also incorporates new practices in printmaking such as copper sulphate etching alongside nitric etching and traditional aquatint, and carries out research into a broad range of print methods such as gum arabic photo-etching, photo-lino and photo-carborundum.

MEMBERSHIP/ACCESS
140 members.
Print membership, associate membership, trial membership, (3 month), and keyholder membership all available. Open Monday to Friday, 10am-5pm, plus Thursday evenings until 9pm.

COURSES/EDUCATION
Three programmes per year covering varied printmaking and print related subjects including master classes by special guest experts. One day, weekend and evening courses as well as week long Easter and Summer Schools. One-to-one tuition also available by arrangement. Regular members' supported sessions, and life drawing / printing days. Hot Bed Press also works with galleries, schools and other arts organisations to run an extensive outreach service, and works with Salford University to offer print provision to students.

EQUIPMENT
Rochat etching press
56 x 106 cm │ 22 x 42 in.

Hawthorn etching press
42 x 92cm │ 16 x 36 in.

Art Equipment etching press
49 x 84 cm │ 18 x 33 in.

Art Equipment resin aquatint booth
(to take plate size) 53 x 61 cm │ 21 x 24 in.

Nitric, ferric and saline-sulphate etching
Fume cabinet 91 x 185 cm │ 36 x 73 in.

Albion relief press
53 x 66 cm │ 21 x 26 in.

Nipping presses x 2
(largest) 30 x 46 cm │ 12 x 18 in.

Marler Elite screen bed
106 x 163 cm │ 42 x 65 in.

Cranco Engineering screen bed
106 x 163 cm │ 42 x 65 in.

All-in-one light box
91 x 116 cm │ 36 x 46 in.

Tilting vacuum frame and light source
124 x 134 cm │ 49 x 53 in.

Letterpress proofing press (plus type)
38 x 63 cm │ 15 x 25 in.)

EXHIBITIONS

Three to four exhibitions organised throughout the year (local, regional and national), as well as bimonthly in-house exhibitions at Hot Bed Press Gallery within the studio/workshop space. A print browser and web gallery also shows members' work. Plans are also underway for an international open-submission print exhibition. Collaborative projects and exchanges undertaken.

MISCELLANEOUS

Hot Bed Press has nine individual artists' studios, all of which have 24-hour access to the print workshop. The workshop also offers printmaking residencies, graduate opportunities/training and printmaking research opportunities, and welcomes exchanges with international print workshops.

OTHER

Hot Bed Press's 9 individual artists' studios all have 24 hour access to the print workshop. Printmaking placements, residencies and research opportunities available.

Hot Bed Bookstars meet at the studio once a month to discuss book arts, create and promote artists books through exhibitions and collaborations.

Inky Cuttlefish Studios (est. 2007)

Lower Ground Floor
5 Blackhorse Lane
Walthamstow
London
E17 6DS

tel   +44 (0)7753 686331 (mob.)
email kschmidt@hotmail.co.uk
       anna.alcock@ukonline.co.uk
web   www.inky-cuttlefish.co.uk

contact
Anna Alcock/Kirsten Schmidt

Opened in September 2007, Inky Cuttlefish Studios is a group of artists' studios, including a photography darkroom and printmaking studio, located a minute from Blackhorse Road Station in north-east London.

MEMBERSHIP/ACCESS
24 members.
Open to the public on Wednesday, Saturday and Sunday, 11am- 4pm, and on Tuesday by appointment.

Open-access users can book in advance to use the studio on Wednesdays and Saturdays from 11am till 4pm. Hire of the printmaking studio at an hourly rate is available to schools and other community groups.

COURSES/EDUCATION
Monthly workshops in a variety of printmaking techniques including etching, photographic screenprinting and collagraph are run on Tuesday evenings from 7 to 9pm. Drop-in art clinics for disabled and elderly people take place one morning a week.

EXHIBITIONS
Exhibitions in the studio space are organised throughout the year, and there is one major touring exhibition per year for invited artists.

EQUIPMENT
Polymetaal etching press (can be used for relief printing)
36 x 60 cm | 15 x 24 in.)
Kimber etching press
71 x 123 cm | 28 x 48 in.

Parker Graphics UV exposure unit
110 x 141 cm | 44 x 55 in.

Dip tanks and bath for etching (ferric chloride)

Hotplate
51 x 61 cm | 20 x 24 in.

Stephenson Blake relief press
36 x 80 cm | 15 x 31 in.

Peter Potter screenprinting table with vacuum
117 x 163 cm | 46 x 64 in.

Peter Potter screenprinting table with vacuum
92 x 137 cm | 36 x 43 in.

Screenprinting table with vacuum
90 x 120 cm | 35 x 47 in.

Washout area with power washer for screenprinting

Screen-rack and drying boards
Fabric printing table
80 x 170 cm | 31 x 66 in.

John Howard Print Studios (est. 2006)

Unit 4
Jubilee Wharf
Commercial Road
Penryn
Cornwall
TR10 8FG

tel   +44 (0)7870 679061 (mob.)
      +44 (0)1326 314006
email john@johnhowardprintstudios.com
web www.johnhowardprintstudios.com

WORKSHOP

John Howard Print Studios 'is a high-quality and vibrant facility set in an iconic eco-building, offering courses, workshops and open access to new and experienced printmakers to develop their skills and expertise'. The Studios offer facilities for printing copper, zinc, steel and aluminium plate, linocuts, woodcuts, collagraphs and monoprints. They can comfortably accommodate ten printmakers at a time.

John is an RE and a member of the Royal Society of Birmingham Artists. He has taught as a visiting lecturer at the University of Central England, the University of Warwick, Coventry University and Birmingham Print Workshop, and is a regular contributor to courses at King Edward's School, Birmingham and University College Falmouth. He is a member of the Penwith Printmakers and exhibits nationally.

MEMBERSHIP/ACCESS
Open-access sessions are available to experienced printmakers. There is an hourly charge but no additional membership or registration fee. Open access usually runs from Tuesday to Thursday, 9.30am-5.30pm, and Saturday, 9.30am-12.30pm, except when courses are running.

COURSES/EDUCATION
Quarterly week-long courses, as well as tailored sessions, are run in a range of printmaking techniques, in groups of no more than eight students.

EQUIPMENT
Rochat etching press
53 x 92cm | 21 x 36 in.

G. Mann and Co. starwheel press
33 x 84 cm | 13 x 33 in.

GunningArts press
51 x 100 cm | 20 x 40 in.

Nitric and ferric etching facilities

Jubilee Stores (est.1998)

Town Quay
Newport
Isle of Wight
PO30 2EF

tel   +44 (0)1983 533151
email info@quayarts.org
web   www.quayarts.org/jubilee.asp

contact
Jacqui Ager   *Classes and*
                     Workshops Manager

Jubilee Stores, owned and run by Quay Arts, is an attractive arts complex overlooking Newport Harbour. As well as a printmaking studio it houses a ceramics workshop, jewellery studio, general workshop and seven private artists' studios. It has printmaking facilities for etching, drypoint, acrylic screenprinting, photopolymer, relief (lino, wood and card), collagraph, monotype, papermaking and book arts. It is also a solvent-free environment. Paper and other materials are available to purchase.

ACCESS
The studio is available for hire by individuals, schools and other groups outside of timetabled classes and workshops. Tuition and technical assistance by arrangement.

COURSES/EDUCATION
One-day, weekend and evening classes and workshops in all aspects of printmaking, papermaking and book arts for all ages and abilities. Summer schools with visiting artists. Outreach sessions for schools, colleges, museums and other groups.

EXHIBITIONS
Various printmaking and book-arts exhibitions and artist's book fairs in Quay Arts galleries and café. Jubilee Stores artists take part in Isle of Wight Open Studios, as well as other events and open days.

EQUIPMENT
Etching press
81 x 136 cm | 32 x 54 in.

Airbrush aquatint – acrylic grounds

Ferric etching

Harrild and Sons 1879 Columbian relief press (platen size)
57 x 86 cm | 23 x 34 in.

Nipping press
25 x 30 cm | 10 x 12 in.

Screenprinting frames for textile and paper
24 x 34 cm | 9½ x 13½ in.

Screenprinting frame for textile and paper
38 x 51 cm | 15 x 20 in.

A4 colour scanner, A0 B&W scanner, PC and A4 colour printer

NB In addition to Jubilee's permanent equipment, other equipment, such as letterpress type and presses, a tabletop etching press and a portable UV exposure unit, is available through visiting tutors.

MISCELLANEOUS
Jubilee Stores' seven individual artists' studios all have 24-hour access to the workshops. All studios have Wi-Fi.

Kew Studio Print Workshop (est.1980)

St. Luke's House
270 Sandycombe Road
Kew
Richmond
TW9 3NP

tel   +353 (0)208 332 2122
email enquiries@kewstudio.org
web   www.kewstudio.org

contact
Sally Hunkin

Part of Kew Studios this is a small etching workshop around the corner from Kew Gardens. Space for two printmakers to work at any one time.

MEMBERSHIP/ACCESS
30 members.
Keyholder membership only, open to all experienced etchers. (Introductory session required.) Day session and evening session tickets available booked in advance. Booking system ensures no more than two etchers in the studio at ant one time.

COURSES/EDUCATION
Etching courses (introductory and advanced), plus individual tuition by arrangement.

EQUIPMENT
Bewick & Wilson etching press
79cm x 120cm | 31 x 48in

Hunter Penrose etching press
61cm x 120cm | 24 x 48in

Nitric and ferric etching

Small resin aquatint box

EXHIBITIONS
The staircase gallery shows members work, including painting and other media from studio artists. Part of Kew Open Studio weekend.

Leicester Print Workshop (est. 1987)

50 St. Stephens Road
Highfields
Leicester
LE2 1GG

tel   +353 (0)116 2553634
email   info@leicesterprintworkshop.com
web   www.leicesterprintworkshop.com

contact
Lucy Phillips   *Director*

WORKSHOP

Close to the centre of Leicester 'The studio offers a high quality experience of printmaking in a supportive environment, with specialist knowledge of traditional and non-traditional techniques, in a well equipped, well lit, ground floor studio.'

MEMBERSHIP/ACCESS
135 members
Full Print, Associate, Taster, Key Holder and Schools Membership available. Technician on hand to support members. Open Tuesday and Thursday 10.00am – 5.00pm, Wednesday 10.00pm – 8.00pm.

COURSES/EDUCATION
Three programmes of courses to members and non-members, covering a range of printmaking techniques for absolute beginners as well as more experienced printmakers. Courses vary from one day courses, evenings and weekend classes. Artists and people working in the creative industries are also invited to take part in talks and demonstrations. An expanding education programme takes printmaking into schools, colleges, museums, galleries and the community, including offsite workshops at The Hub in Lincolnshire and The Rufford Craft Centre in Nottinghamshire. The workshop also offers Corporate Printmaking Days, workshops for teachers and a volunteering programme.

EQUIPMENT
Rochat etching presses x 2
66cm x 121cm | 26 x 48in

Beevers Hydraulic press
51cm x 66cm | 20 x 26in
Resin aquatint booth

Nitric and ferric etching

Nipping press
30cm x 46cm | 12 x 18in

Stone Lithography press
51cm x 91cm | 20 x 36in

Letterpress proofing press plus type
Rollaco portable presses x 3 also available for hire

Natgraph self contained exposure unit
69cm x 100cm | 27 x 40in

A fully equipped framing area is also available for members to mount and frame their own work.

EXHIBITIONS
Exhibitions take place within the region as well as on a national level. Past exhibitions include International Mini Print Show; SmallPrintBigImpression.

MISCELLANEOUS
Leicester Print Workshop also houses 7 artists' studios on two floors above the workshop.

Leinster Print Studio (est.1998)

The Old Convent
Marron's Court
Main Street
Clane
County Kildare
Ireland

tel   +353 (0)86 3558365
email leinsterprint@eircom.net
web   www.leinsterprint.com

contact
Margaret Becker   *Studio Director*

Reopened in 2006 in refurbished premises in a converted convent in Clane, Leinster Print Studio practises green printmaking techniques and was the first safe or green studio in Ireland.

MEMBERSHIP/ACCESS
30 members.
Full and associate membership available. Full membership gives keyholders 24-hour access, while associate entitles the holder to occasional use and is payable by a daily studio fee. Membership application is by submission of work and a CV to the board. A two-month probationary period follows acceptance as a member (during which time the Studio is accessible from Monday to Saturday, 10am-4pm), before 24-hour access is granted.

COURSES/EDUCATION
Printmaking workshops are held in a variety of methods including etching, drypoint, carborundum, lino, woodblock and photo-etch.

Courses and workshops are arranged with primary and secondary schools as well as community groups. A portable press caters for outside workshops. The Studio offers artist-in-residence programmes in printmaking to primary and secondary schools and facilitates an adult-education evening class for 12 students at Scoil Mhuire Secondary School.

EQUIPMENT
Littlejohn etching press
71 x 121 cm | 28 x 48 in.

Lilly & Hewitt
49 x 121 cm | 19 x 48 in.

Tofko etching press
79 x 89 cm | 31 x 35 in.

Small star-wheel etching press
(Furnival & Co.)
38 x 91 cm | 15 x 36 in.

Darkroom and exposure unit

Large workroom

EXHIBITIONS
LPS exhibits regularly across Ireland. Recent exhibitions include an exchange with Seacourt Print Workshop, while the Le Chile twinning project with The Regional Print Centre at Yale College in Wrexham in Wales will include an exhibition at the Graphic Studio Gallery in Dublin in 2009.

Limerick Printmakers (est. 1999)

4 Robert Street
Limerick
Ireland

tel   +353 (0)61 311806
email limerickprintmakers@gmail.com
web   www.limerickprintmakers.com

contact
Melissa O'Brien   *Director and Manager*

Limerick Printmakers was set up by three BA printmaking graduates from the Limerick School of Art and Design – Claire Boland, Kari Fry and Melissa O'Brien – and now benefits from strong links to Limerick School of Art and support from Limerick City Enterprise Board and Arts Council. It is located on the ground floor of a 19th-century grain store in the centre of Limerick.

MEMBERSHIP/ACCESS

Annual, six-month and three-month membership available, plus associate membership and keyholder access. A Friends of Limerick Printmakers scheme also operates. Opening hours are Monday-Friday, 11am-7.30pm, and Saturday, 10am-4pm.

COURSES/EDUCATION

Courses and classes are run in the studio and gallery for the general public and range from etching, drypoint, lithography, collagraph and woodblock printing to drawing, painting, portfolio preparation, arts and crafts. They are for all age groups (adults and children), can be adapted for various levels of skill or experience, and are available weekly or over an intensive period.

EXHIBITIONS

Since 2000 Limerick Printmakers have run a full programme of exhibitions in their own gallery space. The concept is to provide opportunities for all types of artists, emerging as well as more established, to exhibit work. Printmaking is the predominant form in this programme, but all art forms are considered for exhibition.

An annual open-submission print open runs in summer. Exchanges with other print workshops and organisations are welcomed.

EQUIPMENT

Polymetaal etching press bed
1 x 2 m | 39 x 78 in.

Art Equipment etching press bed
60 x 121 cm | 23 x 48 in.

Art Equipment hotplate
50 x 60 cm | 20 x 24 in.

Polymetaal rosin dust box SK-80
(work size) 80 x 100 cm | 32 x 40 in.

UV exposure light unit and darkroom
Radcliff & Sons lithography press
(motorised) 1 x 2 m | 39 x 78 in.

Polymetaal Jl-80 litho press
(bed size) 82 x 114 cm | 32 x 45 in.

Selection of stones
(up to) 80 x 106 cm | 32 x 42 in.

Hand levigator Asbern woodblock-editioning press bed
50 x 68 cm | 19 x 27 in.

H.G. Kippax & Sons silkscreen press
147 x 223 cm | 58 x 88 in.

Filbar silkscreen press
120 x 138 cm | 48 x 55 in.

H.G. Kippax & Sons screenprint table
142 x 152 cm | 56 x 60 in.

UV exposure light unit and darkroom

Natgraph drying cabinet
Fox Graphic silkscreen press
84 x 115 cm ┃ 33 x 46 in.

Fox Graphic silkscreen press
84 x 115 cm ┃ 33 x 46 in.

Precision silkscreen press
110 x 155 cm ┃ 44 x 61 in.

Photography wet room with professional backlit washout booth Fully equipped digital suite

MISCELLANEOUS
A bursary scheme is also available.

londonprintstudio (est. 1974)

425 Harrow Road
London
W10 4RE

tel +44 (0)20 8969 3247
+44 (0)20 8969 8271 (minicom for
deaf and hard-of-hearing customers)
email info@londonprintstudio.org.uk
web www.londonprintstudio.org.uk

contact
John Phillips   *Director*
Louise Thirlwall   *Operations Manager*

John Phillips and Pippa Smith established Paddington Printshop in 1974. In 1991 it became London Print Workshop, as they moved to larger premises, expanded the facilities and established a gallery and digital resources to complement the traditional printmaking facilities. Then in 2000, it was relaunched as londonprintstudio, a custom-designed printmaking and graphic-arts facility. With its accessible studios, residency schemes, innovative education projects, editioning projects and MA and Postgraduate Diploma in Printmaking and Professional Practice (in partnership with Buckinghamshire New University), LPS has become a benchmark for other print workshops.

MEMBERSHIP/ACCESS
Approximately 400 artists.
Annual print studio registration fee allows you to purchase sessional vouchers. You will be given a free induction to the facilities at the beginning of your first session. Open Tuesday-Saturday, 10.30am-1.30pm and 2.30-5.30pm, plus Tuesday and Wednesday evenings, 6.30-9pm. Book sessions in advance. Limited technical support is available.

COURSES/EDUCATION
A range of introductory workshops in printmaking and computer graphics run throughout the year, specifically in screenprinting, stone lithography, etching, photo-etching and digital imaging. One-to-one training is also available in all print and digital media.

LPS will run a Master's (MA) in Printmaking based at London Print Studio from January 2010 in partnership with the Buckinghamshire New University. It is run part time for two days per week for two years and includes visiting lecturers and external visits. All lectures, seminars, tuturials and demonstrations take place at LPS. Students are able to book into the London Print Studio's open-access facilities for their other studio day.

A volunteer trainee programme provides practical work experience and develops skills appropriate to the coordination and running of an open-access artists' resource and gallery.

RESIDENCIES
LPS offers a special residency programme, which runs from 1st June until the end of September. The programme is designed to enable printmakers to expand their portfolio while joining a community of printmakers and exploring London's cultural life. Independent AiR enables unsupported access, while collaborative AiR enables assistance and customised technical support.

EQUIPMENT
Rochat etching press
81 x 121 cm | 32 x 48 in.

Brand press
81 x 121 cm | 32 x 48 in.

Beevers hydraulic press
56 x 76 cm | 22 x 30 in.

Direct Grieg press for stone lithography
66 x 91 cm | 26 x 36 in.

Offset lithography press
66 x 91 cm | 26 x 36 in.

Potavac screenprint tables x 2
76 x 101 cm | 30 x 40 in.

UV light box and darkroom
Selection of screens
(up to) 99 x 144 cm | 39 x 57 in.

Extensive digital suite including large-scale
scanners and printers and dedicated
technical support

EXHIBITIONS
A front-of-house gallery presents
programme of two to three-month
exhibitions of contemporary printmaking
and related art practices. A wide selection
of limited-edition prints is also available.

MISCELLANEOUS
londonprintstudio has been designed to be
fully accessible and includes height-
adjustable sinks, seating and working
surfaces in etching, lithography, block-
printing and digital areas. An induction loop
and sound-enhancement audio loop is
installed, and colour contrasting and tactile
pathways are part of the fabric of the
building so as to assist blind and partially
sighted visitors in navigating the gallery.

LPS initiated and runs globalprintstudios,
an international print-workshop directory, 'a
free online resource to facilitate exchange
and communication within the printmaking
community'. Workshops can enter their
details on this ever-growing database.
Printmakers can search for a workshop
alphabetically, by country, by city or by
services provided. See
www.globalprintstudios.org.

London Printworks Trust (est. 1991)

Unit 7 Piano House
9 Brighton Terrace
London
SW9 8DJ

tel   +44 (0)20 7738 7841
email info@londonprintworks.com
web   www.londonprintworks.com

contact
Faye MacNulty   *Administrator*

The UK's leading textile print resource...which aims to support and promote the advancement of contemporary and experimental printed textiles to a broad and diverse audience, support creative practitioners working in printed textiles, throughout their careers.

MEMBERSHIP/ACCESS
Fully equipped open access textile print and design studio to hire by members and non-members, supported by expert Workshop Co-ordinators. Open Monday to Saturday 10am – 5.30pm

COURSES/EDUCATION
A variety of courses in textile print for beginners and more experienced printers. Typical courses include 5 day introductory screen printing, (involving pigment, polychromatic and heat transfer printing), one day textile induction and repeat pattern printing.

EXHIBITIONS
London Printworks Trust has it's own gallery and runs a specialist exhibition programme that commissions new work from a variety of artists. Artists such as Mark Wallinger, Yinka Shonibari, Adam Chodzco and Bill Woodrow and many more have collaborated onprojects. The Homespun exhibition programme aims to showcase the very best of contemporary and experimental printed textiles.

EQUIPMENT
Print tables with registration bars x 2
6 m x 1.5 | 334 x 59in.

Sample table
3 m x 1.5 | 117 x 59in.

Screen washout area

Baker and steamer

Dye area

Exposure unit
90cm x 120cm | 35 x 47 in.

Heat press A2 42cm x 58cm | 16 x 23in.

Computer design suite

MISCELLANEOUS
The Surface Bursary Scheme supports recent art and design graduates with a grant, one-to-one support, access to London Printworks and free studio space at ASC studios.

SCREEN SERVICE
London Printworks also offers a small scale production service. This includes a screen making service and a fabric printing service for small runs of repeat pattern, t-shirts, banners, cushions and lots more. The LPT Technicians works one to one with each client.

Lorg Fine Art Printmakers (est. 2005)

Unit 8 Ballybane Enterprise Centre
Ballybane
Galway City
Ireland

tel   +353 861 714 877
email lorgprintmakers@gmail.com
web   www.lorgprintmakers.com

Formerly Connaught Association of Printmakers, Lorg was set up in order to create a 24-hour-access print workshop in Galway. A growth in the numbers using the Galway-Mayo Institute of Technology print facilities as part of a print club created a demand for extra facilities. A group of printmaking graduates – Ursula Kelly, Denise McDonagh, Paula Gleeson and Leigh-Anne Seale – together with a number of other local supporters drove a campaign for a print studio in Galway to a successful conclusion, namely, the opening of Lorg Fine Art Printmakers. Lorg aims to 'heighten the awareness of printmaking as an accessible, unique and innovative art form', and encourages digital image-making, multimedia printmaking and the use of other recent innovations in printmaking.

MEMBERSHIP/ACCESS
125 members.
Various levels of membership are available: associate (access during open hours), part-time (six-month) and full-time (24-hour access). Open Tuesday to Saturday, 11am-6pm.

COURSES/EDUCATION
Courses are run for beginners, intermediate and advanced printmakers. The invited artists programme continues to welcome guest printmakers to give talks and demonstrations. Lorg Printmakers also offer two bursaries annually to graduates of the Galway-Mayo Institute of Technology.

EQUIPMENT
Natgraph hand-screenprint table
102 x 152 cm | 40 x 60 in.

Natgraph self-contained exposure unit
(max. frame size) 102 x 152 cm | 40 x 60 in.

2 light boxes
66 x 122 cm | 26 x 48 in.

Washout room with Kärcher power hose & backlit washout booth

Polymetaal JW 100 etching presses x 2
100 x 200 cm | 40 x 80 in.

Vertical etching tank

Hotplate
63 x 76 cm | 25 x 30 in.

Light box
66 x 122 cm | 26 x 48 in.

Acid room with acrylic-resist booth

Furnival offset lithographic press
(max. print size) 51 x 61 cm | 20 x 24 in.

Apple Mac G4 with dual-screen digital-editing suite including, Final Cut Pro HD, IMovie, IDVD and DVD Studio Pro

Epson Stylus 9800 44in. B0+ Printer High Speed 8/9

Equipment available for rental: Epson EMP 62+ projector 2000 ANSI lumens, SVGA (accessories include Mac adapter); Canon EOS digital stills camera 400D 18-55 kit 10.1 MPix DSLR; Sony HDR-FX1HDV 1080i camcorder – high-definition video handycam with 3 x 1 megapixel CCDs, Carl Zeiss® Vario-Sonnar T* lens and a host of manual features.

EXHIBITIONS

Lorg is involved in many projects, showing members' work in various venues in Galway and further afield, and encouraging exchanges. 'We strive to collaborate with as many artists' studios and other arts organisations where possible.' Exhibitions and projects have previously included involvement in the Galway Arts Festival and the Tulca Season of Visual Art. Lorg aim to keep printmaking dynamic and contemporary with projects that in the past have included exhibitions in non-standard spaces such as billboards or by putting children's prints on the sides of buses.

Lovers Knot (est. 2007)

22-27 The Oval
Bethnal Green
London
EC2 9DT

tel +44 (0)7796094980 Ian Steadman
     +44 (0)7910941188 Graham Hughes
email ianjsteadman@btopenworld.com
      graham.hughes@rca.ac.uk

Set up by Ian Steadman, a lecturer from Middlesex, and Graham Hughes a print tutor at The Royal College of Art, Lovers' Knot is well equipped to cope with large scale prints. Membership is limited to 2 people to keep it exclusive.

MEMBERSHIP/ACCESS
Open access Tuesday and Thursday 6.00pm – 10.00pm.

COURSES/EDUCATION
Etching and screenprinting evening classes available Tues 6.00pm – 10.00pm, Wednesday 6.00pm – 9.00pm, Friday, 6.00pm – 9.00pm

EQUIPMENT
Large scale intaglio press
107cm x 200cm | 42 x 79in

Winstone stone litho press
60cm x 95cm | 23 x 37in

Oil and water based screenprinting
165cm x 390cm | 65 x 115in

Maplebeck Press (est. 2005)

Maplebeck Farmhouse
Maplebeck
nr. Newark
Nottinghamshire
NG22 0BS

tel   +44 (0)1636 636825
email pf@maplepress.co.uk

contact
Patricia Ferguson   *Owner*

A private press beautifully situated in converted stables, Maplebeck is a fine example of how individuals can contribute to the overall provision of printmaking by opening their doors and offering support and advice as well as excellent facilities for a few 'regulars'. The space has been designed to great effect and is a pleasure to use.

MEMBERSHIP/ACCESS
12 regular users.
Open on a seasonal basis for up to three days a week, plus an evening session.

COURSES/EDUCATION
There are introductory courses in etching, collagraph and relief printing. Course participants are then welcome to sign up to become 'members.

Using a small portable press, they can also take printmaking out to schools and groups.

EQUIPMENT
Rochat etching press
81m x 137 cm | 32 x 54 in.

Nitric and ferric etching

Resin aquatint

Small vice press

MISCELLANEOUS
Maplebeck Press has also set up Newark Printmakers' Group, who meet at Millgate Museum, Newark, which houses a complete printers' shop on the top floor.

Milton Keynes Printmakers (est. 1988)

South Pavilion
Courtyard Arts Centre
Great Linford
Milton Keynes
MK14 5DZ

tel   +44 (0)844 3578293
email info@mkprintmakers.co.uk
web   www.mkprintmakers.co.uk

contact
Di Oliver   *Chair*

WORKSHOP

Situated in an 18th-century pavilion, a listed building located in the beautiful surroundings of the parkland of Great Linford Manor (now a recording studio in private ownership), the South Pavilion is part of Artworks-MK, a charitable trust running an arts centre in the Manor complex. This includes a gallery/theatre, as well as ceramics, jewellery and woodworking areas, and artists' studios in the almshouses.

MEMBERSHIP/ACCESS
30 members.
Membership is for keyholders only, so members must have a proven track record in printmaking. New members are accepted on submission of a portfolio and CV. Members are required to take part in the running of the group.

COURSES/EDUCATION
There are ongoing series of classes offering instruction in monoprint, collagraph and drypoint, as well as occasional masterclasses by guest tutors in subjects including book-making, etching, photopolymer printing, transfer printing and wood engraving.

EQUIPMENT
Bewick & Wilson etching press
61 x 121 cm | 24 x 48 in.

Lawrence portable etching press
30 x 61 cm | 12 x 24 in.

UV light box/exposure uni
76 x 91 cm | 30 x 36 in.

Bewick & Wilson hotplate
51 x 66 cm | 20 x 26 in.

Ferric and nitric available, with extraction booth

EXHIBITIONS
Members have an active exhibitions programme and an extensive profile of local and national shows. They exhibit regularly both as a group and as individuals. International exchanges have also been run in the past and are welcomed in the future.

Morley College Print Room (est. c 1967)

Morley College
61 Westminster Bridge Road
London
SE1 7HT

tel   +44 (0)20 7450 1842
email enquiries@morleycollege.ac.uk
web   www.morleycollege.ac.uk

contact
Frank Connely   Head of Printmaking
frank.connelly@morleycollege.ac.uk

Morley College is 'one of the oldest adult education colleges in the country' having been set up in the 1880s. It runs many courses including languages, music & drama, humanities and visual arts. As well as its courses it has an open access element allowing ex-students and visiting printmakers to make use of the print facilities. There are good facilities for etching/ intaglio, stone/plate lithography and relief printing.

MEMBERSHIP/ACCESS
The open access print workshop usually runs for 6 weeks during term time. The workshop is aimed at all artists/ printmakers who have extensive experience of printmaking or who have studied printmaking at Morley. Those who are less experienced are encouraged to enrol onto one of the regular courses, which are aimed at all levels (see below).

COURSES/EDUCATION
Rolling programme of courses in beginner, intermediate and advanced printmaking, including 'traditional', 'new' and 'photo-etching'. These run in blocks of 9, 10, 11 or 12 weeks during term time. Beginners complete an introductory course that includes monoprint, intaglio (drypoint, etching, collagraphs, photo-etching), relief print (lino/woodcut). Intermediate and advanced students pursue personal project work in chosen media and are also introduced to new methods, as appropriate. The Summer school focuses on shorter 'taster' courses as an opportunity to concentrate on the particular or to introduce new methods and techniques. All classes are taught by practising artists.

EQUIPMENT
Rochat etching press
68cm x 110cm | 27" x 44" (Max. Print size)

D & J Grieg Etching Press
38cm x 95cm | 15" x 38" (Max. Print size)

Bendini etching press
53cm x 70cm | 21" x 28" (Max. Print size-for monoprint)

Resin aquatint booth
to take plate size 53cm x 70cm | 21" x 28"

Nitric etching (some ferric by demand)

Fume cabinet

Photo etching (aqua blue developer)

Hopkins & Cole relief press
45cm x 60cm | 18" x 24"(Max. Print size)

W.Notting relief press
12" x 18" (Max. Print Size)

Tilting vacuum frame and light source
70cm x 80cm | 28" x 32"

Nakashini Offset Litho Press
59cm x 40cm | 28" (Plate size: 23.5" x 16")

Stone Litho Press
70cm x 53cm | 28" x21"

OTHER
All students are taught to work independently and to a professional standard. They have opportunities to discuss and question other artists' work, including that of peers, national and international artists and new trends in printmaking. They are also taught to develop critical decision-making skills in relation to both their own work and as a member of a group.

They are encouraged to submit work to open exhibitions externally throughout the year and there are also opportunities to organise and take part in exhibitions at the Morley Gallery.

North Notts Non-toxic Print Workshop (est. 2006)

Studio 4
West Workshops
Harley Foundation
Welbeck
Worksop
Nottinghamshire
S80 3LW

tel   +44 (0)1246 822997 or
       +44 (0)7761 62 7078
email sarahgodfrey73@hotmail.com
web   www.nontoxicprintmaking.co.uk

contact
Sarah Godfrey

Set in the Welbeck Estate behind the excellent Harley Gallery, the workshop is part of an extensive range of individual artists' studios. Its aim is to 'encourage an awareness and provide opportunity for people to experience for themselves non-toxic printmaking practices, through provision of high-quality exhibitions and interesting and engaging art workshops'. It is run by Sarah Godfrey who 'welcomes people of all ages and ability to the workshop with the attitude art is for all'.

MEMBERSHIP/ACCESS
Limited open-access facility available to those who have attended an induction to the workshop. These take the form of pre-booked days as and when they are required by visiting artists.

COURSES/EDUCATION
Workshops include non-toxic Intaglio-Type (using ImagON film as developed by Prof. Keith Howard),* monoprint/monotype, drypoint, woodcut/lino, and collagraph/carborundum. Workshops are suitable for all levels, from the complete beginner to the professional. The amount of people attending is kept to a minimum in order to give each person enough time and space to gain as much as possible from the experience. Sarah is also available to visit schools, art societies and groups to provide demonstrations and workshops.

EQUIPMENT
Large etching press (make unknown)
59 x 91 cm | 23 x 36 in.

Intaglio etching press
36 x 61 cm | 14 x 24 in.

Natgraph UV exposure uni
69 x 100 cm | 27 x 40 in.

MISCELLANEOUS
Sarah also has a printmaking consultancy business through which she provides expertise and training for colleges and other print studios with regards to the setting up of non-toxic printmaking practices.

*NB Sarah does not use acid, but prefers the non-etch Intaglio-Type as an environmentally friendly approach to printmaking; she also uses exclusively water-based inks.

Northern Print Studio (est. 1994)

Stepney Bank
Ouseburn
Newcastle upon Tyne
NE1 2NP

tel   +44 (0)191 261 7000
email enquiry@northernprint.org.uk
web   www.northernprint.org.uk

contact
Anna Wilkinson   *Director*

WORKSHOP

In autumn 2006 Northern Print, a not-for-profit studio and gallery revenue-funded by The Arts Council, moved from Fish Quay, North Shields to new facilities in Ouseburn in Newcastle upon Tyne. The new facilities are housed across two floors in 280 sq. m (3000 sq. ft) of renovated building. NPS have been a flagship print workshop for some years, with residencies, partnerships and innovative projects in printmaking and an enviable education/outreach programme. The move to new premises helps reinforce and build on its existing reputation as a major resource and advocate of printmaking.

MEMBERSHIP/ACCESS
170 members.
Standard membership, but also graduate membership – a free membership for those who have graduated within the previous 12 months. Open Tuesday to Saturday, 10am to 5pm, with late-night opening on Thursday until 9pm; the gallery is open Wednesday-Friday, 11am-5pm, and Saturday,12 noon-4pm.

COURSES/EDUCATION
'We aim to make printmaking accessible to everyone through a programme of classes and courses. We offer professional training in all aspects of printmaking as well as introductory courses for beginners. There is also a schools and groups education programme, and we hold frequent events for children and families.' Projects are frequently developed in partnership with other arts and non-arts organisations and have engaged with subjects as diverse as science and art, heritage, geography and industry.

EQUIPMENT
Bewick & Wilson electric press
106 x 178 cm │ 42 x 70 in.

Polymetaal press (JSV-60)
59 x 120 cm │ 23 x 47 in.

Electric Polymetaal press (JWEV-80)
79 x 160 cm │ 31 x 63 in.

Rochat etching press
66 x 122 cm │ 26 x 48 in.

Albion relief press
32 x 45 cm │ 12 x 18 in.

Kippax 3-D Handbed screen table
112 x 155 cm │ 44 x 61 in.

Kippax semi-automatic screen bed
107 x 140 cm │ 42 x 55 in.

Small portable etching press available for outreach

Digital suite with A3 inkjet printer

Education room

Editioning room

Darkroom with enlarger

EXHIBITIONS
NPS has its own gallery space and a dynamic programme of print exhibitions. Members are also encouraged to take part in exhibitions. A corporate sales service is available to work in conjunction with businesses for a bespoke art package.

EDITIONING

A separate room/press, available to artists, is set aside for the editioning service. NPS has a wide experience of collaborating with artists on contract printing and co-publication.

MISCELLANEOUS

The gallery is also available for hire as a venue for events and corporate hospitality.

North Star Printmakers (est.1977)

North Star Studios
65 Ditchling Road
Brighton
East Sussex

tel   +44 (0)1273 601041
email info@northstarprintmakers.co.uk
web   www.northstarprintmakers.co.uk

WORKSHOP

North Star Studios is a printmaking co-operative situated in the centre of Brighton, 5 minutes walk from Brighton station and the heart of the North Laine. The studios comprise of 5 main areas - etching, lithography, screenprinting, relief and photography.

MEMBERSHIP/ACCESS
17 members.
Each member of the studio is a key holder enabling access to North Star 24 hours, 7 days a week to all areas and disciplines.

EDUCATION/COURSES
As a co-operative we exhibit on a regular basis at numerous venues including North Star itself.

EQUIPMENT
Etching press (Dowling Design)
65cm x 135cm | 26in x 54in

George Mann & Co. off-set lithography press
57cm x 85cm | 22in x 33in

Relief press
70cm x 132cm | 27in x 51in

Screen bed
120cm x 165cm | 47in x 65in

Nitric etching

Resin aquatint box

Photography dark room

EXHIBITIONS
'As a co-operative we exhibit on a regular basis at numerous venues including North Star itself.' The studio opens its doors annually to the public as part of the Open Houses for the Brighton Festival in May.

Oaks Editions Lithography Studio (est. 1998)

The Old Stables
Oaks Park
Croydon Lane
Sutton
SM7 3BA

tel   +44 (0)20 8542 4541
      (no phone at studio)
email simonburder@oaksfineart.co.uk
web   www.oaksfineart.co.uk

Oaks Editions Lithography Studio is a professional artist-printmaker's workshop, fully equipped with two direct presses for stone lithography. It is part of Oaks Park Studios, converted stable buildings on the former estate of the Earl of Derby, now an attractive public park. There is a café conveniently placed next door.

MEMBERSHIP/ACCESS
Primarily an editioning workshop, there are also a small number of regulars who use it, to produce an edition of prints or having completed a course at the Studio. This is purely by 'mutual arrangement', with the owner, Simon Burder, in attendance.

COURSES/EDUCATION
Stone lithography courses are organised several times a year, both at weekends and on weekdays. They are suitable for artists with or without previous experience of printmaking. Other course formats and dates are negotiable: for example, a recent one-day course was run for curators from the Word & Image Department of the V&A Museum. Lithography demonstrations are also given. One-to-one tuition is also available, with exclusive use of the studio at these times.

EQUIPMENT
Krause direct litho press
56 x 76cm | 22 x 30 in.

Winstone semi-automatic direct litho press
56 x 76 cm | 22 x 30 in.

Around 20 stones
(various sizes up to) 56 x 76 cm | 22 x 30 in.)

Flat-bed galley press (letterpress & lino)
36 x 56 cm | 14 x 22 in.

Intaglio tabletop press
51 x 101 cm | 20 x 40 in.

Hotplate

Stone moving trolley

EXHIBITIONS
Studio artists regularly exhibit both nationally and internationally.

EDITIONING
Oaks Editions Lithography is able to offer a collaborative printing service to suit the individual artist. All projects are discussed fully and an estimate made which can take account of varying levels of involvement with the production of editions. Simon Burder has worked with many artists over the last 20 years, and is widely respected, with work having featured in various printmaking books. He graduated from Exeter College of Art and was awarded a French Government Scholarship to study lithography at the École des Beaux-Arts. He has continued to work primarily with stone lithography and has shown regularly in Britain and abroad. He also teaches at City Lit, Putney School of Art and Sutton College of Learning for Adults.

Ochre Print Studio (est. 2007)

Lockwood Centre
9-13 Westfield Road
Slyfield Industrial Estate
Guildford
Surrey
GU1 1RR

tel   +44 (0)7988 229763
email info@ochreprintstudio.co.uk
web   www.ochreprintstudio.co.uk

Ochre was originally set up by Julie Hoyle and Angela Poole. The studio occupies a large space, the envy of many print workshops, and is expanding to include a 'non-toxic etching' facility. A team of artists run a number of other facilities at the centre, including a glass kiln, a ceramics studio and an editing suite, all with the stated aim to 'encourage a lively inclusive arts community where skills are shared, ideas are exchanged and experimentation can be enjoyed by all.'

MEMBERSHIP/ACCESS
The studio is open Tuesdays, 6-9pm, and Saturdays 10-4pm.

COURSES/EDUCATION
Varied evening and weekend beginners' and intermediate courses, as well as masterclasses, taught by a number of visiting experienced facilitators. Workshops are also available for schools and people with learning difficulties.

EQUIPMENT
Etching press
84 x 120 cm | 33 x 48 in.

Bradbury Wilkinson etching press
56 x 121 cm | 22 x 48 in.

2 x Pottervac screenprint bed
111 x 161 cm | 44 x 64 in.

Mylar screenprint bed
86 x 111 cm | 34 x 44 in.

Kippax screenprint bed
61 x 81 cm | 24 x 32 in.

Large-format exposure unit (vacuumed print-down frame)

Textile-printing facilities with two large padded tables
Small screen bed (ideal for book arts)

Small book-arts relief press

Adana press

Large-format inkjet

and film printing service

Oxford Printmakers Cooperative (est. 1976)

The Christadelphian Church Hall
Tynedale Road
Oxford
OX4 1JL

tel +44 (0)1865 726472
email oxfordprintmakers@hotmail.co.uk
web www.oxfordprintmakers.co.uk

MEMBERSHIP/ACCESS

Full (keyholder, 24-hour access), standard (access 18 hours a day), associate and day/hourly membership. Open Mondays, 4-8pm, Tuesdays, 10.30am-6.30pm, Saturdays, 11am-5pm. The workshop is not staffed at other times. All new members are required to do 20 probationary hours before being admitted.

COURSES/EDUCATION

A range of short courses on print processes such as etching, lithography, collagraph, mixed-media printmaking, monoprinting, papermaking, relief printing, screenprinting and viscosity etching, plus safe etching based on the Edinburgh Print Workshop model. The studio has had many demonstrations from visiting artists, notably Helen Chadwick, William Hayter and Krishna Reddy. Community outreach work is also offered, taking a portable etching press to schools and community groups for taster sessions in printmaking. The OPC occasionally takes on school students for one week's work experience. This is negotiated with the school and the hours are arranged between student and technician.

EQUIPMENT

Rochat etching press
81 x 163 cm | 32 x 65 in.

Rochat etching press
66 x 121 cm | 26 x 48 in.

Portable etching press
41 x 61 cm | 16 x 24 in.

Resin aquatint booth fume cupboard for nitric etching

Albion relief press
56 x 84 cm | 22 x 33 in.

Two nipping presses
(largest) 41 x 54 cm | 16 x 21 in.

Furnival direct litho press
56 x 84 cm | 22 x 33 in.

Selection of stones

Photolitho plates also in stock

Adelco vacuum bed
51 x 76 cm | 20 x 30 in.

A number of portable hinged boards

Darkroom for photo-etch and photoscreen

EXHIBITIONS

Over the years, Oxford Printmakers has been involved in many exhibitions in the UK and overseas.

MISCELLANEOUS

Consultancy and advice available as well as a print-process and print-supply database which many people refer to. Links with other print workshops in the UK and abroad have involved residencies and exchanges.

Peacock Visual Arts (est. 1974)

21 Castle Street
Aberdeen
AB11 5BQ

tel   +44 (0)1224 639539
email info@peacockvisualarts.co.uk
web   www.peacockvisualarts.co.uk

Established as Peacock Printmakers (Aberdeen) Ltd. In 2001 it was renamed Peacock Visual Arts to reflect its current status, having expanded to include video production facilities, photography and digital media suites in 'the widest range of visual arts production facilities openly available in Scotland'. The print workshop is set on two floors, with screenprinting on the upper floor and etching, lithography and relief on the lower floor. All are set in a spacious warehouse accommodating 14 staff and a team of volunteers.

MEMBERSHIP/ACCESS
Open Tuesday to Saturday, 9.30am-5.30pm. There is no membership as such, just a daily hire charge.

COURSES/EDUCATION
Courses in screenprinting, etching, stone lithography and relief printing, as well as photography, digital media and video.

EQUIPMENT
Rochat etching press
60 x 100 cm | 23 x 39 in.

Electric etching press
130 x 165 cm | 51 x 65 in.

Nitric and ferric etching

Acid bath (various sizes of tray)
(up to) 165 x 130 cm | 51 x 65 in.

Acrylic aquatint spray booth
89 x 142 cm | 35 x 56 in.

Hotplates x 2
61 x 76 cm | 24 x 30 in.

Metal guillotine (plates)
(cutting width) 91 cm | 36 in.

Mann Direct litho press
(stone & plate litho, plus Toyobo intaglio)
65 x 90 cm | 25 x 35 in.

Columbian relief press
50 x 60 cm | 19 x 23 in.

Paper guillotine x 2
(cutting width – largest) 122 cm | 48 in.

Water bath x 2
(largest) 104 x 132 cm | 41 x 52 in.

Kippax screen bed
150 x 221 cm | 59 x 87 in.

Kippax screen bed
1@ 124 x 150 cm | 49 x 59 in.
2@ 99 x 145 cm | 39 x 57 in.

Kippax screen bed (for editioning)
124 x 145 cm | 49 x 76 in

UV exposure light (5kW bulb)

Exposure table (glass tilting bed)
185 x 236 cm | 73 x 93 in

Light box
76 x 106 cm | 30 x 42 in

Various plan chests for hire (x 51)
up to 89 x 127 cm | 35 x 50 in.

Digital suite and video

Photography darkroom

EXHIBITIONS

There is a programme of changing exhibitions in both the main gallery and shop. 'We organise an annual programme of national and international contemporary-art exhibitions, as well as talks, critical debates and workshops.' A shop also sells original prints and original artworks from regional, national and international artists.

MISCELLANEOUS

Peacock Visual Arts have put forward a proposal for a centre for contemporary art to be set in a new iconic building in Aberdeen's Union Terrace Gardens. Aberdeen City Council has now, in principle, given their backing to the project.

Poole Printmakers (est. 1991)

5 Bowling Green Alley
Poole
Dorset
BH15 1AG

email Lizcotton123@hotmail.com

WORKSHOP

Set in a lovely, restored 17th-century cartshed 'with flagstoned yard and a rural air', near the centre of Poole, this workshop oozes 'olde worlde' charm and prides itself on its history. It is run as a cooperative on a voluntary basis.

MEMBERSHIP/ACCESS
47 members.
Full keyholder membership plus a friends scheme.

COURSES/EDUCATION
Regular courses are available for beginners and those wishing to learn new processes in woodcut, wood engraving, lino, screenprint, lithography, etching and drypoint. Local schools use the workshop to expand their pupils' experience, and Poole Printmakers have worked with special needs groups on long-term education projects.

EQUIPMENT
Tofko etching press
56 x 89 cm │ 22 x 35 in.

Hopkinson & Cope Albion relief press
31 x 41 cm │ 12 x 16 in.

Hopkinson & Cope Albion relief press
61 x 76 cm │ 24 x 30 in.

Two small vice presses

Ferric etching facilities

Solar-plate etching

EXHIBITIONS
The studio usually holds four or five exhibitions every year at local venues. It is also involved on an annual basis in Dorset Art Week and Poole Art Week.

Porthmeor Print Workshop (est. 1995)

The Penwith Gallery
Black Road West
St Ives
Cornwall
TR26 1NL

tel   +44 (0)1736 799194
email rachael@kantaris.com
web   www.kantaris.com/rachael/
       workshop.htm

contact
Rachael Kantaris

Situated amongst the backstreets of St Ives in a converted barn, the workshop is close to the beautiful seafront and galleries that make this such a tourist area. The workshop has very good natural light and is well laid out. It has a very good creative environment, with lots of charm and character.

MEMBERSHIP/ACCESS
Open access, with separate hire charges members' and non-members'. Open Saturday, Monday and Wednesday 10.30 am – 5.30 pm and Tuesday 10.30 am – 9.30 pm.

COURSES/EDUCATION
Two to three courses per year in collagraph and monoprinting.

EQUIPMENT
Rochat etching press
66cm x 76mm ｜ 26 x 30 in

Star-wheel etching presses
66cm x 76mm ｜ 26 x 30 in

Etching press
66cm x 76mm ｜ 26 x 30 in
Colombian relief press

EXHIBITIONS
All members have an exhibition each year in the 'gallery' space at the front of the workshop.

Print Club (est. Sept 2007)

Unit 3
Miller's Avenue
Dalston
London
E8 2DS

tel   +44 (0) 7894 033787 (mob.) or
       +44 (0) 7780 853757 (mob.)
email info@printclublondon.com
web   www.printclublondon.com

contact
Fred Higginson   *Director*
Rose Stallard   *Creative Director*

WORKSHOP

Set up in 2007 by Fred Higginson (sculptor) and Rose Stallard (illustrator), Print Club is designed to work as a members' water-based screenprinting club enabling illustrators and designers to produce posters, T-shirts, record covers and all things screenprinted.

The trend for screenprinting in the UK died down in the late eighties but is gaining momentum again. Print Club aims to revive screenprinting by providing a laidback yet productive, affordable environment, enabling designers to go from laptop to inky hands.

MEMBERSHIP/ACCESS
40 members.
New members are welcome. Open 24 hours a day, 7 days a week. If you have a basic knowledge of screenprinting or have completed a beginner's workshop you can become a member at Print Club (as long as there is space available).

COURSES/EDUCATION
If you have little or no previous screenprinting experience Print Club runs a short workshop in both paper and T-shirt printing to get you started. It also runs courses off site in conjunction with Rough Trade Records, while its Pull a Sicky workshop is aimed at getting design and creative companies to come and hang out at Print Club for a day of team building, creative thinking and T-shirt printing.

EXHIBITIONS
Print Club runs a couple of big shows every year which bring together a mixture of established and emerging illustrators and designers for a bonanza of hand-pulled, screenprinted posters.

EQUIPMENT
Vacuum beds x 2
76 x 102 cm | 30 x 40 in.

Vacuum beds x 2
102 x 152 cm | 40 x 60 in.

Parker Exposure unit A0 plus (max. paper size)

Washout/screen-coating room

2- or 4-colour T-shirt carousel

T-shirt tunnel dryer

Heat press

A3 black & white photocopier

A0 light box

G3 and black & white A4 printer

Screen/paper/ink storage

MISCELLANEOUS
Print Club has an online shop selling members' and invited artists' work. It also runs a creative service under the name Tuckshop, which offers illustration, design, and short-run bespoke screenprinting.

Print Market Workshop (est. 1997)

Chapter Arts Centre
Market Road
Canton
Cardiff
CF5 1QE

tel   +44 (0)7775 707875
email pete@printmarketworkshop.co.uk
web   www.printmarketworkshop.co.uk

contact
Pete Williams or Lou Thornton

Set up by Pete Williams and Lou Thornton just outside Cardiff City Centre, Print Market Workshop is well equipped, and Pete and Lou are renowned for their innovative work, not least the large-scale woodcut commissions for the Wales Millennium Centre, as well as their work with schools. However, following a recent re-organisation of the Chapter Arts Centre, which saw a move to another site within the building, Pete is looking to move the workshop to larger premises in Cardiff.

MEMBERSHIP/ACCESS
Print Market Workshop operates an open-access policy for two days every week, though booking is essential.

COURSES/EDUCATION
A range of weekend courses are run by Pete and Lou, along with various guest tutors, in screenprinting, acrylic-resist etching, stone lithography, drypoint, monoprinting and paper lithography. Projects with schools and community organisations are undertaken, and have proven to be dynamic and on a large scale.

EQUIPMENT
Rollaco etching press
(approx.) 46 x 91 cm | 18 x 36 in.

Converted mangle press
(approx.) 61 x 121 cm | 24 x 48 in.

Stone lithography press

Ferric etching

Silkscreen vacuum bed (large)

EXHIBITIONS
The exhibition programme includes international art fairs and a strong relationship with both the Howard Gardens Gallery and CBAT Gallery in Cardiff Bay. International exhibitions have included those in the USA and India and, more recently, China, Italy, Germany and Norway. Print Market Workshop regard exhibitions as 'crucial to our aim of establishing print as a contemporary and developing practice'.

EDITIONING
The workshop has an established editioning service, with artists working with the Print Market to develop new work and to produce final images.

MISCELLANEOUS
The workshop owes much of its success to the external commissions and projects it undertakes, which support and underpin the workshop as a facility.

Prospect Studios

137-141 Burnley Road East
Waterfoot
Rossendale
BB4 9DP

tel   +44 (0)7757186327
email abirch@ambirch.freeserve.co.uk

An artists' studio occupying three floors, located half a mile from the centre of Waterfoot and two miles from the M66. There is a direct bus from Manchester.

MEMBERSHIP/ACCESS

Access is limited to weekend classes, which take place from 10am to 4pm Saturday and Sunday. There are 20-30 regular users attending weekend classes on a regular basis.

EQUIPMENT

Art Equipment etching press
46 x 84 cm | 18 x 33 in.

Art equipment relief press
46 x 100 cm | 18 x 40 in.

Main processes: nitric-acid etch, resin aquatint with zinc plates

Class members also work in drypoint, collagraph, woodcut and linocut.

COURSES/EDUCATION

Individual tuition and group workshops by arrangement, with groups limited to a maximum of nine people. Weekend classes take place once a month. Accommodation can be arranged locally. Classes suitable for beginners as well as artists looking to develop their work into print. Alan also runs workshops for schools and galleries such as the Whitworth Art Gallery and other galleries around Greater Manchester.

EXHIBITIONS

Class members have organised exhibitions as well as exhibiting prints at fairs throughout the North-west. They have also won print awards and been selected for various national print exhibitions.

Red Hot Press (est. 2004)

The Corn Exchange
Old Cattle Market
Terminus Terrace
Southampton
SO14 3FE

tel   Sarah Mander on 07790 870558
        (mob.) or Katherine Anteney on
        07814 016563 (mob.)
email   inforhp@redhotpress.org.uk
web   www.redhotpress.org.uk

Set up by two Southampton-based printmakers, Sarah Mander and Katherine Anteney, Red Hot Press is situated in an Edwardian building in a small business area near the centre of Southampton. It is small but well laid out and uncluttered, with facilities for saline-sulphate etching, drypoint, collagraph and relief printing. 'We try to run the workshop as safely as possible, cutting out the use of solvents to clean up with, and using safer washable inks and safe etching techniques.'

MEMBERSHIP/ACCESS
30 members.
Full annual membership (renewable every September) as well as non-member schemes for hire of the workshop facilities on a daily and half-day basis. 'People have to do an induction to use the workshop, and once we are happy that they can use the facilities safely we allow them to hire the workshop unsupervised. We have supervised practice days (one per month) for people with some printmaking experience who need technical support using the facility.'

COURSES/EDUCATION
Regular courses in linocut and woodcut (Japanese and western), monoprinting, drypoint, saline-sulphate etching, collagraph and bookbinding. There are also tailored workshops for schools and colleges, as well as a bi-monthly get-together called Cuppa Culture, with artist talks, demonstrations and an opportunity for people to show their work.

EQUIPMENT
Art Equipment etching press
122 x 61 cm | 48 x 24 in.

Galley press for relief printing
58 x 43 cm | 23 x 17 in.

Portable relief press
30 x 21 cm | 8 x 12 in.

Letterpress x 2 (for printing type)

EXHIBITIONS
Annual members' exhibition, usually in Southampton. Members exhibit nationally and internationally.

MISCELLANEOUS
Commissions undertaken, including editioning. Team-building days are also provided for businesses, as well as workshops for schools and colleges.

Ropewalk Contemporary Art & Craft (est. 2000)

The Printmaking Studio
Maltkiln Road
Barton-upon-Humber
North Lincolnshire
DN18 5JT

tel   +44 (0)1652 660380 (reception)
email melissa@the-ropewalk.supanet.com,
      (education and workshops)
web   www.the-ropewalk.co.uk

contact
Tim Needham

WORKSHOP

A print workshop set within a contemporary craft centre which was extensively redeveloped in 2000 and 2005, and now houses artists' studios and creative industries businesses, as well as three gallery spaces.

MEMBERSHIP/ACCESS
25 members.
Access to the print studio is available on either an hourly, sessional or day rate. Regular sessions with the Ropewalk Print Group are held on Wednesdays between 12.30pm and 4.30pm

COURSES/EDUCATION
Occasional print courses and taster courses as part of a larger programme of art and craft classes. Educational workshop service available to schools and groups, delivered by experienced artists, including tailor-made training sessions for business. In-house printmaker Tim Needham is also available to offer technical support on a day rate if required.

EQUIPMENT
Art Equipment floor-standing etching press
24 x 49 cm | 9 x 19 in.

Portable etching press
31 x 61 cm | 12 x 24 in.

Hotplate
51 x 61 cm | 20 x 24 in.

Aquatint booth
43 x 43 cm | 17 x 17 in.

Fume cupboard
30 x 55 cm | 12 x 22 in.

Ferric etching for copper and zinc

EXHIBITIONS
The large gallery houses a changing programme of contemporary art exhibitions as well as national touring exhibitions from The Hayward. Submissions for shows are accepted throughout the year. Exhibitions also include the British Miniature Print Exhibition on tour, exchange exhibitions with workshops such as Edinburgh Printmakers and Artichoke Print Workshop plus one-person shows by local and national printmakers.

MISCELLANEOUS
A photography darkroom is annexed to the print room, with three quality enlargers and wet-room processing.

Seacourt Print Workshop (est. 1980)

Unit 33, Dunlop Industrial units
8 Ballo Drive
Bangor
Northern Ireland

tel   0298 914 60595
email   robertpeters@seacourt-ni.org
web   www.seacourt-ni.org.uk

WORKSHOP

Moved to current premises in 2006, having previously been in the basement of the Carnegie Library since 1989. Seacourt has been very active with residencies and projects over the years. 'Seacourt strives, whenever possible, to use safe and non-toxic materials and methods. It was the first print workshop in Ireland to adopt Acrylic-Resist Etching techniques, as promoted by Edinburgh Printmakers.'

MEMBERSHIP/ACCESS
37 members
Membership schemes include keyholder, non-key-holder and irregular users.
Open Monday – Friday 9.00am – 5.00pm.

COURSES/EDUCATION
8 week courses and weekend courses available in a range of print media including drypoint, collagraphs, etching, screenprinting, general printmaking, and photo-intaglio. One-to-one tuition also available in any of the above techniques and lithography.

EQUIPMENT
Harry Rochat etching presses
66cm x 116cm ┃ 26 x 46in

Harry Rochat etching press
81cm x 158cm ┃ 32 x 63in

Guillotine for cutting metal plates

Polymetaal direct litho press
76cm x 101cm ┃ 30 x 40in

Motor-driven litho press (make unkown)
76cm x 101cm ┃ 30 x 40in
John Grieg direct hand press
8cm x 61cm ┃ 15 x 24in

A selection of limestone litho stones, aluminium plates and photo-positive plates are also available

Columbian Press
51cm x 66cm ┃ 20 x 26in

A hand-operated 24 x 32in cylinder proofing press

A number of book presses of various sizes
Vacuum Printing Table with squeegee arm, available printing surface 1 x 1.5 metres

A self-contained Exposure Unit for exposing plates or screens, available exposure surface 48 x 60in

A back-lit Washout Booth and Power Washer

Several portable screenprinting units
Digital suite

EXHIBITIONS
At least two regular exhibitions a year for members. Seacourt actively seeks exchanges and partnerships and works/exhibits with other workshops in Ireland, and has also established international links with similar studios in Europe and America to facilitate the exchange of information, ideas and art.

MISCELLANEOUS
Annual international residency scheme has attracted printmakers from countries such as USA, Sweden. Seacourt is always interested in hearing artists' proposals for residencies.

Sheffield Print Workshop (2008)

50 Upper Albert Road
Sheffield
S8 9HS

tel   +44 (0)114 258 0110
       +44 (0)7749 216291 (mob.)
email peterpainterprint@btinternet.com
web   www.peterpainterprintmaker.co.uk

contact
Contact: Peter York

WORKSHOP

This is a new workshop situated in the leafy suburb of Meersbrook two miles to the south of Sheffield city centre. spread over three rooms offering experienced printers the access and facilities to explore their work, and classes for those brand new to printmaking. Offers safe etching on copper, aluminium and steel, woodcut, linocut, drypoint, mezzotint, a range of collagraph techniques plus ImagOn intaglio-type photo-etching.

ACCESS/ MEMBERSHIP
Open Monday and Wednesday 6.30pm - 9.30pm, Friday 9.30am – 12.30pm/1.00pm – 4.00pm. (Times change seasonally, so it's worth checking the website.)

COURSES/EDUCATION
Weekend classes once a month, plus week long holiday and summer schools in etching, photo-etching relief printing, collagraph and collagraphs. Classes are limited to 6 places. Classes are also given to art groups, schools and community groups.

EQUIPMENT
Polymetaal etching press
80cm x 130cm ┃ 32in x 52in

Small portable bench press to print up to A4

Full range of tools, equipment, inks and paper available

Sidney Nolan Trust (est. 1990)

The Rodd
Presteigne
LD8 2LL
Wales

tel   +44 (0)1544 267362
email sidneynolantrust@therodd.org
web   www.sidneynolantrust.org

contact
Anthony Plant   *Trust Administrator*

The Rodd is an historic manor house set in beautiful countryside in the Border Marshes. Sidney Nolan lived here between 1983 and his death in 1992. In 1985 he set up a trust to support artists and musicians. The print facility was set up some years after his death in the large barn, and promotes solar-plate printmaking, or flexography.

MEMBERSHIP/ACCESS
30 members.
The Sidney Nolan Trust supports a group of artist-printmakers who use the Trust's printmaking studio and exhibit at Trust exhibitions.

COURSES/EDUCATION
Regular seminars and workshops including drypoint, collagraph, solar-plate, saline-sulphate etch and book arts. The Trust promotes and teaches techniques that avoid the use of hazardous acids and solvents. It also works with partner groups – usually either a community/art group, a museum/gallery or a secondary school – to deliver its outreach programme.

EQUIPMENT
Kimber etching press
71 x 121 cm | 28 x 48 in.

EXHIBITIONS
Annual exhibition held in the Tithe Barn as well as international exchange exhibitions (which have included an exchange/residency with Grafikinnustofan in Reykjavik in 2007).

Snap Studio (est. 2007)

20-21 Lower Park Row
Bristol
BS1 5BN

tel   +44 (0)1173 763564
email snap@snapstudio.org.uk
web   www.snapstudio.org.uk

Snap was set up by eight Bristol-based 'print-centric' artists, who exist in a symbiotic, cooperative relationship that enhances their own creative practices while boosting their combined public profile through the growth and promotion of Snap's facilities, activities and network of creative practitioners. While the individual members of Snap retain their identity as creative practitioners, the cooperative is founded on three major collective ideas: cooperation, promotion and networking.

MEMBERSHIP/ACCESS
Membership of the cooperative is limited, but includes a studio, gallery and shop space. Members share responsibility for the running, maintenance and expansion of the idea of Snap. Expressions of interest in joining Snap are always welcome. 'In time we hope to open out our facilities and exhibition space to other artists, as well as to full members, by offering associate memberships.'

COURSES/EDUCATION
Regular short courses (one-day and two-day) in screenprinting and bookbinding.

EQUIPMENT
Portable table top screen-beds x 3

60cm x 80cm | 23 x 31 in

Exposure unit
60cm x 80cm | 23 x 31 in

EXHIBITIONS
With their own gallery space and lots of energy and dynamism to shows and events it is well wort a visit.

Soulisquoy Printmakers (est. 1983)

Print studio:	Contact address:	tel	+44 (0)1856 879900
Soulisquoy Studio	c/o Buckquoy		+44 (0)1856 761508
Pickaquoy Centre	Harray	email	carol.dunbar@btinternet.com
Muddisdale Road	Orkney		
Kirkwall	KW17 2JS	contact	
Orkney		Carol Dunbar	*Chair*
KW15 1RR			

Soulisquoy Printmakers was established in 1983 by a group of enthusiastic professional printmakers based in Orkney who wished to create a studio facility. For over 15 years the workshop was housed in a former wartime building on the local industrial estate in Kirkwall. In the late 1990s a new purpose-built sports and arts complex, the Pickaquoy Centre, was constructed closer to the centre of Kirkwall, and the workshop has been based at there ever since. Soulisquoy Printmakers is dedicated to the promotion of printmaking and providing access to traditional techniques to professional artists, individuals and groups. 'Since moving to the Pickaquoy Centre our processes are all acrylic or water-based. We use copper and ferric chloride. We continue to use oil-based inks but clean up with environmentally friendly products.'

MEMBERSHIP/ACCESS

26 active members.
There is a small annual membership fee and also a supporters and friends scheme. The workshop studio is available during the opening hours of the Pickaquoy Centre, usually 7am-10pm on weekdays and 10am-8pm at weekends. Non-Soulisquoy members are required by the Pickaquoy Centre to undertake an induction session prior to using the studio; this can be arranged by contacting Carol Dunbar.

COURSES/EDUCATION

Soulisquoy regularly run workshops and classes, details of which are emailed to members and advertised in the local press. They have an established record in providing residency opportunities and initiating printmaking projects.

EQUIPMENT

Etching press
53 x 122 cm | 21 x 48 in.

Etching press
25 x 46 cm | 10 x 18 in.

Columbian relief press

Range of lead and wooden type

Kippax UV vacuum bed
120 x169 cm | 47 x 66 in.

Screenprinting table
120 x169 cm | 47 x 66 in.
Ultraviolet exposure unit

EXHIBITIONS

Soulisquoy hold an annual exhibition, the location and date of which varies from year to year.

South Hill Park Printmaking Studio (est. 2002)

Ringmead
Bracknell
Berkshire
RG12 7PA

tel   +44 (0)1344 416255
email ??@southhillpark.org.uk
web   www.southhillpark.org.uk

WORKSHOP

Set in a beautiful 18th-century mansion converted into an arts centre in 1973. In 2002 a major refurbishment was completed, including the new crafts courtyard, ceramics studio, jewellery studio, cinema, digital-art studio and printmaking studio. It is a very active and well-supported venue. The printmaking studio is beautifully designed with glass frontage and great lighting, and is a pleasure to print in.

MEMBERSHIP/ACCESS
Open access on Wednesday evenings and Friday afternoons and some Saturdays. Workshop available for hire by members and non-members.

COURSES/EDUCATION
Courses include monoprint/carborundum, plate lithography and general printmaking classes. They run as part of a large education programme at the arts centre.

EQUIPMENT
Rochat etching Press
61 x 91 cm │ 24 x 36 in.

Columbian relief press
61 x 86 cm │ 24 x 34 in.

Stone lithography press
48 x 63 cm │ 19 x 25 in.

Art Equipment hotplate
51 x 61 cm │ 20 x 24 in.)

Ferric etching

Resin aquatint

EXHIBITIONS
The centre has its own gallery, which has a varied programme of exhibitions.

Spike Island Printmakers (est. 1976)

133 Cumberland Road
Bristol
BS1 6UX

tel   +44 (0)117 9290135
email info@spikeprintstudio.org
web   www.spikeprintstudio.org

contact
Irena Czapska   *Studio Administrator*

WORKSHOP

Spike Island Printmakers (SIP) was originally set up as Bristol Printmakers' Workshop. It is now situated in Spike Island Artspace, a converted tea-packing factory at the edge of Bristol's harbourside; an international arts centre which has undergone major redevelopment and houses over 70 artists' studios, vast gallery spaces, and a programme of residencies and fellowships. It is 'the largest open-access print studio in the South West and provides exceptional resources for traditional printmaking processes'.

MEMBERSHIP/ACCESS
130 members
A variety of memberships allow for flexible access and membership rates. Full membership (key-holder for 3 days a week access), Standard Member, Student Member and Artspace member, (at different rates); access during technician's hours (currently Mon, Tues and Fridays) or with experienced keyholder. Associate Membership also available for those who can print elsewhere but want to exhibit with SIP.

Open access times; Monday - Friday 10am - 6pm, (Tues until 9pm).

COURSES/EDUCATION
Extensive course programme in all print media including water-based screenprinting, etching, wood-cut, engraving and solar-plate. Courses range from weekend to 10 week evening courses. Specific courses/tutorials by request.

EQUIPMENT
1 Large format Tofko press
120cm x 200cm | 48 x 78in

3 Traditional heavy roll presses
70cm x 120cm | 28 x 48in largest

2 Inking hot plates

Ferric chloride and copper sulphate etching baths for copper, steel, znc and stainless steel

Various sized etching baths up to 100 x 200cm | 39 x 78in

Aquatint Resin box.
Separate and ventilated solvents cleaning room.

4 Natgraph hand bench tables
80cm x 110cm | 32 x 44in

1 large format hand bench, approx 110 x 80cm with squeegee arm

2 Medium and small scale tables for accuracy and fine registration

Screens 110 x 160 cm variety of mesh sizes from 150 – 12 strands per inch

Natgraph Ultra Violet 1.6kw exposure unit with vacuum print down frame

Back lit wash out booth

Albion Press (1842) relief press
50cm x 70cm | 20 x 28in

Gem roller proofing press
50cm x 70cm | 20 x 28in

Van de Cook large format semi-automated relief proofing press.

Designated photo-etch darkroom with Parker Graphics vacuum bed and UV lamp box, for developing Toyobo photo-polymer Gravure Plates

Digital suite with printers up to A3

EXHIBITIONS
In-house exhibitions and external exhibitions by members. We have selected exhibitions and invited artists and curators.

EDITIONING
Full editioning programme launched in December 2007. Master Printer, Martyn Grimmer has broad experience of working on editions and collaborative projects.

MISCELLANEOUS
Lark Trust Bursary for recent graduates.

St Barnabas Press (est. 1992)

Belfast Yard
Coldhams Road
Cambridge
CB1 3EW

tel +44 (0)1223 413792
email james@stbarnabaspress.com
info@stbarnabaspress.com
web www.stbarnabaspress.com

contact
James Hill

The Press was founded by master printmaker James Hill in 1992 on St Barnabas Road, Cambridge. In 2001 the Press moved to its current premises at Belfast Yard: 420 sq. m (4500 sq. ft) of space with a mezzanine floor, with a further 90 sq. m (1000 sq. ft) recently added to create a permanent gallery space. The Press supports etching, lithography, screenprint and relief-printing processes and offers expertise in multimedia and new printing technologies. There is scope for preparation and manipulation of images on computer for transfer to photo-print processes. The Press is entirely self-financed, through sales of art produced there and earnings from the services it provides to artists and the local community.

MEMBERSHIP/ACCESS
75 members.
There are flexible membership and access schemes to allow those with some printmaking skill to use the facilities of the Press with support from skilled print technicians; these are standard, open-access and keyholder. The Press is open from Monday to Friday, 9.30am-6pm, Saturday,10.30am-4pm, manned with a technician in attendance?, and Sundays and other times by arrangement.

COURSES/EDUCATION
These range from taster days to short, intensive summer courses to termly courses (seven or ten weeks – autumn, winter and spring) in all printmaking techniques. There are mixed ability classes for novices and printmakers with some

experience. Techniques available include etching, screenprinting, relief printing and lithography. The aim is to give newcomers a basic competency in printmaking, and assist those with some experience to develop and extend their range. One-to-one tuition is also available through the 'teaching flexi-card scheme', and with the tabletop presses for screenprinting and etching, The Press also conduct outreach courses for young children and those in secondary schools.

COURSES ABROAD
An annual excursion to Beijing, in China, and Tibet has been running since 2003 and includes masterclasses and visits to the printmaking department of Beijing Central Academy Fine Art Institute, the workshop of He Kun, in Simao, South China workshop in the south and many other places of artistic merit usually connected with printmaking.

EQUIPMENT
Etching press x 3
66 x 151 cm | 26 x 60 in.

Tabletop etching press
Columbian press
51 x 76 cm | 20 x 30 in.

Albion press
51 x 76 cm | 20 x 30 in.

Screenprint vacuum bed
101 x 151 cm | 40 x 60 in.

Screenprint vacuum bed
151 x 250 cm | 60 x 80 in.

Screenprint vacuum bed
100 x 200 cm | 39 x 78 in.

Small stone litho press

Imperial stone litho press

Larger work can be accommodated on one
of the etching presses

Darkroom for indirect and direct
photostencil screenprinting, photo-etching,
relief printing and photolithography

Digital scanning and black & white
processing 620 mm | 24½ in. wide and 'as
long as you like' Framing equipment

EXHIBITIONS

Small and large gallery spaces in the
mezzanine contain a rolling programme of
new works by resident artists for sale, and
there is a programme of exhibitions at the
Press throughout the year, including some
featuring international artists.

EDITIONING SERVICES

Emphasis in recent years has been on
collaborative editioning projects with
artists, and the publication of original
prints, and on the promotion of work of the
resident artists. St Barnabas Press offers
editioning by contract with artists, and also
publishes its own editions of folios and
individual works to the public.

FRAMING

St Barnabas Press now has facilities to do
in-house framing to the high standards that
artists and collectors expect, using only
acid-free materials and amazing, reflection-
free glass (Mirogard®).

MISCELLANEOUS

The studio also houses 16 artists on the
mezzanines, who are mainly but not
exclusively printmakers.

Swansea Print Workshop (est. 1998)

19A Clarence Street
Swansea
SA1 3QR

tel +44 (0)1792 464418
email mail@swanseaprintworkshop.org.uk
web www.swanseaprintworkshop.org.uk
see also:
www.dylanthomasprints.comc

Swansea Print Workshop was set up in 1998 by a small group of artists 'to provide much-needed professional printmaking and drawing facilities in the Swansea area. It is now a major contributor to printmaking in South Wales, providing access to technical support, unique open-access facilities and a regular programme of events which underpins contemporary practice at all levels.' SWP is currently engaged in raising support for a relocation to a major redevelopment in the city. The new facility would incorporate a gallery, artists' studios and a large print workshop. (See: www.kingslanewarehouse.co.uk)

The workshop is committed to a technology which extends the range of creative possibilities for artists without using many of the toxic chemicals traditionally associated with printmaking. This approach, pioneered by Keith Howard in Canada and the Edinburgh Print Workshop, has many benefits, including a low-hazard, environmentally friendly workshop free of intrusive ventilation and spirit-based cleaning products.

MEMBERSHIP/ACCESS
126 members.
Ordinary and full membership plus non-members' access rates. There are open-access sessions on three days a week for members. A regular printmakers' forum meeting and talks by invited artists provide a platform for the exchange of information and discussion of work in progress.

The workshop is all on the ground level, including disabled toilet facilities. Handouts and other printed information are available on request in large-format print, and their website is fully DDA-compliant.

COURSES/EDUCATION
Masterclasses, advanced, intermediate and introductory courses in a range of intaglio and relief processes: etching and related techniques, drypoint, aquatint, chine collé, photo-etch and non-etch photogravure. Other techniques offered include linocuts and woodcuts, three-colour reduction monotype, screenprinting and photo screenprint, collagraph, cyanotype and digital print techniques.

Regular courses are offered, while one-to-one tuition and bespoke advanced support for individuals can be arranged with experienced printmakers. Swansea Print Workshop also runs accredited courses for Swansea University, provides INSET training sessions and has an extensive outreach programme for schools and colleges. Two life-drawing groups operate weekly.

EQUIPMENT
Radcliffe etching press
91 x 182 cm | 36 x 72 in.

Inverleith etching press
38 x 76 cm | 15 x 30 in.

Littlejohn etching press
53 x 91 cm | 21 x 36 in.

Portable Tofko etching presses x 2

Columbian relief press
61 x 91 cm | 24 x 36 in.

Screenprinting press
129 x 171 cm | 51 x 68 in.

UV exposure unit for light-sensitive emulsions on screens, etching plates and fabrics

Darkroom equipped for all light-based print processes

EXHIBITIONS
Swansea Print Workshop puts on an annual members' exhibition with established local, national and international links with other arts organisations and educational establishments. It exhibits its members' work collectively in addition to their individual activities. Recent exhibitions have included those in Pakistan and the USA.

EDITIONING
The Workshop provides an editioning service for artists by arrangement.

MISCELLANEOUS
A large drawing studio adjacent to the press room is for the use of groups or individual artists. This is equipped with full-length mirrors ranged along one wall, directional lighting, demountable work tables, easels and a digital projector. All facilities can be hired by arrangement, either for one-off activities or on a regular basis for independently run courses.

Taigh Chearsabhagh Print Workshop & Darkroom (est. 1998)

Taigh Chearsabhagh Museum & Arts Centre
Lochmaddy
North Uist
Western Isles
SCOTLAND
HS6 5AA

tel   +44 (0)1876 500293
email admin@taigh-chearsabhagh.org
web   www.taigh-chearsabhagh.org

This is the only print workshop and darkroom in the Outer Hebrides and Skye, off the North West coast of Scotland. It is part of a thriving Arts Centre and Museum, the focus for creative and cultural activities in the Uists. Its location, on the most westerly inhabited island in Scotland provides a dramatic and inspiring setting. (A daily flight from Glasgow to Benbecula takes one hour. Alternatively you can travel by ferry from Skye or from Oban to South Uist.)

MEMBERSHIP/ACCESS

Annual membership available with sessions for half day or full day on a pre-booked basis at a very reasonable rate. The workshops are suitable for one artist to use at a time and are equipped for block, intaglio using Copper Sulphate. (Basic inks, developer, cleaning materials and newsprint are available free of charge.)_You can buy printing papers and camera film in the shop.

EDUCATION

Occasional weekend courses in acrylic resist etching run by visiting tutors such as Alfons Byautus from Edinburgh Printmakers.

Taigh-Chearsabhagh Art Centre also offers a national Certificate in Art & Design in association with Lews College, Stornoway and a BA Fine Art, level 1 (Certificate of Higher Education in Fine Art) and Level 2 (Diploma of Higher Education in Fine Art), in partnership with Moray College in Elgin. You can choose to pursue the full B.A.

course which runs for 1 academic year; (running from September to May), or study individual components such as printmaking, photography, animation and textiles.

EQUIPMENT

Rochat etching press
53cm x 105cm | 21 x 42in

Acrylic resist etching

Fully equipped darkroom

MISCELLANEOUS

As well as a museum, galleries, studios and workshop spaces, a cafe and shop are also housed in the building. A self-contained flat is also available for artists to rent.

Tamar Print Workshop

Cherrybrook House
Tavistock
Devon
PL19 0LA

tel   +44 (0)1822 810329
email mary@gulwork.wanadoo.co.uk

contact
Mary Gillet

WORKSHOP

An independent studio run by artist Mary Gillett on the edge of Dartmoor and the Tamar Valley World Heritage Site.

MEMBERSHIP/ACCESS
Regular sessions arranged to enable small groups to use the facilities. Rather than formal instruction, the emphasis is on the exchange of ideas and feedback generated by informal discussion. Beginners are guided through some of the basic traditional etching processes. The more advanced may arrive with a specific project or idea to work with at their own pace and within their own context.

COURSES/EDUCATION
Courses run two or three times a year and are taught by Mary Gillett. Tuition is non-prescriptive, with emphasis on guidance within the context of each individual's needs, abilities and ideas. With two small presses for outreach work, Mary also runs courses from village halls on Dartmoor with poet and author Roselle Angwin, and contributes to community workshops with ceramicist Jennie Hale of Workshop Under the Sky. Monoprints and collagraphs can be printed on all presses.

EXHIBITIONS
Group exhibitions are organised in the region throughout the year, including participation in the annual Drawn to the Valley Open Studios event.

EQUIPMENT
Rochat etching press
66 x 122 cm | 26 x 48 in.

Hunter Penrose Littlejohn table press
46 x 92 cm | 18 x 36 in.

Tofko portable proofing press (small)

Rollaco portable press (small)

Offset litho press for monoprinting
56 x 64 cm | 22 x 25 in.

Traditional aquatint box (takes plates up to)
49 x 60 cm | 19 x 23½ in.

Trays for etching(take plates up to)
49 x 60 cm | 19 x 23½ in.

Acrylic-resist techniques are combined with traditional etching. A weak solution of nitric acid is used on zinc, and Edinburgh Etch solution on copper

The Art House (est. 2008)

Drury Lane
Wakefield
WF1 2TE

tel   +44 (0)1924 377740
email info@the-arthouse.org.uk
web   www.the-arthouse.org.uk

contact
Liz Whitehouse   *Director*

In 1994 a small group of disabled and non-disabled artists came together to plan the creation of a workspace to welcome them all equally. The new Art House is a new build in the centre of Wakefield with exemplary access. It houses a number of artists' studios and a residential flat. The print room is part of a 65 sq. m (700 sq. ft) space which incorporates flexible space for creating art.

MEMBERSHIP/ACCESS
Membership of Art House is required, including an induction before anyone can use the facilities. There are dedicated open-access sessions with technician support twice weekly. At other times use of the facilities must be booked in advance. Weekday, evening and weekend sessions are all available.

COURSES/EDUCATION
Artist members will be able to book to use the printmaking facilities for a small fee, and will also be able to hire the room to deliver classes and workshops. Many projects are also being planned, including some 'Introduction to Printmaking' classes. 'Professional development and training is central to our support for visual artists. We consult members on a regular basis to ensure that what we provide is what they need.'

EQUIPMENT
Equipped for intaglio and relief printmaking and for general art activity, the 65 sq. m (700 sq. ft) community studio is available for hire to artists, trainers and community arts organisations. It can be used either for general art activities or for intaglio and relief printmaking. The studio has a Halepress M80 motor-driven press with a bed size of 80 x 140 cm (32 x 55 in.), safe etching equipment and facilities, and height-adjustable tables, together with general art equipment. Technician assistance is available. The facilities make the print room particularly suitable for editioning, as well as for delivering masterclasses or intaglio print teaching/training.

EXHIBITIONS
Each year the Art House aims to offer opportunities for member artists to show their work through a range of exhibitions and other events at accessible venues nationwide.

MISCELLANEOUS
The Art House wants artists to travel from across the UK and abroad to use the workspace. Therefore there are two short-term studios for hire as well as a three-bedroom flat with a communal kitchen/living area. The studios and accommodation are intended for any artist who would like to use them, including artists with disabilities. The flat has one double and two single bedrooms, and so provides very flexible accommodation. In the case of disabled artists, it can accommodate one artist with partner and/or one artist with a professional carer. One of the short-term studios is provided with printmaking facilities for individual use by residents, including a Rollaco press (prints up to A3).

The Print Shed (est. 2006)

Swinmoor House
Madley
Hereford
HR2 9JD

tel   +44 (0)7796 673123
email theprintshed@swinmoor.net

contact
Jill Barneby

WORKSHOP

Owned and run by Jill Barneby, a recent graduate in printmaking. Four small outhouses converted for printmaking and framing, with plans for a gallery space, the studio is very reasonably priced. It works on a non-toxic basis, using ferric and solar-plate etching.

MEMBERSHIP/ACCESS
Members can book to use the studio on a daily or half-daily basis, though they must first attend a free induction session. Up to four people can use the studio in any given session. Members wishing to have exclusive use of the studio can arrange this for an increased daily/half-day charge. There is no open access – sessions must be booked. Non-members can also use the workshop, though at a higher daily rate than members.

The 'drawing studio' upstairs can also be used for plate preparation, drawing, coffee, etc. Discounted framing is available.

COURSES/EDUCATION
There are courses for beginners and experienced printers in collagraph, drypoint (both paper drypoint and aluminium), linocut and multiple linocut, as well as reduction cutting for the more ambitious. Print is combined with textile, etching – non-toxic, solar-plate, monoprint and 'lithosketch'. Courses are run by Jill Barneby and occasional special-guest printmakers, and are kept to a maximum of four or five students. Small school groups are also catered for with bespoke printmaking classes.

EQUIPMENT
Rollaco etching press
61 x 121cm | 24 x 48 in.

Intaglio Printmaker tabletop press for use in the studio or for hire

Large sink for paper-soaking
61 x 121cm | 24 x 48 in.

Hotplate
31 x 38 cm | 12 x 15 in.

Nipping press (old cast-iron one), great for making cards and small linocuts

EXHIBITIONS
Plans are in place for the next phase of development, with a converted space next to the workshop to be turned into a small gallery. A website gallery is also being planned.

West Yorkshire Print Workshop (est. 1981)

75A Huddersfield Road
Mirfield
West Yorkshire
WF14 8AT

tel   +44 (0)1924 497646
email info@wypw.org
web   www.wypw.org

contact
Kathryn Desforges   *Administrator*

MEMBERSHIP/ACCESS

120 members.

'The print workshop at WYPW is an open-access workshop that aims to provide high-quality printmaking facilities in which both the professional printmakers and beginners can work comfortably. We can offer facilities for etching (traditional and non-toxic), relief printing, collagraph, silkscreen printing (paper and textiles), black & white photography and a digital imaging suite.'

Standard membership for access during opening times Tuesdays, 10.30am-10pm, Wednesdays, 10.30am-6pm, and Thursdays, 10.30am-6pm) and keyholder membership (24-hour access) for experienced printmakers (by application only).

EDUCATION/COURSES

A rolling programme of workshops in printmaking and related arts runs on weekends or evenings. Courses include an introduction to printmaking, collagraph, etching, screenprinting, textile printing, waterless lithography and black & white photography. Tailor-made courses are offered to schools and community groups, and WYPW also runs a programme of free creative workshops on Saturday mornings for children aged 8-14.

EQUIPMENT

Print room

Rochat etching press
70 x 120 cm | 30 x 48 in.

Polymetaal etching press
46 x 90 cm | 18 x 36 in.

Paper bath
76 x 106 cm | 30 x 42 in.

Plate room

Resin aquatint box (holds plates up to approx.) 55 x 55 cm | 22 x 22 in.

Hotplate
61 x 76 cm | 24 x 30 in.

Ferric, nitric and copper-sulphate etching facilities with laboratory-standard filter extraction

Screen room

Kippax screenprint bed x 2
(approx.) 97 x 145 cm | 38 x 58 in.

Textile printing table
110 by 190 cm | 44 x 86 in.

Vacuum exposure unit
148 x 163 cm | 59 x 65 in.

Darkroom

Darkroom facilities for b&w photography

2 Durst M370 BW enlargers

EXHIBITIONS

The Workshop has its own good-sized gallery showing a variety of exhibitions including those by groups and solo artists, and there is also a permanent selection of members' prints available. Entrance to exhibitions is free. Members' exhibitions are also held at other venues.

MISCELLANEOUS

The Workshop also has nine artists' studios available. The shop sells a comprehensive range of printmaking papers and sundries.

Wrexham Regional Print Centre (est. 2002)

Memorial Arts Building
Yale College
Grove Park
Wrexham
Wales
LL12 7AA

tel   +44 (0)1978 311794 (ext. 2286) or
      +44 (0)7813 437205
email printcentre@yale-wrexham.ac.uk.
web   www.yale-wrexham.co‹····ac?····›.uk/
      facilities/facilities_printcentre
      _whatson.htm

contact
Steffan Jones-Hughes

WORKSHOP

Part of Yale College, the centre has been offering open-access facilities to artists and designers from across Wales and beyond since 2002. It is a joint venture between Yale College and the Arts Council of Wales. The nature of this workshop as part of the college gives it a particular dynamic. The programme is varied and extensive.

MEMBERSHIP/ACCESS
100 members, with an additional community of 800 printmakers who receive bulletins and information. Open access for members on Saturdays, 9.30am-12pm, and Wednesdays, 10am-4.30pm Additional sessions are also available – contact the centre for details. Booking in advance is essential. To use the workshop you must be an experienced printmaker, or have successfully completed one of Regional Print Centre's workshop classes in printmaking techniques.

EDUCATION/COURSES
A varied range of short and 10-week courses offered in printmaking and related media including screenprinting, solar-plate, photopolymer etching, etc. Past workshops have also included print surgeries and artists' talks from high-profile artists.

A Professional Certificate/Diploma in Printmaking also available, a comprehensive programme which helps learners to develop the skills needed to be a professional artist-printmaker. It can be studied part-time over two years and is

aimed at artists and designers with printmaking experience. 'The course is wide-ranging, and artists have been involved in projects in a variety of locations, developing funding applications, finding exhibition opportunities, curating projects, all in addition to developing their own creative practice.'

The Centre offers a programme of in-house education and outreach workshops with a mobile press for art groups, community groups, schools and colleges. The outreach programme can be brought to any school in North Wales, The Wirral or Cheshire. Work in the Welsh language can also be arranged, and all work can be linked to the National Curriculum.

EQUIPMENT
Rochat etching press
76cm x 101cm ❘ 30 x 40 in.

Swedish etching press
40 x 61 cm ❘ 10 x 24 in.

Star-wheel press
76 x 101 cm ❘ 30 x 40 in.

Vice presses x 4

Screenprint bed

Light boxes x 3
(largest) 150 x 200 cm ❘ 40 x 79 in.

Textile print tables – suitable
for sampling up to 3 m | 10 ft

Photo-etching

Nitric, ferric and saline-sulphate etching
plus photopolymer etching

Resin aquatint

EXHIBITIONS
The Regional Print Centre organises
exhibitions by invited printmakers and
groups. Previous exhibitions have included
a Paul Peter Piech (work from the archive)
touring show 2006-2009, an ongoing print
exchange with Irish and Welsh artists in
collaboration with Leinster Print Studio,
which will result in a tour in 2008-10,
entitled Aspects of Landscape, and the
Postcard Project. There is also an annual
show of professional printmakers in Yale
Memorial Gallery, which in previous years
has gone by the names Hot (2008), Impress
(2007), and First Edition (2006). Wrexham
Print International is organised by Oriel
Wrecsam (Wrexham Arts Centre) and is
shown biennially in the Memorial Gallery
and Oriel Wrecsam.

MISCELLANEOUS
A number of residencies over the past few
years have included printmakers from
Brazil, California, Chicago, Berlin, Trois
Rivières, Quebec and Cracow.

Wyards Print & Artworks Ltd (est. 1997)

99 Ospringe Road
Faversham
Kent
ME13 7LG

tel +44 (0)1795 590680
web www.wyards.com

Set in a converted 19th-century factory warehouse, Wyards is owned and run by Cathy Moore, who has restored the building, and lives next door in the Bridge House. The workshop is well laid out and provides a comfortable and professional printmaking environment to work in.

MEMBERSHIP/ACCESS

30 members.
Experienced printmakers can book the workshop for a daily fee. Open Wednesday-Saturday, 10am-6pm (book a morning and/or afternoon session). The workshop has complete disabled access.

COURSES/EDUCATION

Wyards' education programme provides printmaking classes for adults, schools, art clubs and learning-disability groups, life-drawing sessions (printmaking and life drawing combined), watercolour and monoprinting classes. Saturday classes run throughout the year on a rotational basis, including special guest printmakers. One-to-one tuition is also available.

EQUIPMENT

Hunter Penrose etching press
71 x 122 cm | 28 x 42 in.

Kimber etching press
107 x 153 cm | 40 x 55 in.

Colombian relief press
57 x 87 cm | 22 x 34 in.

Vertical dip tanks x 2 (copper and steel)
64 x 72 cm | 25 x 28 in.

Ferric and nitric acid

Resin aquatint (housed outside the workshop)

Gas hotplate

Selection of letterpress

EXHIBITIONS

A spacious and well-lit gallery adjoining the workshop houses a changing programme of exhibitions in contemporary graphic and fine art from local, national and international artists throughout the year.

OTHER

Editioning of limited-edition etchings undertaken – single plate or multiple, monochrome or colour.

York Print Studio (est. 2006)

31 The Village
Stockton on the Forest
York
YO32 9HF

Contact address:
11 Elm Park Vale
Stockton Lane
York
YO31 1DU

tel +44 (0)1904 421743
email catherinesutcliffefuller@hotmail.com

A private studio set in an undisturbed rural location with views over a small farmyard. Separate space for sketching, painting and drawing. 'For individual artists who wish to make etch and relief prints as big as A1.'

MEMBERSHIP/ACCESS
The studio is available to experienced printmakers to hire on a daily basis, but longer terms can also be discussed. It is set up for one artist to use at a time, and there are a number of regular users who rent the space on a daily basis. There is no current membership scheme.

COURSES/EDUCATION
Inexperienced printmakers may wish to take advantage of printmaking lessons, in which Catherine can teach the skills required to safely use all of the available equipment.

EQUIPMENT
Rollaco etching press (custom-made)
76 x 126 cm | 30 x 50 in.

Aquatint booth

Large nitric-acid bath

Metal-cutting guillotine

Europe

AUSTRIA

Internationale Sommerakademie für Bildende Kunst
Franziskanergasse 5a
PO Box 18
5010 Salzburg
Austria
+43 662 842113 or 843727
office@summeracademy.at
www.summeracademy.at

Print courses at the International Summer Academy of Fine Arts. The academy is on two sites: Hohensalzburg Fortress and the Old Salt Factory.

Weekstatten für Druckgraphik an der Kuenstlereischen VHS
Lazarettgasse 27
Vienna 1190
Austria

sergius.kodera@univie.ac.at
Lithography, screenprinting, relief printing, etc.

BELGIUM

Ateliers Malou ASBL
97 Rue Voot
1200 Brussels
+32 (0)2 770 92 50
ateliers.malou@scarlet.be
www.ateliersmalou.be

Artists' collective art studios with occasional print courses.

Frans Masereel Centre
Zaardendijk 20
2460 Kasterlee
Belgium

+32 (0)1 485 22 50/52
(Contact: Ivan Durt, Artistic Co-ordinator)
fransmasereelcentrum@vlaanderen.be
www.fransmasereelcentrum.be

Flemish centre for the graphic arts, with the aim of bringing artists into contact with every aspect of the printed image by means of residences, workshops, demonstrations and exhibitions. It is visited annually by more than 100 artists, both young and established. The unique rotunda workshop also has artist chalets to support three-week residencies, from January to November. Masterclasses are run once or twice a year.

Kasba Atelier de Gravure
Rue Middelbourg, 126
Watermael Boisfort
1170 Brussels
www.estampe.be/kasba

Well-equipped spacious workshop offering intaglio, lithography and typography in Moorish house restored in 1996, promoting advocacy in engraving and international exchange. Also houses Encreux Collectif, a group of artists promoting book arts.

See also:

Centre de la Gravure et de l'Image Imprimée
(Centre for Engraving and the Printed Image)
10 rue des Amours
B-7100 La Louvière
Belgium
+32 (0)6 427 87 27
is@centredelagravure.be
www.centredelagravure.be

Print gallery showing contemporary printmaking with extensive collection available for research plus library containing over 10,000 books on printmaking and a well-stocked shop. An education department also runs printmaking workshops, mainly for children.

Estampe

Rue Tourette, 128
6000 Charleroi
Belgium
studio@estampe.be
www.estampe.be
Contact: Hugues Przysiuda

Home of Estampe Bookmarks exchange – established in 1999. News forum and virtual gallery for printmaking plus good links pages. (see also Print Opens section).

Museum Platin-Moretus

Vrijdagmarkt 22
2000 Antwerp
+32 (0)3 221 14 50/51
museum.plantin.moretus@stad.ant
werpen.be
www.museum.antwerpen.be/plantin_/
moretus

Large typographic museum with preserved 16th -century letterpress printers' workshop and letter foundry, and two of the oldest presses in the world. There is also a library with 25,000 books including a Gutenburg Bible.

FRANCE

Manifestampe-Fédération Nationale de l'Estampe

c/o Michel Cornu
29 résidence Circé
Rue du Bois Guyot
77350 Le Mée sur Seine

contact@manifestampe.org
www.manifestampe.org

National Federation of Printmakers representing 2000 members and promoting printmaking. The name is a composite word meaning a 'manifesto for print'. There is a very good links page on the website to other associations, ateliers and exhibitions.

Amac Chamalières

Rue des Saulées
(nr. Associations House)
63400 Chamalières
+33(0)4 73 37 86 71
amac1@tiscali.fr
www.amac-chamalieres.com
(Contact: Marie Naud)

Engraving, etching, aquatint, drypoint, monotype, printing … etc. Also organises Chamalières Print Triennial.

Atelier 63

54 Rue Daguerre
Montparnasse
75014 Paris
+33 (0)1 43 22 21 78
(Contact: Joëlle Serve)
www.connectworks.co.uk/atelier63/introe.ht
ml

An international place of work and training in etching, engraving, drypoint and mezzotint with a well-equipped studio in the heart of Paris. Open September to June with different levels of access, between 4 and 20 hours a week. In 1983, Joëlle Serve also set up Trace, an association of engravers.

Atelier à Bras

5 rue de la Gardelle
Castelreng 11300
Aude
France
+33(0)6 33 43 70 36
apwbee@gmail.com or
atelierabras@hotmail.com
www.apwb.org

Relief printing and intaglio studio run by renowned printmaker Matthew Hilton; open five days a month under supervision /tuition. Printmaking holidays in printing without a press and printing outside.

Atelier Bordas

2 Rue de la Roquette
Paris 75011
+33 (0)1 47 00 31 61
(Contact: Franck or Cécile)
mail@atelierbordas.com
www.atelierbordas.com

Open access with lithography, block printing, monoprinting and digital printmaking; also research, editioning and publishing.

Atelier Contrepoint
10 rue Didot
75014 Paris
+33(0)1-45-43-85-01
(Contact: Hector Saunier/Juan Valladares)
contrepoint@mac.com
www.ateliercontrepoint.com

Formerly Atelier 17, and renamed Atelier Contrepoint after S.W. Hayter's death in 1988, the workshop 'is best defined as an experimental etching studio frequented by artists and students from all corners of the world. A place of exchange and apprenticeship'.

Atelier de Gravure
Bea Nevoux
25 rue Lafayette
56-200 la Gacilly
France
+33 (0)6 82 70 61 09
bea.nevoux@bleu-nuit.fr
www.bleu-nuit.fr
Engraving studio with courses in etching, aquatint and drypoint.

Atelier de Gravure
Auretie Amiot
amiotteare@hotmail.com
www.atelier-etching.com

Creative space deticated to graphic arts based in Metz with mobile workshop visits to ??? and events across the region of Larraine.

Atelier de Gravure Brito
Maison Jan Brito
Avenue du Général de Gaulle
35-550 Pipriac
Contact via:
bea.nevoux@bleu-nuit.fr
See: www.manifestampe.org

Elementary and advanced etching, aquatint and drypoint with Master Printer Jan Brito.

Atelier de Lithographie
The Masserie
46330 Saint-Gery
France
+33(0)565312558
michel-herbaut@atalierdelithographie.com
www.atalierdelithographie.com

The workshop offers courses in stone lithography.

Atelier de L'Orme
Métiers de l'estampe
16 rue de l'Orme
75019 Paris
+33(0)1 53 72 47 53
(Contact: Alice Menecier)
contact@atelierdelorme.com
http://www.atelierdelorme.com

Etching and lithography workshop run by Alice Menecier and Emmanuelle Mellot, with courses in etching and lithography.

Atelier Montmiral
Rue Gambetta
Castelnau de Montmiral
81140 France
+33(0)5 63 40 51 55
bmnewth@yahoo.co.uk
www.ateliermontmiral.com

Printmaking and painting courses run by Mick and Bunny Newth in renovated 20th-century school in hilltop village. Etching, relief, screenprinting and book-making.

Atelier du Safranier
2 bis Rue du Cannet
06600 Antibes
+33 (0)4 93 34 53 72
Atelier.du.Safranier@wanadoo.fr
www.chez.com/ateliersafranier

Etching, monotype and lithography courses throughout the year.

Centre Art Graphique de La Métairie Bruyère
89240 Parly
rld.art@wanadoo.fr
asso@aux4ventsdelart.org
http://www.la-metairie.fr

Centre National de l'Estampe et de l'Art Imprimé (CNEAI)
Maison Levanneur
Ile des Impressionnistes
78400 Chatou
+33 (0)1 39 52 45 35
cneai@cneai.com
www.cneai.com

Set up in the Fournaise hamlet used by Renoir, Derain and Vlaminck, the centre now promotes and publishes multiples in the wider sense and works with artists and schools to create ollaborative projects centred around print. It also has a large course programme.

Gravicel (le Salon de Gravure)
18 rue de Brigode
59000 Lille
+33 (0)3 20 40 19 06
(Contact: Isabelle Cellier)
gravicel@yahoo.fr
See: www.manifestampe.org/PDF/Graveur
(pdf only)

Etching studio that also organises a themed print biennial.

Hastings Etching Workshop
Voillerousse
09500 St Felix de Tournegat
Ariège
+33 (0)5 61 69 39 43
martinware@whitevarnish.com
members.aol.com/hastingsetching/
(Contact: Martin Ware (RCA))

Hastings Print Workshop moved to France in 2004 and runs courses in etching and monoprinting in a large converted barn south of Toulouse.

La Taille Douce – Atelier Françoise Bricaut
9 rue Ernestine
75018 Paris
+33(0)-06-84-49-28-32
francoisebricaut@free.fr
www.francoisebricaut.free.fr/

Etching workshop at the foot of Montmartre run by Françoise Bricaut, a former pupil of S.W. Hayter. The workshop is open to beginners and professionals. English is spoken.

Les Ateliers de la Scierie
Association
Route de Saint-Beaulize
12540 Fondamente
+33 (0)5 65 99 33 81
(Contact: Sophie Vigneau)
sophie.vigneau@free.fr
www.ateliersdelascierie.fr

Workshops for adults in etching, book-making, etc. Residencies and accommodation available.

L'Empreinte
40 rue Saint-Michel
69007 Lyon
(Contact: Martian Aymé)
martian.ayme@wanadoo.fr
http://www.lempreinte-gravure.com

Association of etchers in Lyon, working around two presses, with workshops, exhibitions and editioning projects organised.

L'Estampe de Chaville
23 rue Carnot
92370 Chaville
+33 (0)1 47 09 68 65
estampedechaville@online.fr
www.estampedechaville.online.fr

Etching studio which welcomes artists from the suburbs of Paris as well as many international artists. Organises exhibitions and workshops. Established in 1977, it was under threat of closure at the time of writing the book, though also looking for support.

Les Ateliers Moret
8 rue Saint-Victor
75005 Paris
+33 (0)1 43 26 51 67
(Contact: Daniel Moret)
lesateliersmoret@wanadoo.fr
www.lesateliersmoret.free.fr

Etching and engraving workshop with courses, etc.

Maison de la Gravure Méditerranée
105 chemin des Mendrous
34170 Castelnau le Lez
info@maisondelagravure.eu
http://maisondelagravure.free.fr

The atelier of the Association of
Mediterranean Engraving. Courses,
masterclasses, editions and education in
schools. Equipment and support for co-
limited printmaking in residency;
applications by portfolio. Good links page.

Taille12 – Morsure27
Art Visuel
12 rue du Dr Chanoine
Chalet des pénitents
Vernonnet
27200 Vernon
BP 304
+33 (0)2 32 51 88 33
(Contact: Ulrike Vidalain)
www.taille12-morsure27.site.voila.fr

Etching workshop and gallery established
in 1996. Exchanges with the likes of Open
Bite Printmakers in Australia.

Torben Bo Halbirk's Studio
80-82 rue du Chemin Vert
75011 Paris
+33 (0)1 43 55 92 37
afleurdencre@torbenbohalbirk.com
www.torbenbohalbirk.com

Originally set up to promote Franco-Danish
exchange in printmaking, it has now
extended to working with etchers from all
over the world. The workshop has been
able to establish relationships with a dozen
workshops in Europe, and others in South
Africa and Argentina. It is also behind the
construction of two new projects: a summer
workshop on the Croatian island of Krk; and
the launching of Imprint, a workshop
collective in Luxembourg.

see also:

Art du Timbre Gravé
Association
Les Essertines
71220 Vérosvres

+33 (0)3 85 24 88 63
(Contact: Pierre Albuisson)
artdutimbregrave@wanadoo.fr
http://www.artdutimbregrave.com

Association of engravers.

Art Trek
PO Box 1103
Bolinas
CA 94924
USA
carol@arttreks.com
www.arttreks.com

Printmaking courses (and painting
holidays) in St Jeannet and Antibes, French
Polynesia, etc.

Cedric Green
cedricgreen@club-internet.fr
www.greenart.info

Electro-etch courses and at St Front-la-
Rivière in the Dordogne, given by a pioneer
in alternative and green printmaking
techniques. Site with many links.

Graver Maintenant
(Engraving Now)
www.graver.maintenant.free.fr

An association of artists and amateurs
interested in printmaking in all its forms,
they also promote print and organise an
annual exhibition/trade fair.

JGC (Jeune Gravure Contemporaine)
(Young Contemporary Printmaking
Association)
16 rue Grégoire de Tours
75006 Paris
+33 (0)1 53 10 82 59
andre.beguin.free.fr/html/jgc/index.htm

Association founded in 1929.

Le Bois Gravé
3 rue Crétet
75009 Paris
+33 (0)1 42 80 30 59
(Contact: Claude Bouret)
bouretc@wanadoo.fr

Contemporary woodcut.

Le Chant de l'Encre
6 place Thomas
63000 Clermont-Ferrand
m.brugerolles@wanadoo.fr
www.artsenbalade.com
Association of printmakers with annual
open-studios event.

Le Trait-Graveurs d'aujourd'hui
le.trait@wanadoo.fr
Etchers' association.

Musée de Gravelines
Château – Arsenal
59820 Gravelines
+33 (0)3 28 51 81 00
www.ville-gravelines.fr

Museum of printmaking including
workshops, demonstrations, internships
and a publishing facility.

URDLA Association
207 rue Francis de Pressensé
BP 1235
69608 Villeurbanne cedex
+33(0)4 72 65 33 34
(Contact: Cyril Noirjean)
urdla@urdla.com
http://www.urdla.com

International centre of prints and books.

USEFUL WEBSITES

www.nouvellesdelestampe.fr
French print magazine.

www.presse-estampe.com
For French presses.

www.trace-multiples.fr
Trace Biennial run by Atelier 63.

www.estampe.net
Print links on personal site of André Beguin.

www.mai-68.org
Socialist site with a revolutionary zeal;
really interesting poster activities.

imaginaction.over-
blog.org/pages/Quelques_liens-
346193.html

GERMANY

Artwerk-Werkart
Manuelle Siebdruckwerkstatt für Kunstler
Schleissheimerstr. 45 RGB
D-80797
München
+49 (0)89127 388 58
gesapuell@t-online.de
www.druckgrafik.de

Screenprinting workshop.

Atelier Dorothea Koch
Gugelstr. 89 R
90459 Nürnberg
+49 (0)911/994 4700
atelier@dorotheakoch.de
www.dorotheakoch.de

Personal studio of Dorothea Koch, with
open studio on Mondays, plus courses and
editioning. Etching and drypoint.

Bielefelder Handpresse
Spindelstr. 41
D-33604 Bielefeld
+49(0)521 13 16 53
rotermund5@aol.com

Supports and promotes printmaking in the
Bielefield region.

Druckstelle
Werkstatt für kunstlerische Drucktechniken
Manteuffelstr. 103
D-10997 Berlin
(Contact: Eva Pietzcker & Miriam Zegrer)
info@druckstelle.info
www.druckstelle.info
(Good site in English)

Facilties for intaglio, woodblock and
screenprint, and also a darkroom.
Particularly interested in alternative
printing techniques.

Druckwerkstatt eV
Friedensallee 44
D-22765 Hamburg
+49 (0)40 333 102 37
(Contact: Gerten Goldbeck)
gertengoldbeck@gmx.de
www.druckwerkstattev.de

Lithography, intaglio and screenprinting.

Grafikwerkstatt Dresden
Junghansstr. 3
01277 Dresden
+49 (0)351 319 050 30
grafikwerkstatt.dresden@t-online.de
www.dresden.de

Large well-equipped workshop founded in
1958, based in a former camera factory
with etching, lithography, 'algraphy', relief
printing and book-making. Courses run
plus accommodation available.

Hundsdruck
Gesellschaft zur Forderung Kunstlerischer
Druckgrafik e.v.
Kaltmuhlweg 12
83026 Rosenheim
+49(0)8031-67429
hundsdruck@gmx.de
(Contact: Andreas Opperer & Brigitte
Reich)

Letterpress, bookbinding and design.
Courses and workshops delivered.

IMPRESSION Werkstatt für Tiefdruck
Gewerbegebiet Steinkirchen
Robert-Koch-Str. 2
82162 Planegg
+ 49 (0)89 21938663
(Contact: Melissa MayerGalbraith &
Thomas Sebening)
z@druckgrafik.de
www.druckgrafik.de

Well-equipped workshop for relief and
intaglio.

Katelhon KG
Katelhonstr. 8
59519 Mohnesee
(Contact: Klaus Judes)

Klaus-Juedes@t-online.de
Lithography, relief and intaglio. Privately
owned workshop with open access and
editioning.

Kolner Graphikwerkstatt e.v.
Im Sionstal 17
50678 Köln
+49 (0)221/310 04 25
info@graphikwerkstatt.de
www.grafikwerkstatt.de

Gallery workshop in Cologne offering
courses in etching.

**Druckwerkstatt im Kulturwerk des bbk
berlin GMBH**
Mariannenplatz 2
10997 Berlin
+49 (0)30 614015 70
druckwerkstatt@bbk-kulturwerk.de
www.bbk-kulturwerk.de
(Contact: Mathias Mrowka)

Large workshop established in 1955 with
workshops for letterpress, etching,
lithography, silkscreen, bookbinding,
papermaking, photography and digital
media. Part of the Professional Association
of Berlin Artists, the workshop inhabits a
very large and impressive building.

Kulturzentrum Alte Feuerwache
Bruckenstr. 2-4
D-68167 Mannheim
+49 (0)621 336 13 36
Email: info@bbk-mannheim.de
www.bbk-mannheim.de
Print workshop in arts centre based in an
old fire station. Lithography, intaglio and
relief. Courses run.

Steindruck München
Lithographiewerkstatt im Münchner
Künstlerhaus am Lenbachplatz
Lenbachplatz 8
D-80333
München
+49 (0)89 599 18 459
steindruck-munchen@druckgrafik.de

Scholarship in lithography workshop in
Munich Art Gallery including free

accommodation. Electric and hand presses available.

Internationale Senefelder-Stiftung
c/o MAN Roland Druckmaschinen AG
PO Box 10 12 64
63012 Offenbach
+49(0)69 8305 29 62
info@senefelderstiftung.com
www.senefelderstiftung.com

A foundation set up in 1971 to celebrate the 200th birthday of Alois Senefelder, it supports young lithographers and promotes lithography, etc. Triennial award for outstanding achievement in lithography; next one in 2011.

Stiftung Werkstattmuseum für Druckkunst Leipzig
(Museum for the Printing Arts, Leipzig)
Nonnenstraße 38
04229 Leipzig
+49 (0)341 2 31 62 0
info@druckkunst-museum.de
www.druckkunst-museum.de

Large museum dedicated to type, including hands-on workshops.

Atelier Kystprik
Ellernbrook
24235 Stein
+49 (0) 4343 7014
(Contact: Birgit Rautenberg-Sturm)
atelier@kystprik.de
www.kystprik.de

Personal studio of Birgit Rautenberg-Stum. Runs occasional workshops.

USEFUL WEBSITES

www.buchdruckkunst.de
Letterpress/book-arts site.

www.forumbookart.com
Book arts in Hamburg.

www.grafikboerse.de
Large printmaking site with links to artists, galleries, etc.

www.gutenberg.de/museum.htm
Museum of Johannes Gutenberg in Mainz.

www.netzwerk-druckgrafik.de/messe.htm
Network site for International Salon for Original Graphics, a symposium held biennially in Hamburg.

Tapir Print Studio (Germany)
c/o Julian Wolfart
Christburger Strasse 39
10405 Berlin
Germany
+49 (0)160 9556 6040
info@tapirstudio.org
www.tapirstudio.org

GREECE

Greek Printmakers' Association
4 Lebesi Str
Makrigianni 11742
Athens
+30 210922 8370
(Contact: Nikos Stavrakantonakis, Secretary)
info@haraktes.org
www.haraktes.org

The Aegean Center for the Fine Arts
Pharos 84400
Cyclades
+30 22840 23 287
studyart@aegeancenter.org
www.aegeancenter.org

Independent school of art running term-long courses, including accommodation on the Greek island of Pharos with printmaking centring on etching.

Neapolis Engraving Centre
Thessalonika
(Contact: Zenaphan Zachinis Artistic Director)
DETPAN@neapoli.gr
karaart.com/greekart/neapoli-printmaking/neapoli-printmaking.html

Established in 1997, this centre 'of the highest specifications' is based in the art centre in the renovated Ilios Factory, and is supported by Neapoli Municipality. International links are welcomed.

Rhodes Modern Greek Art Museum
Nestorideion Palaca
Gabriel Haritos Square
Rhodes 85100
+30 224 103 6646
neapinakothiki@mgamuseum.gr
www.mgamuseum.gr
(Contact: Dr Mary Kampouropolou,
President)

Engraving workshop set up in September
2008 alongside the inaugural exhibition of
the Triennale of Engraving in the
Mediterranean.

Athens School of Art
42 Patision Street
10 682 Athens
+30 210 38 97 131
(Contact: Mrs Valeria Tsantila)
llp.asfa.gr
www.erasmus.asfa.gr

Print department reopened in 2004 and
includes typography. It also has an Erasmus
scheme.

Aristotelian University of Thessalonika
Dept of Fine & Applied Arts
54124 Thessalonika
+30 2310 99 6000
www.auth.gr

Largest university in Greece with large
printmaking department. It also has an
Erasmus scheme.
NB The following conversation with Nikos
Stavrakantonakis, Secretary of the Greek
Printmakers' Association, reveals a lot
about the way in which printmaking is
generally accessed in Greece.

'In Athens we don't have any open access in
workshops. But we always try to find a
printing workshop between our members ...
Usually if an artist wants to print they are
welcomed to print as guests in our members'
workshops. Sometimes they pay a small rent,
sometimes not. Depends from the person.'

Neapolis Engraving Centre
http://karaartcom/gtrakart/neapoli-
printmaking/neapoli-printmaking.html

HOLLAND

Vereniging Voor Originale Grafiek (VOG)
(The Association for Original Print)
Info@vereniging-voor-originele-grafiek.nl
www.vereniging-voor-originele-grafiek.nl

Association supporting and promoting
original printmaking, founded in 1993.
Extensive website profiling printmaking in
the Netherlands.

Amsterdams Grafisch Atelier (AGA)
Laurierstraat 109
1016 PL Amsterdam
+31 (0)20-6252186
contact Jeroen vanden Maagdenberg
amsterdams.grafisch.atelier@planet.nl
www.amsterdamsgrafischatelier.nl

Very well equipped studio with lithography,
etching, silkscreen, relief printing and
digital facilities. The workshop specialises
in printing techniques that are
environmentally friendly. International
exchanges with Japan, U.S.A. and Latin
America. The atelier invites artists to offer
project proposals. The AGA initiates
courses, masterclasses, productions,
exhibitions, innovative projects, exchanges,
and Artists in Residence (A.I.R.) projects.

Atelier Aad Hekker
Kerkstraat 187
1017 GH
Amsterdam
+31 (0)20 626 67 30
heckerlitho@xs4all.nl
www.hekkerlitho.nl
(Contact: Aad Hecker)

Lithography studio (stone and offset) in
converted hayloft in 300-year-old coach
house in Amsterdam. Printer-publisher with
an emphasis on collaboration between
artist and printer. Workshops and courses
for artists and art students, plus open days
and exhibitions.

See also

www.lithographica.nl
Atelier 'De Goede Moet'

Hogeweg 2
6621 BN
Dreumel
+31 (0)48 757 04 44

Atelier De Werkplaats
Hendrik van Deventerstraat 1
2563 XP
Den Haag
+31 (0)70 364 56 33

Atelier De Wijde Doelen
Biltstraat 333
3572 AS
Utrecht
+31 (0)30 233 1836
info@wijdedoelen.nl
www.wijdedoelen.nl

Art centre for people with disabilities, with ceramic and print facilities.

Atelier Jan Naezer
Ledeganckplein 7
2524 CP
Den Haag
+31 (0)70 364 56 33
info@atelierjannaezer.nl
www.atelierjannaezer.nl

Studio of Jan Naezer. With courses in lithography and etching (with environmentally friendly ethos), as well as painting and drawing, the studio is a recognised centre of learning.

Experimenteel Grafisch Werkcentrum
Schoolstraat 3
9441 PE
Orvelte
+31 (0)59 332 22 25

Grafiek Orvelte
www.grafiek-orvelte.nl

Etching, lithography, book-making, etc.

Grafisch Atelier Alkmaar
Doelenstraat 23
1811 KX
Alkmaar
+31 (0)72 512 80 75
www.grafischatelieralkmaar.nl

Lithography, etching, relief printing, screenprinting and letterpress.

Grafisch Atelier Arnhem
Mariënburghstraat 12
6811 CS
Arnhem
+31 (0) 26 443 81 41

Grafisch Atelier Breda
Nieuwe Veste
Molenstraat 6
4811 GS
Breda
+31 (0)76 529 96 00

Grafisch Atelier Daglicht
(Daylight Print Workshop)
De Rondom 18
5612 AP
Eindhoven
+31 (0)40 247 55 38
daglicht@planet.nl
www.grafisch-atelier-daglicht.nl

Located in the Meulensteen Art Centre at the Technical University in Eindhoven. Facilities for lithography, etching, silkscreen, etc. in spacious workshop.

Grafisch Atelier Den Bosch
Boschveldweg 471
Willem II Fabriek
5211 VK
Den Bosch
+31 (0)73 613 42 77
info@gadenbosch.nl
www.gadenbosch.nl

Open-access lithography, screenprint and etching studio.

Grafisch Atelier Friesland
St Anthonystraat 4
8911 DV
Leeuwarden
+31 (0)58 215 31 10
(Contact: Herman Noordermeer)
info@grafischatelierfriesland.nl
www.grafischatelierfriesland.nl

Etching, lithography, relief, letterpress and screenprinting workshop offering courses, exhibitions and international projects.

Grafisch Atelier Nebesto
Herkenberg 8
6231 LK
Meerssen
+31 (0)43 365 21 97

Grafisch Atelier Utrecht
Werkplaats voor beeldende kunstenaars
(Workshop for visual arts)
Plompetorengracht 4
3512 CC
Utrecht
+31(0)30 231 85 82
info@gau.nu

Well-equipped studio offering facilities in etching, lithography, screenprinting and digital media. Courses and exhibition space available.

Grafisch Centrum Groningen
Warmoesstraat 41
9724 JJ
Groningen
+31 (0)50 542 07 42
(Contact: Hans Horn)
info@grafischcentrumgroningen.nl
www.grafischcentrumgroningen.nl
Etching, lithography, typography, silkscreen, book-making and papermaking in busy, active workshop.

Grafisch Collectief Thoets
Nassaukade 321
1053 LS
Amsterdam

+31 (0)20 618 35 43
thoets@thoets.nl
www.thoets.nl

Stone lithography, intaglio, relief and silkscreen. Essentially a collective of seven printmakers. (Annual open day usually in March.)

Grafisch Werkcentrum & Uitgeverij Oost
Molukkenstraat 200-P1
1098 TW
Amsterdam
+31 (0)20 465 18 41

info@grafischwerkcentrum.nl
www.grafischworkcentrum.nl

Lettepress, relief printing, bookbinding and intaglio. Extensive education programme including adult and children's workshops, lectures and masterclasses. Studio is available to rent on daily, weekly or monthly basis.

Grafische Werkplaats Ars Aemula Naturae
Pieterskerkgracht 9-A
2311 SZ
Leiden
+31 (0)71 514 07 84
info2arsaemula.nl
www.arsaemula.nl

Art academy established in the 17th Century. Courses include lithography.

Grafische Werkplaats De Wittenburg
Wittenburgstraat 6
6901 AN
Zevenaar
+31 (0)31 652 67 22

Grafische Werkplaats 'Drukkerij Fontijn'
Avenue Concordia 99-101
3062 LE
Rotterdam
+31(0)10 477 77 77

Grafische Werkplaats Pictura
Voorstraat 190-92
3311 ES
Dordrecht
+31 (0)78 614 98 22
info@pictura.nl
www.pictura.nl/werkplaats.htm

Etching, lithography and screenprinting in association/academy established in 1774, with gallery and many other contemporary art activities.

Grafische Werkplaats Prints (GWP)
Prinsessegracht 16
2512 GA
Den Haag
+31 (0)70 360 93 87
info@grafischewerkplaats.nl
www.grafischewerkplaats.nl

Etching, lithography, relief printing and silkscreen as well as digital printing and photography. Based in The Hague, it is one of the few workshops for large-scale printing in Holland. Grafiewinkel Inkt, a print gallery that emerged out of GWP, is only a few doors down the street (see: www.grafiewinkelinkt.nl).

Gerrit Rietveld Academie Grafische Werkplaats
Frederik Roeskestraat 96
1076 ED
Amsterdam
+31 (0)20 571 16 28
(Contact: Sytze Folkertsma, Print Studio Admin.)
wmulder@grac.nl (International Relations)
www.gerritrietveldacademie.nl

Independent college with lithography, relief and etching facilities. International students welcome. Courses offered.

Kreatief Centrum Grafische Werkplaats Hof 88
Elizabethof 2
7607 ZD
Almelo
+31 (0)52 159 22 08

Kunstatelier Legeland
Akkerstraat 27
5615 HP
Eindhoven
+31 (0)40 245 52 82

Kreatieve Werkgroep Arnhem
Kemperbergerweg 813
6816 RW
Schaarsbergen
+31 (0)26 445 61 59

Open Atelier
Morsstraat 56
2312 BN
Leiden
+31 (0)71 512 43 72

Open Ateliers
Piekstraat 15
3071 EL
Rotterdam

+31 (0)10 297 30 70

Plaatsmaken/Stichting Het Grafisch Centrum
Emmastraat 73
6828 HD
Arnhem
+31 (0)26 351 56 97
info@plaatsmaken.nl
www.plaatsmaken.nl

Professional facilities for lithography, etching, relief, silkscreen, video and digital media. To be eligible to work at Plaatsmaken a professional CV and work proposal are required. Residencies via SLAK (see: www.slak.nl)

Stichting Grafisch Atelier Kampen
Hofstraat 78
8261 BB
Kampen
+31(0)38 332 34 35
info@grafisch-atelier.nl
www.grafisch-atelier.nl
Workshop established in 1984 facilities for etching, relief, screenprint and lithography.

Stichting Grafische Ateliers Maastricht
Romeinse Baan 299
6215 SK
Maastricht
+31 (0)43 347 30 30
artesjok@planet.nl
www.grafischateliermaastricht.nl

Etching, screenprinting, stone and offset lithography, letterpress and relief printing.

Stichting Grafisch Atelier 't Gooi'
Naarderstraat 14
1211 AL
Hilversum
+31 (0)35 621 62 62
gag@planet.nl
www.gaghilversum.nl

One of the oldest workshops in the Netherlands, (est. in 1968), it offers facilities for etching, relief printing, lithography, screenprinting, letterpress and book-making.

Stichting Grafisch Atelier Twente
Walstraat 8-10
7511 GH
Enschede
+31 (0)53 430 33 89
info@grafischateliertwente
www.grafischateliertwente.nl

Facilities for screenprint, etching and relief printing. Gallery shows print exhibitions throughout the year.

**Stichting Grafische Werkplaats
De Bange Duivel**
Haagweg 4
2311 AA
Leiden
+31 (0)71 514 88 00
kantoor@kunstcentrumhaagweg4.nl
www.kunstcentrumhaagweg4.nl

Large artists' studio complex with 60 studios, including two professional print studios: the first, Lokaal 07, has lithography, etching and relief; the other, De Bange Duivel, specialises in screenprinting.

WBK Vrije Academie
Paviljoensgracht 20-24
2512 BP
Den Haag
+31 (0)70 363 89 68
(Contact: Thomas Ankum & John de Rijke)
info@vrijeacademie.org
www.vrijeacademie.org

Daily access in well-equipped academy, with technical support available from Tuesday to Thursday. Lithography, letterpress, etching, screenprinting, photopolymer and digital printing available. A wide range of courses are on offer.

see also:

**Gemeenschap Beeldende
Kunstenaars GBK**
Postbus 307
6800 AH
Arnhem
+31(0)26 443 00 34
info@gbk.nl

www.gbk.nl
Largest artists' association in the Netherlands with own large art centre.

Polymetaal
Evertsenstraat 69 C
2315 SK
Leiden
PO Box 694
Leiden
2300 AR
+31 (0)71 522 26 81
info@polymetaal.nl
www.polymetaal.nl

Polymetaal is the major press manufacturer in Holland. Once a month it runs courses in 'non-toxic' etching, with five-day workshops in water-based printing held once a year.

Stichting Lettergieten 1983
Postal address:
Postbus 33
1550 AA
Westzaan
Museum address:
Jacobus van Waertstraat 53
1551 CJ
Westzaan
+31 (0)75 628 57 53
museum@lettergieten.nl
www.lettergieten.nl

Letterpress museum, still casting type and offering print demonstrations.

Stichting Weerdruk
Entrepotdok 42a
1018 AD
Amsterdam
+31 (0)20 620 79 98
(Contact: Martin Veltman & Frans Lasès)
info@weerdruk.nl
www.boekwerkinuitvoering.nl

Large bookwork and typography project.

Trans Artists
www.transartists.nl

Large site detailing international

residencies, arts organisations, etc. in the Netherlands.

Werkplaats Steendrukkerij Amsterdam
Lauriergracht 80
1016 RM
Amsterdam
+31 (0)20 624 14 91
www.steendrukkerij.com

Printmaking gallery with print workshop behind.

ITALY

Bottega del Tintoretto
(also known as Stamperia del Tintoretto)
Fondamente dei Mori 3400
Venice 30121
+39 (0)41 722 081
(Contact: Roberto Mazzetto)
tintoretto@tin.it
www.tintorettovenezia.it

Former home of Tintoretto established as an open-access print studio in 1986. Cultural events, exhibitions, conferences, theoretical and practical courses and seminars are organised. Courses cover a wide range of practices, from traditional methods to the latest innovations including bookbinding, papermaking, engraving and lithography.

Centro per L'Incisione e la Grafica d'Arte
(The Centre for Engraving and Graphic Art)
Via Regina Elena 3
00060 Formello (Roma)
+39 (0)69 088541
centroincisione@comunediformello.it
www.comunediformello.it/
centroincisione.asp

Inaugurated in 2003, the centre organises exhibitions, conferences, courses and seminars open to all: experts in the field or simple enthusiasts.

Il Bisonte
International School of Printmaking
Via San Niccolò 24r
28-50125

Florence
+39 (0)55 234 25 85
info@ilbisonte.it
www.ilbisonte.it

Established in 1959 and based in the ancient stables of the Palazzo Serristori in San Niccolò in Florence. Intensive workshops focusing on specific techniques, with access to print the archive of major artists who have printed at Il Bisonte plus specialist printmaking library. Conferences, seminars and exhibitions also organised. Individual and group open-studio access.

Kaus Associazione Keishiro
International Centre for Artistic Engraving
Arte Urbino
Via Saffi 41-61029
Urbino (PU)
+39 338 162 7150
fenice@abanet.it
www.kaus.it

Beautiful centre for printmaking specialising in etching/engraving, book-making and woodcut, set in hanging gardens of the monastery of Santa Clara with the support of the Academy of Fine Arts, and the State Art Institute, in Urbino. Extensive international links. Residential courses and symposium. Personal or targeted work and innovative/historical research welcomed and supported.

Mulano Sietti Istituto for Art & Culture
Via della Badia
55-59026 Montepiano di Vernio
Toscana
+39 (0)574 959532
info@artevacanza.it
www.artevacanza.it

Summer courses in villa in the Appenine Mountains in Northern Tuscany, with vocational courses in etching, drypoint, screenprint and woodcut.

Progretto Ecate
Via Palestro 7
22100 Como
elana@progrettoegate.com
www.progrettoecate.com

A small not-for-profit guild providing educational resources in printmaking for artists and members of the public. Offers an impressively broad range of courses including etching, artist's books, botanical printmaking, digital image-making and Japanese woodblock.

Rigalto Studio & Print Workshop
Voc. Petrosso 70
Pietrafitta
06060 Perugia
Umbria
+39 75 83 91 27
(Contact: Antonio Muratore)
rigaltostudios@hotmail.com
www.rigaltostudios.netfirms.com

Print workshop with facilities for etching, woodblock, lino and collagraphs. Situated half way between Florence and Rome in a stone farmhouse and tower dating from 1600. Self contained apartments for hire as holiday lets allow access to the workshop.

Santa Reparata International School of Art
Via San Gallo 30
50129 Florence
+39 (0)55 462 7374
rolsen@santareparata.org
www.santareparata.org
(Contact: Rebecca Olsen, Director)

Based in the middle of Florence with extensive new print facilities. Graduate and undergraduate study. The majority of students are American, but there are students from all over the world.

Scuola Internazionale di Grafica
Cannaregio
Calle Seconda del Cristo 1798
30121 Venice
+39 (0)41 721 950
(Contact: Matilde Dolcetti, Director)
info@scuolagrafiica.it
www.scuolagrafica.it

Extensive printmaking facilities. Independent studio residencies in printmaking, painting and drawing all year round (four to eight weeks).

Accommodation and studio space are provided.

The Artists International Print Project is also run every year by Mike Taylor and Simon Marsh of Paupers Press in London, inviting renowned artists to produce new work in the print studios.

Studio Camnitzer
Melchiade 1
Valdottavo
Lucca 001
+39-516-466-6975
(also c/o 124 Susquehanna Avenue, Great Neck, NY 11021, USA)
studiocamnitzer@gmail.com
www.studio-camnitzer.com

Formerly run by Luis Camnitzer, this studio residence for artists specialises in photo-etching and in using new Ecoresist-60, an Italian liquid photo-emulsion. It situated in an 18th-century farmhouse near Lucca in Tuscany. Technical advice is available from the Director, Michael Hanning. An editioning service is also available.

Venice Printmaking Workshop
6281A Cannaregio
Fondamente Nove
Venice 30131
+39 (0)41 52 43 807
(Contact: Gianfranco Gorini)
info@veniceprintmaking.it
www.veniceprintmaking.it

Impressively equipped print studio devoted to large-format printmaking and editions of artist's books. Four-week international residencies by application, limited to eight people at any one time. The studio also organises an international biennial of large-format contemporary printmaking.

See also:

La Tana Spazio dal 1999
+39 340 3167140
latanaspaziodal1999@tiscali.it
www.utenti.lycos.it/latana1999

International association of book arts which

organises major exhibitions annually, promotes an annual Review of International Book Artists.

La Stamperia d'Arte della Fratelli Alinari
www.collotipie.alinari.it
Based in Florence, this is the only studio in the world with a working collotype workshop. Collotype is a traditional process, not dissimilar to photogravure, producing prints from glass using a light-sensitive gelatin.

Print Show
www.print.it
Website with articles and forum on contemporary printmaking.

Scuola Superiore del'Arte Applicata del Castello Sforzesco
Via Giusti 42
20154 Milan
+39 02 34932021
info@scuolaartecastellosforzesco.it
www.scuolaartecastellosforzesco.it

Art school for traditional crafts such as mosaics, and including printmaking. Short courses available.

LUXEMBOURG

5 Leemerwee
L-1954
Luxembourg
+352 25 09 51
atempreinte@yahoo.fr or
aempriente@netscape.net
mywebpage.netscape.com/AEmpreinte

Etching studio established in 1994. The collective's printmakers organise individual and group exhibitions.

PORTUGAL

Agua Forte Association de Gravura
Rua de Santo Amaro à Estrela 41
Rés-do-Chão Esqº/Frente
1200-801
Lisbon
+351 213956295

agaf@aguaforte.com
www.agua-forte.com

Etching, photopolymer, collagraphs, etc. The workshop adopts non-toxic techniques, and welcomes cultural exchanges for the dissemination of traditional and experimental etching techniques. Courses have also been run in screenprinting and relief printing.

ARCO
Centro de Art & Communicaçao Visual
Rue de Santiago 18
1100-494
Lisbon
+351 21880 10 10
secretaria@arco.pt
www.arco.pt

Large art college with summer courses, youth programmes and evening classes in well-equipped print studio. Typography also on offer.

Diferença Communicação Visual
Rue Sao Filipe Nery 42 CV
1250-227
Lisbon
+351 213 832 193
Workshop/gallery.

Núcleo de Gravura do Grupo Recreativo e Cultural de Alijó
(Alijó Centre for Printmaking)
AV. Teixeira de Sousa, nº 15
5070-012 Alijó
+351 259 958 036
info@douro-gravura.org
www.douro-gravura.org

Etching/ intaglio workshop. Courses, exhibitions and international exchange, including organising the Bienial Internacional de Gravura.

Tavira Print Workshop
Contact: Bartolomew Dos Santos
Escadinhas Alto de Santanal
Tavira 8800
+351 281 325997

Intaglio and stone lithographt open-access by arrangement.

SPAIN

Augotinto
C/ Ourense No. 11
Bajo
27004
Lugo
augatinta@augatinta.com
www.augatinta.com/
+34 (0) 982 240 281

Etching, aquatint, photo-etching, relief printing and book-making. Emphasis on non-toxic methods. Courses throughout the year. Also supplier of presses and materials.

Centro Andaluz de Art Seriado
Área de Cultura del Excmo. Ayuntamiento
Palacio Abacial
Carrera de las Mercedes
23680 Alcalá la Real (Jaén)
+34 (0) 953 587 041
http://inicia.es/de/arteseriado/
cultura@alcalalareal.es

Intaglio and screenprinting workshop with courses including masterclasses in non-toxic etching and screenprinting. Artists welcomed from around the world.

Centro Murciano de Arte Gráfica y de la Estampa Contemporánea
Canalejas 8
Caravaca de la Cruz
CP 30400 (Murcia)
+34 (0) 968 70 30 66
(Contact: Carmelo Rubio or Paco Mora)
cmagecjardinico@yahoo.es
http://www.jardinico.org

Etching, lithography and silkscreen workshops among others including iron forge, photography and ceramics. Courses include electro-etch, offset litho and photoscreen.

El Almez a El Lledoner
C/ Raval de les Cases Noves 9
17137 Viladamat
Spain
+34 (0)972 78 83 70
info@ellledoner.com

www.elledoner.com

Screenprinting studio.

Fuentetodos
Ayuntamiento de Fuentetodos
c/o Cortes de Aragón 7
50142
Zaragoza

+34(0) 976 143 867
www.fuentetodos.org
info@fuentetodos.org

Museum of etching near the birthplace of Goya; gallery of graphic art with courses in etching and aquatint, etc. in picturesque medieval town.

Fundación CIEC (Centro Internacional de la Estampa Contemporánea)
Rúa do Castro 2
15300 Betanzos (A Coruña)
+34 (0) 981 77 29 64
(Contact: Omar Kessel/Ruben Pardo)
ciec@fundacionciec.com
www.fundacionciec.com
Major printmaking centre in lovely building founded by artist Jesús Núñez, with print courses in lithography, screenprinting, relief and etching, plus a gallery. Great website in Spanish (Castellano).

Fundació Pilar i Joan Miró a Mallorca
C. Saridakis 29
07015 Palma
Mallorca
+34 971 70 02 06
tallers@fpjmiro.org
www.miro.palmademallorca.es

Foundation created by the donation by Joan Miró and his family of four workshops where he had worked from 1956 until his death in 1983. Engraving, lithography, silkscreen, ceramics, photography and digital workshops available as a 'springboard for experimentation' for young artists and more established ones to carry out projects, exchange ideas, etc. Course programme in various techniques including engraving, silkscreen, digital media and art therapy. The Foundation also offers Pilar Juncosa and

Sotheby's Grants and Awards for research/education into Miró himself, for innovation, and for training, experimentation and creation in the graphic-art workshops.

Taller Gravura
C/ntra Stra de las Dolores de San Juan Coronel 3, 1º
29005 Malaga
+34 (0) 952 210141
gravura@gravura.es
www.gravura.es

Etching studio established in 1979 by Paco Aguilar. Etching courses offered.

Museo del Grabado Español Contemporáneo
C/ Hospital Bazán s/n
29601 Marbella (Málaga)

+34 (0) 952 76 57 41
info@museodelgrabado.com
www.museodelgrabado.com

Located in the beautiful former Hospital Bazán in the old town of Marbella, the museum houses an important collection of modern prints and runs courses in etching, as well as art lectures, concerts and drawing competitions. The museum also organises the annual National Engraving Awards.

Taller de Grabado, Gran Canaria
(Gran Canaria Etching Workshop)
Historiador Fernando Armas 10
Urbanización Zurbarán
35017 Las Palmas de Gran Canaria
+34 (0)928 170 151
www.portal.grancanaria.com/portal/centros
.cult

Etching workshop which also runs an open printmaking competition.

Alberto Papel y Grabado
El Recreo 72
Las Caldas 33174
Oviedo
+34 (0) 985 798359
Etching courses offered

Calcografía Nacional
Alcalá 13
28014 Madrid
+34 (0) 91 532 1543
calcografia@calcografianacional.com
www.calcografianacional.com

Spain's national archive of etchings and engravings, including an important collection of work by Goya and other Spanish artists. The print studio is open to visitors.

Estampería
San Sebastiàn 6
07760 Ciutadella de Menorca
+34 (0)971 386 451
www.murtraedicions.com

Printers/publishers run by Jordi Roses or Pilar Lloret. Very good website with print dictionary/glossary.

USEFUL SITES

www.spanishprintmakers.com
(a subsidiary of www.worldprintmakers.com)
Good site for Spanish printmakers and a forum for printmaking exhibitions, etc.

http://usuarios.lycos.es/mdocampo/id30.htm
Useful list of print courses.

SWITZERLAND

Atelier Aquaforte
Av Ed.-Rod 24
1007 Lausanne
aquaforte.blogspot.com

Studio run by Monique Lazega offering courses and access throughout the year.

Ateliers d'Impression
Atelier de St-Prex
Grand'Rue 15
1162 St-Prex

Workshop for engraving and intaglio established in 1968. Visits and workshops on request.

Atelier Raynald Métraux
Côtes-de-Montbenon 6
1003 Lausanne
+41(0)21 311 16 66
info@atelier-metraux.com
www.atelier-metraux.com

Editioner-printer specialising in lithography, offering occasional lithography courses; an excellent opportunity to work with a professional master printer.

GE Grave
Atelier Genevois de Gravure
17 route de Malagnou
CH-1208 Genève
+41 (0)22 700 62 85
gegrave@bluewin.ch
www.ateliergegrave.ch

Established in 1966, under the patronage of Max Ernst, the workshop caters for intaglio and relief. It also runs courses in traditional and innovative printmaking. The workshop has its own gallery and external exhibition programme, and tailored editioning is also available.

Radieratelier Daniel Scheidegger
Obere Hauptgasse 87
CH-3600 Thun
www.radieratelier.ch

Courses in etching, drypoint and aquatint. Darkroom also available. Open studio on Thursday evenings.

Tom Blaess Printshop – Gallery
Uferweg 10b
Altenberg
3013 Bern
+41 (0)79 222 46 61
blaess@cns.ch
www.tomblaess.com

Printer and publisher of original lithographs and mixed-media monotypes from contemporary international artists. Monotype workshops run regularly at weekends in light and airy professional printshop with printer Tom Blaess.

See also:

www.estampes.ch

Portal for printmaking in Switzerland including galleries, dealers and glossary of print.

EASTERN EUROPE

INTRODUCTION

Eastern Europe has a strong tradition of printmaking, both as a craft and as a tool of political activism – indeed, as a medium for propaganda. Printmaking has not been generally practised in open-access workshops in the same manner as in the UK, but has nevertheless continued in many forms through artist groups and in the academies and universities. Although the picture of printmaking is changing along with the political landscape of Europe itself, it is still hard to find out about printmaking in countries as familiar as the Czech Republic, Romania and Croatia. The IMPACT International Print Conference that took place in Estonia in 2007 (and before that in Poland/Germany in 2005) has helped bring printmaking in Eastern Europe to the attention of printmakers in the UK. The oldest printmaking biennials/triennials in the world, in Cracow and Ljubljana, have been leading lights in promoting and sustaining printmaking that crosses cultural and political boundaries, and extending the hand of knowledge and exchange.

At this point, I have to admit that whilst printmaking is blossoming (particularly lithography, letterpress and etching), it is to my disappointment that I have not been able to include in the following list more print workshops and organisations in Eastern Europe. Whether this indicates a difference in the way printmaking is practised in these countries, or whether it is simply a result of workshops being less active in promoting themselves on the internet, will be something I expect to discover in time. I have to console myself that this may be the start of a long journey – but take it as read that the relative size of this list is due in no small part to my own ignorance of printmaking in Eastern Europe, and that there is undoubtedly a lot more going on.

CZECH REPUBLIC

The Academy of Fine Arts, Prague
U Akademie 4
170 22 Prague 7
+420 220 408 200
www.avu.cz

Dílna Ručního Papíru o.s.
Velká Dominikánská 33
412 01 Litoměřice
Tel.: +420 724 092 279
(Contact: Irena Styrandová)
Irena.Styrandova@seznam.cz

Handmade-paper workshop in beautiful fortified royal town of Litoměřice in the Czech central mountain area nicknamed the Garden of Bohemia. Courses and exhibitions on papermaking and the art of paper.

See also:

International Biennial of Graphic Design Brno
This long-established graphics biennial (the oldest in the world), held at the Morovian gallery in Brno, showcases print and typography with a changing theme/emphasis at each event.
www.maravska-galarie.cz

Inter-Kontakt-Grafik
PO Box 30
110 01 Prague 1
+420 224 212 139
galerie@mbox.vol.cz
www.ikg.cz

Formed by the Association of Free Printmakers in 1993, Inter-Kontakt-Grafik is 'an international networking centre' which established the International Triennial of Graphic Arts (next event 2010), a themed triennial with participation by invitation only. IKG also organise the national competitions: the Print of the Year, an annual national graphic-arts competitive

exhibition (since 1994); and the Vladimír Boudník Award, a lifetime achievement award given to a living Czech printmaker (since 1995).

Grapheion
www.grapheion.cz

International printmaking magazine based in Prague.

ESTONIA

Graafikakoda
(Workshop of Estonian Printmakers)
Vabaduse väljak 6
10146 Tallinn
+372 6446872/+372 5569 6086
(Contact: Loit Joekalda)
loitj@online.ee
www.estograph.ee

The workshop is a very active etching and lithography studio with a traditional style. It has litho stones and an old Krause litho press, as well as a large etching press, two smaller etching presses, and a press for relief prints. It is in the centre of Tallinn near the wonderfully bohemian Kuku Club. From here Loit also runs the Eesti Vabagraafikute Ühendus (Association of Estonian Printmakers).

Eesti Litograafiakeskus
(Estonian Lithographic Centre)
Parnu mnt 154-228 Tallinn
+372 5560 4631
(Contact: Jaak Visnap & Kadri Alesmaa)
litokeskus@gmail.com
www.hot.ee/litokeskus

Contemporary lithography workshop offering sales of art, courses, 'work on special order'. The workshop is run by a young and active group of printmakers and situated in a large industrial unit on the outskirts of Tallinn.

MTÜ Kultuuritehas Polymeer
martin@kultuuritehas.ee
www.trykikoda.kultuuritehas.ee

This amazing typesetting workshop prints many posters for the arts in Tallinn (plus business cards and letterheads, etc., all in traditional typesetting – see website for images). The workshop is run by a young group of printers, and houses a large collection of type and printing machinery. It is situated in a huge industrial warehouse on the outskirts of Tallinn. They undertake commissions and contract printing as well as running summer workshops.

See also:

Eesti Kunstiakadeemia
(Estonian Academy of Arts)
Tartu mnt 1
Tallinn 10145
+372 626 7314
(Contact: Urmas Viik, Head of Department)
graafika@artun.ee
www.artun.ee

The Graphic Art Department has facilities for intaglio, letterpress, lithography and digital technologies. The Academy welcomes international students through the Erasmus exchange programme and several other European institutional exchange networks.

Tallinn International Print Triennial
(Contact: Mrs Mare Pedanik, Secretary)
+372 6022 6002
tallinn@triennial.ee
www.triennial.ee

HUNGARY

Magyar Rezkarcolo – es Litografusmuveszek Egyesulete
(Art Union of Hungarian Engravers and Lithographers)
H-1092 Raday U. 31/K
Budapest
+36 1 456 0535
grafikai@axelero.hu
www.rezcarc.hu or www.etching.hu

Originally the Union of Hungarian Etchers, founded in 1921, the workshop is set in the dynamic cultural area of Budapest. A non-profit-making organisation, its main goal is the cultivation and presentation of traditional printmaking methods. Facilities for etching, intaglio, relief and lithography. Its own art gallery, the Art Galleria IX, is situated a block away on the same street. Exchange exhibitions arranged with the likes of the New York Society of Etchers, Trace (Paris) and Taidegraafikot (Finland).

MACEDONIA

City Museum of Skopje – Open Graphic Art Studio
str. M.H. Jasmin bb, Skopje
+3892 3114 742
(see www.skopjeonline.com.mk)

The Open Graphic Art Studio was established in 1997 and since then has hosted about 70 local and international events. The gallery and the studio are part of the programme and are housed in the building that is home to the City Museum of Skopje in the centre of Skopje. The studio is a space of 60 sq. m (646 sq. ft), occupying part of the former railway station that was half-destroyed by the catastrophic earthquake of 1963. It has a silkscreen lab and an etching press.

See also:

International Graphic Triennial – Bitola
Institute and Museum, Bitola
st. Kliment Ohridski bb
7000 Bitola
+389 47 233 187
grafik@freemail.org.mk or
muzej@muzejbt.org.mk
www.muzejbt.org.mk

Faculty of Fine Arts, Skopje/Macedonia
"Bitpazarska" bb
1000 Skopje
(Dean: Professor Dimitar Malidanov)
flu@ukim.edu.mk
www.flu.ukim.edu.mk

Printmaking department within fine-arts faculty.

POLAND

The Association of Polish Artists and Designers
00-496 Warsaw
ul. Nowyswiat 7/6
+48 22 621 01 37
biuro@zpap.pl
www.zpap.org.pl

Represents over 8500 artists, and advocates for the arts.

Academy of Fine Arts, Katowice
Department of Graphic Arts – Chair of Graphic Arts
17 Koszarowa Street
40-068 Katowice
+48 32 608 67 39
dzial_nauczania@aspkat.edu.pl
www.asp.katowice.pl

Academy with a strong history and pedigree in graphic arts, with newly renovated print studios.

Academy of Fine Arts, Cracow
ul. Humberta 3
31-121 Cracow
+48 12 632 13 31
(Contact: Andrzej Pietsch, Head of Department)

Large department of graphic arts including lithography, relief print, etching, intaglio and screenprinting studios.

Academy of Fine Arts, Poznas
Al. Marcinkowskiego 29
60-967 Poznas
+48 61 855 25 21
(Contact: Prof. Stefan Ficner, Head of Department)
office@asp.poznan.pl
www.asp.poznan.pl

Academy of Fine Arts, Warsaw
ul. Krakowskie Przedmiescie 5
00-068 Warsaw
grafika@asp.waw.pl
www.asp.waw.pl

Academy of Fine Arts, Wroclaw
Eugeniutz Geppert
ul. Plac Polski 3/4
50-156 Wroclaw
+48 71 343 80 31/32/33/34
info@asp.wroc.pl
www.asp.wroc.pl

European Academy of Arts, Warsaw
Pawilon Cytadeli WarszawskieJ
ul. Skaza_ców 25
01-532 Warsaw
(tel./fax) +48 22 839 93 90
(Contact: EAS Prof. Ryszard Osadczy, Dean of the Graphics Department)
dziekanat@eas.edu.pl
www.eas.edu.pl

Non-state private school established in 1992.

Maria Curie-Skodowska University in Lublin
Faculty of Arts
Al. Kranicka 2
20-718 Lublin
(tel./fax) + 48 81 524 53 91/533 51 74
art@umcs.lublin.pl
http://art.umcs.lublin.pl/

Nicolaus Copernicus University
Faculty of Fine Arts
ul. Sienkiewicza 30/32
87-100 Torun
+48 56 611-38-10
kontakt@umk.pl
www.umk.pl

See also:

Silesian University Department of Art in Cieszyn
www.wart.us.edu.pl

ROMANIA

Asociacia Culturala˘ "Graphite"
Str. Augustin Pacha

Organises the International MiniPrint exhibition, Graphium.
www.omnigraphies.com

Intercontinental Biennial of Small Graphics
Fundatia "Inter-Art" Foundation
Aiud/Stefan Balog
515200 – Aiud
C.P. 40/Judetul Alba
www.neme.org/main/359/biennial-of-small-graphics

RUSSIA

St Petersburg Print Studio
Moskovskii Prospect 7
Unit 8
St Petersburg
Russia
pbelyi@hotmail.com
Founded in 2002 by Peter Belyi, the workshop has a large etching press. SPPS is 'dedicated to stimulating the cultural processes that take place in St Petersburg and to raising the status and understanding of printmaking.' St Petersburg Print Studio is currently negotiating with the Russian State Museum to move premises within the Engineers Castle, St Petersburg.

THE RUSSIAN ACADEMY OF ARTS
The creative workshops of the Russian Academy of Arts are 'creative and research laboratories for studying the processes and prospects of modern fine-arts development and the adoption of new technologies.' The in-depth training can be both an independent option of an extra for further professional education and a part of the programme for advanced training, or a refresher course see www.rah.ru

V. Surikov Moscow State Academy Art Institute
30 Tovarisheski Pereulok
109004 Moscow
+7 495 912 3932
artinst@mail.ru

The faculty of graphic art has three workshops: easel drawing, graphic design and posters, book illustrations. The curriculum includes not only painting and drawing lessons, but also the study of different publishing processes and graphic

techniques: etching, lithography, linocut, xylography, serigraphy.

The Russian Academy of Arts also has creative workshops in graphic art alongside painting and sculpture.

Graphic Art Workshop, St Petersburg
2a the 3rd line of Vasilievski Island
St Petersburg

Headed by Ilya Bogdesco.

Graphic Art Workshop, Krasnoyarsk
195 Krasnoyarski Rabochi Prospect
Krasnayarsk

Headed by German Pashtov.

Graphic Art Workshop; Moscow
16 Eropkinski Pereulok, apt. 5-6
Moscow

Headed by Alexei Shmarinov.

SLOVENIA

International Centre of Graphic Arts (MGLC)
(Mednarodni Graficni Likovni Center)
Grad Tivoli
Pod turnom 3
1000 Ljubljana
+386 (0)1 241 38 00
lili.sturm@mglc-lj.si
www.mglc-lj.si

Set in Tivoli Mansion, MGLC is an institution devoted to the promotion and printing of the graphic arts, conducting various printing programmes in its print workshops, which are equipped for producing prints in the techniques of silkscreening, lithography, woodcutting, etching, drypoint, aquatint, mezzotint and combinations of these. The workshops produce works in graphic techniques of many Slovenian and foreign artists. Demonstrations and workshops in printmaking techniques are organised for groups by prior arrangement. MGLC also organise the Ljubljana International Print Biennial, one of the oldest print biennials in the world.

SCANDINAVIA

DENMARK

The Danish Association of Graphics
Danish Grafikeres House
Solvegade 14
1307 Copenhagen K
+45 33 13 31 85
epost@danskegrafikere.dk
www.danske-grafikere.dk

Atelier Agerbo
Svenstrupvej 12
2700 Brønshøj
+45 38 79 03 65
atelier@agerbo.dk
www.agerbo.dk

Blending traditional and experimental print media including zinc and copper etching and photopolymer.

Det Grafiske Vaerksted
(The Design Workshop)
Norregade 35
9800 Hjorring
+45 98 90 00 11
dgv@has.dk
www.hgv.dk

Stone and offset plate litho plus etching studio. Apartment for visiting artists. A large print archive is also housed in Sindal Public Library.

Fluxprint
Struenseegade 15
5.sal
2200 Copenhagen N
+45 35 82 20 44
print@fluxprint.com
www.fluxprint.com
(Contact: Bjarne Soerensen Werner)

Graphic workshop for digital print for artists.

Fyns Grafiske Vaerkstad
(Funen Graphic Workshop)
Hans Jensens Straede 18-20
5000 Odense C
+45 6613 9973

fynsgrafiskevaerksted@mail.dk
www.fynsgv.dk

Relief printing, lithography and gravure. Shop selling members' work.

Grafiske Gruppe
(Graphic Group Havarthigaardens Workshop)
Havarthivej 6
2840 Holte
+45 42 35 74 ⟵···are there a couple of digits missing from this phone number?···⟶
(Contact: Finn Jensen)
fje@mail.tele.dk
www.grafiskgruppe.dk

Intaglio, photopolymer film and litho.

Hoejbjerg PhotoGrafiske Vaerksted
(Hoejbjerg PhotoGraphic Workshop)
Oddervej 80 C
DK-8270
Højbjerg
+45 86 72 54 39
(Contact: Inger Lise Rasmussen)
Ilr@aarhus.dk
www.aarhuskommune.dk/view/borger/kult
ur_fritid/kultur/hoejbjerg_fotografiske_vae
rksted

Equipped to cover traditional intaglio, analogue photography, photogravure and digital photography. Their mission; is 'to explore the potential area between photography, graphic art and the digital universe'.

Kobenhavns Grafiske Vaerksted
Fabrikken for Kunst og Design
(The Factory of Art & Design)
Sundholmsvej 46
2300 Copenhagen S
+45 32 54 94 24
www.ffkd.dk

Artists' co-operative/studio base in Copenhagen, with 50 studios including print facilities (as well as photo, wood, iron, textiles, stereographic and ceramics). Artist-in-residence scheme and annual alternative art fair.

Skovhuset Graphic Workshop
skovhuset@furesoe.dk
www.skovhus-kunst.dk

Statens Vaerksteder for Kunst og Handvaerk
(Statens Workshop for Art & Craft)
Gl. Dok Parkhus
Strandgade 27B
1401 Kbh.
Copenhagen
+45 3296 0510
www.kum.dk

Storstrøms Amts Grafiske Vaerksted
(The Graphic Arts Print Workshop)
Grønnegade Kaserne Kulturcenter
Sygestalde 15 C
4700 Næstved
+45 55 73 75 78
(Contact: Jan Kiowsky)
grafisk-kunst@mail.dk
www.grafisk-kunst.dk (good links page)

Etching, lithography, photogravure, relief and computer graphics in ex-army barracks.

Vestsjællands Arbejdende Kunstværksteders VAK
(Vestsjællands Working Art Workshops)
Graphic Workshop
Teglværksvej 22
4450 Jyderup
+45 59 27 70 77
vak@vak-kunstvaerksteder.dk
www. vak-kunstvaerksteder.dk

Zinc and copper etching/aquatint, photopolymer gravure, etc.

See also:

Grafisk Eksperimentarium
v. Henrik Boegh
Trepkasgade 8
2100 Copenhagen
+45 35 35 39 07
www.artbag.dk
www.grafiskeksperimentarium.dk

The website of Henrik Boegh, specialising in non-toxic intaglio. Henrik has taken part in the development of non-toxic intaglio

since 1995, is the author of a book on subject, and runs a mail-order shop selling materials and equipment. Also, courses offered in studio in Andalucian mountain town of Capilieri.

FAROE ISLANDS

Faeroernes Grafiske Vaerksted
(Faroese Graphic Workshop)
Orman Vidarlund 1
Post Box 1210
FO 110 Torshavn
+298 31 63 86
(Contact: Jan Andersson)
Faroe Islands Art Museum (www.art.fo).
Stone-litho printers. International residencies.

FINLAND

The Association of Finnish Printmakers
Erottajankatu 9B
00130 Helsinki
+358 9 700 285 01
info@taidegraafikot.fi
www.taidegraafikot.fi

Grafiikandaja Himmelblau
Finlaysoninkuja 9
Fin-33210-Tampere
Finland
+358 (0)3 213 3050
himmelblua@himmelblau.fi
www.himmelblau.fi

Etching and photo-etching

Joensuu Print Workshop
Kontopolku 2
80110 Joensuu
Finland
+358 (0)13 267 5317
www.jns.fi/grafikanpaja

Workshop established in 1992 with facilities for etching, stone lithography and screenprint. Courses offered.

Jyvaskylan Centre for Printmaking
Hannikaisenkatu 39

40100 Jyvaskyla
Finland
+358 14624 817
jukka.partanen@jkl.fi
www.jyvaskyla.fi/taidemuseo/grafiikkake
skus

Etching, relief printing and lithography set
in beautiful municipal building.
Established international residency
scheme (including accommodation)
'dedicated to creating and promoting
international contacts'. Gallery Harmonia
and Centre for Creative Photography also
in same building.

Lahden Taidegraafikotry
(The Graphic Association of Lahti)
Taidepanimo
Paijanteenkatu 11
14140 Lahti
Finland
+358 3 783 2837
info@lahdentaidegraafikot.fi
www.lahdentaidegraafikot.fi

'Suitable for many kinds of metal graphic
arts'.

Maltinranta Art Center
(Tampere Artists' Association)
Kuninkankaju 2
33210 Tampere
Finland
+358 (0)3 214 9214
info@tampereen-taiteilijaseuta.fi
www.tampereen-taiteilijaseuta.fi

Litho, screen and 'various forms of metal
graphics'.

Vaasan Taidegraafikot ry
(The Graphic Artist Association of Vaasa
Print Workshop)
Ludysitalo/Laivanvarustajankatu
65170 Vaasa
Finland
(Contact: Johanna Lemettinen)
info@vaasantaidegraafikot.fi
www.vaasantaidegraafikot.fi

'Metal graphics' and lithography.

Turun Taidegraafikot
(Turku Graphic Arts)
Helsinginkatu 15
20500 Turku
Finland
+358 (0) 2 2329996
hg@turun-taidegraafikot.fi
www.turun-taidegraafikot.fi
Intaglio and lithography.

ICELAND

Félagio Islensk Grafík
The Icelandic Printmakers' Association
Tryggvagötu 17
Hafnarmegin
101 Reykjavík Sími 552 2866
PO Box 857
121 Reykjavík
www.islenskgrafik.is

The Association has its own workshop and
organises exhibitions and co-ordinates
projects in all aspects of printmaking.

NORWAY

The Association of Norwegian Printmakers
Tollebugaten 24
N-0157
Oslo
firmapost@norske-grafikere.no
www.norske-grafikere.no

Established in 1919 by Edvard Munch.

Fellerverskedet Myren Graffik
Myrbakken 5
Kristiansand 4624
Norway
(Contact: Håkon Grønlien or Asbjørn
Hollerud)
pjonpjon@hotmail.com

Grafisk Verksted Naestved
(Naestved Graphic Arts Workshop)
Grønnegade Barracks Cultural
"Sygestalden" 15 C
4700 Næstved
Norway
+47 55 73 75 78

(Contact: Jan Kiowsky, Workshop Leader)
grafisk-kunst@mail.dk
www.grafisk-kunst.dk

Etching, lithography, photogravure, linocuts, woodcuts, computer graphic and other related processes in small studio.

Lademoen Kunstnerverksteder
(Lademoen Fine Art Studios)
Mellomveien 5
N-7042
Trondheim
Norway
+47 73 51 35 15
(Contact: Kristina C. Karlsen, Administrator)
ladamoen@online.no
www.lademoen.no

Norske Grafikeres Verksted
(Norwegian Printmakers' Studio)
Fyrstikkalleen 17
0661 Oslo
Norway
+47 22 68 14 57
ngrver@online.no
www.norskegrafikeresverksted.no

Lithography, engraving, woodcut, photo and digital media. International exchanges since 2001.

See also:

Kunstverket
Tromsøgata 5b
N-0565 Oslo
Norway
+47 23 23 41 50
(Contact: Petter Morken, Gallery Director; Kjell Johansson, Workshop Manager)
Egallerist@kunstverket.no
www.kunstverket.no
www.grafisk-stentrykk.com

Art gallery specialising in prints and multiples and linked/located alongside Grafisk Stentrykk lithography studio printers/editioners.

Atelier Nord
Lakkegata 55D
N-0187 Oslo

Norway
+47 23 06 08 80
office@anart.no
www.anart.no
Contemporary arts centre with production facilities and project rooms including digital media, etc.

SWEDEN

Grafiska Sallskapet
The Swedish Association of Printmakers
Hornsgatan 6
118 20 Stockholm
+46 (0)8 643 88 04
galleri@grafiskasallskapet.se
www.grafiskasallskapet.org (links page to all workshops – follow 'linkar')
Founded in 1910 and now with 430 active members, the Association has its own gallery, organises international exhibitions and produces its own newsletter, PRINTNEWS.

Algarden Verkstad
(formerly Boras Printmaking Workshop)
Algardsvagen 33
S-506-30
Boras
+46 (0)33 419860
info@algarden.se
www.algarden.se
(Contact: Christina Lindeberg)

Beautifully situated in a 17th-century mill and outbuildings by the River Viskan, there are facilities for lithography, screenprinting, intaglio digital and glass in three workshop spaces. Gallery for national and international printmakers. Welcomes guest printmakers.

Bild och Form i Västbergslagen
(Image & Form i Västbergslagen)
Östra Storgatan 26 A
771 00 Ludvika
+46 (0) 240 126 40
frans.v.b@telia.com
Contact Frans van Brüggen
+46 (0)240 80787

Bildverkstan
(Image Studio)
Vänortsgatan 9 e

431 33 Mölndal
+46 (0)31 76 09 30
(Contact : Marie Palmgren)
marie.palmgren@hotmail.com

Bolaget Vardagsbilder HB
(Every Picture Company)
Norra Forsäkergatan 29
431 63 Mölndal
+46 (0)31 87 12 18
vardagsbilder@ramverk.se
www.ramverk.se/vardagsbilder

Lithography workshop (offset and stone)
following the heritage and ethos of Alois
Senefelder, updated with digital input.

Charlottensburggruppen Verkstaden
Bollgatan 12
171-38 Solna Stockholm
+46 (0)75522116
(Contact: Jan Thunholm)

Falu Konstgrafiska Verkstad
(The Print Workshop in Falun)
Blindgatan 44
791 72 Falun
Sweden
+46 (0)23 82453
amodhir@hotmail.com
www.falu.nu

Lithography, relief, intaglio, screenprinting
and digital print. 'In addition we offer the
possibility of working with non-toxic graphic
techniques and materials.'

Fengefors Medieverkstad
(Fengefors Media Workshop)
Dalsland
Fabriksvägen 2
664 95 Fengefors
malin@notquite.se
www.notquite.se

Digital media workshop.

Gävle Konstgrafiker
Tredje Tvärgatan 3
802 84 Gävle
+46 26 12 80 21
gavle_konstgrafiker@spray.se
www.gavlekonstgrafiker.com

Etching, lithography, screenprinting,
photoscreen and enamelling. International
exchanges organised and guest rooms
available.

Grafik 99
Bildverket
Gustaf Adolfs väg 3
392 38 Kalmar
+46 (0)480 470128/470439
margithoffman@yahoo.se
www.grafik99.com
(Contact: Margit Hoffman)

Etching, intaglio and engraving.

Grafikens Hus
International Centre For Fine Art Printmaking
Gripsholms Kungsladugård
S-647 31 Mariefred
+46 (0)159 23160
(Contact: Lars-Goran Malmqvist)
info@grafikenshus.se
www.grafikenshus.se

Set in Royal Barn of Gripsholms Castle in
Mariefred, the centre houses exhibition halls,
workshops, collections, a library, conference
rooms, a shop and café. The workshops have
resources for etching, lithography, relief
printing and screenprinting. Also
photomechanical techniques and computer
printing. The centre also has a workshop for
making handmade paper and for book-
making.

Grafikgruppen Visby
Ryska Gränd 18 621 56
Visby
Gotland
+46 (0)498 2144 24
info@grafikgruppen.se
www.grafikgruppen.se

Collective workshop offers courses in
screenprinting, etching phototransfer,
computer graphics and experimental video.

Grafikverkstaden Simrishamn
(Simrishamn Graphic Workshop)
Lindhagagatan 3
272 36 Simrishamn
(Tel & fax) +46 (0)414 737 16

(Contact: Vera Ohlsson)
grafik@okraft.nu
www.grafikverkstaden.com

Open workshop for experiments in graphics and glass. Alternative methods of graphics, no solvents. Equipment for relief, intaglio, screenprinting and handmade books.

Grafiska Sällskapets Koppargrafiska Verkstad
Fiskargatan 1
116 45 Stockholm
+46 (0)8 644 37 59
(Contact: Ulrika Jevbratt)
ulrika@jevbratt.net
www.grafiskasallskapet.se

The Swedish Association of Printmakers' own workshop includes etching, photopolymer and digital facilities. Apartment available for guest printmakers.

Grafiska Verkstaden
Stationsgatan 38
951 34 Luleå
+46 (0)920 298 00
(Contact: Brita Weglin)
brita.weglin@telia.com

Karlskoga Grafikverkstad
Per Lagerhjelmg 4
691 31 Karlskoga
+46 (0)586 592 40
(Contact: Göran Persson)
goran.persson@karlskoga.se

K.I.K. Lindöateljéerna
Lindövägen 11
392 30 Kalmar
+46 (0)480 105 95
(Contact: Anders Lonn, Monica Strandberg)
kikalmar@yahoo.se

Sweden has a national network of artists and literary collective workshops, known as KKVs. The network currently includes 25 workshops and around 3700 artists. Each workshop has a specific focus, but in general they incorporate sculpture, printmaking, ceramics, glass, textiles among other disciplines. See www.kkv-riks.se for more details and links.

The following are KKVs with printmaking.

KKV-Bohuslan
Kollektiva Konstnärsverkstan
(Collective Artists' Workshop)
Gerlesborg Skärholmen
450 70 Hamburgsund
Bohuslan
+46 (0)523 542 20
(Contact: Ann-Charlotte Enoksson)
info@kkv-b.se
www.kkv-b.se

Intaglio workshop and textile printing studio in large artists' collective, which also has sculpture and ceramics workshops.

KKV-Gaffel
Gaffel Atelje Konstnärsverkstad
(Gaffel Workshop Studios)
Industrihuset Fabrics
Main Street 11_13
806 45 Gävle
+46 (0)26 10 74 30
gaffelverkstan@gmail.com
www.gaffelverkstan.com

Paper and textile screenprinting.

KKV-Göteborg
Banehagsgatan 1
Uppgång O
414 51 Göteborg
+46 (0)31 24 68 13
(Contact: Vladimir Stoces)
kkvgbg@swipnet.se
www.kkvgbg.se

Screenprint, lithography and intaglio plus textiles workshop in large 'artists & literary collective workshop' alongside ceramics, glass, enamelling, sculpture and embroidery.

KKV Grafik-Malmo
Västmanlandsgatan 3 plan 5
214 30 Malmö
+46 (0)40 18 57 31
(Contact: Arnold Hagstrom)
postmaster@kkvgrafikmalmo.se
www.kkvgrafikmalmo.se

Intaglio, lithography, relief printing,

screenprinting and black & white photo laboratory.

KKV-Harnosand
Kastellgatan 58
871 33 Härnösand
+46 (0)611 23633
(Contact: Kerstin Lindstrom/Lisa W. Carlson)
kkv.harnosand@tele2.se
www.home.swipnet.se/kkvharnosand

Intaglio, screenprinting, letterpress, bookmaking, papermaking, photography and digital media.

Kiruna Konstkollektiv
c/o Thorneus
Tennisvägen 18
981 33 Kiruna
+46 0980 154 49
(Contact: Solveig Thorneus)

KKV-Lulea
Kronan
Hus H5
974 42 Luleå
(Tel/fax) +46 (0)920 45 45 62
margot.bergman@kulturen.lulea.se
www.kkvlulea.se

Etching/aquatint workshop as well as digital facilities alongside sculpture and ceramics workshops.

KKV-Nordvästra Skåne
(Collective Artists and Literary Workshop in North-west Skane)
Höja Landsväg 32
262 93 Ängelholm
+46 (0)431 882 09
(Contact: Else Ekblom)
lage.lofdahl@spray.se
www.kkv-engelholm.se

Metal graphics, lithography, screenprinting and textile printing, etc. Gallery plus external exhibitions.

KKV-Orebro
Bevarrinsgatan 9B
703-65 Orebro
+46 (0)19 31 28 95

larspers.carina@roxang.se
(Contact: Larspers Carina Roxang)

KKV-Ornskoldsvik
Kulturfabriken
Malargrand 3
892-00 Domsjo
+46 (0)600 532 91
(Contact: Jan K. Persson)
okkv@telie.com
www.okkv.se

KKV-Östersunds
Kollektiva Grafikverkstad
(Östersunds Collective Print Workshop)
Härkevägen 5
SE-832 96 Östersund
Froson
+46 (0)63 43157
(Contact: Odd Larsson)
oddlarsson@hem.utfors.se
www.algonet.se/~herke/grafiken.html

Screenprinting, relief, letterpress and intaglio, including photopolymer/Image-On. Safer methods in printing and newer techniques used.

KKV-Sormland i Nyköping
Behmbrogatan 5
611 34 Nyköping
+46 (0)155 28 96 20
(Contact: Bernt Westlund)
kkvsormland@hotmail.com
www.geocities.com/kkvse/index.htm
Etching, lithography, relief printing and letterpress, alongside sculpture workshop.

KKV-Stockholm Nacka
Planiavägen 28-30
131 34 Nacka
+46 (0)87 16 98 06
(Contact: Eva Lindgren/Perry Stein)
kkv@kkv.nu
www.kkv.nu

Based in a large industrial building with about 800 artist members. Workshops for copper etching, litho, metal, papermaking, repro, screen, photography and fabric. Also monumental sculpture, wood, concrete, bronze, computer, ceramics and enamel.

KVV-Sundsvalls
Paviljongvägen 11
852 40 Sundsvall
+46 (0)60 61 16 81
(Contact: Martin Enander)
info@sundsvallskollektivverkstad.se
www.sundsvallskollektivverkstad.se

Artists' collective based in former hospital, with facilities for metal graphics and screenprinting as well as sculpture, ceramics and photography.

KKV-i Vasteras
Regattagaan 43
723-48 Vasteras
+46 (0)21 80 41 51
(Contact: Nina Ihren)

KKV-Vaxjo
Italienska Palatset (Italian Palace – formerly Smaland KKV)
J.F. Liedholms väg 17
352 34 Växjö
+46 (0)47 159 96
(Contact: Tomas Fouckt)
tomasfouckt@hotmail.com
www.italienskapalatset.se/kkv.php

Graphics, ceramics, paper, wood, computer, video, with glass studio currently being built.

KKV Tuoddar-Villan
Bolagsvägen 8
971 00 Malmberget
+46-(0)970-246-70
(Contact: Marlene Fors, Barbro Törngren)
barbro.toerngren@telia.com

KKV-Värmland
Kasernhöjden 25
Box 1031
651 15 Karlstad
+46 (0)54 15 92 97
(Contact: Rolf Gustafsson)
konstkkv@swipnet.se
www.kkvvarmland.se

Intaglio, photopolymer, lithography and screenprinting.

Konstgrafiska Verkstaden i Dalsland
(Dasland Graphic Arts Workshop)
Malin Palm St
Bodane 142
662-98 Tosse
Dasland
+46 (0)532 24041
(Contact: Lisbeth Fürdell)
Lisbeth.fyrdell@telia.com
www.grafikverkstan.se

Situated in former brewery, the workshop has a facilities for intaglio/etching/aquatint, photogravure and darkroom.

Konstepidemins Väg
(The Epidemic of Art)
413 14 Göteborg
+46 (0)31 82 85 58 031
www.konstepidemin.se

100 studios in 10 buildings on former site of Hospital of Epidemic Diseases.

Kretsen Grafikverkstad
Södertälje Konstnärskrets
Gamla Flickskolan Orionkullen
Västra Kanalgatan
151 71 Södertälje
+46 (0)8 550 214 23
(Contact: Olaf Sandahl, Workshop Manager)
kretsen@kretsen.info
www.kretsen.info

Lithography, etching, relief, collagraphs.

Krogen Amerika
Läroverksgatan 5
582 27 Linköping
+46 (0)13 31 22 85
(Contact: Berit Hammarbäck)
grafiken@telia.com
www.krogenamerika.se

Small workshop with gallery next door.

Litografiska Akademin
(Lithographic Academy)
Konstlitografiska Verkstaden
Vulcanön
522 34 Tidaholm
+46 502 143 34/126 06
(Contact: Lars Lundqvist)

lito@helliden.fhsk.se
www.lithonet.org

Incorporating The Collective Lithography
Workshop, a master-printer editioning
service, the Museum of Lithographic Art,
Helliden Graphic School and the paper
workshop.

Marks Konstgrafiska Verkstad
Frytslavägen 8
511 56 Kinnahult
+46 (0)320 155 24
(Contact: Tor Udd)
tor_udd@hotmail.com

Umea Kommunala Verkstader
Vastra Strandgatan 9
902 46 Umea
+46 (0)90 16 34 46
(Contact: Mats Eriksson)

Uppsala Konstnarskollektiv Verkstad
Ekebyvagen 10a8
752 63 Uppsala
+46 (0)18 54 29 66
(Contact: Ralf Viberg)

Varberg Konstnärsförening Grafikgruppen
Hamnmagasinet
Sjöallén 6
432 44 Varberg
+46 (0)340 896 15
(Contact: Tommy Bolander)
konstnarsforening@hotmail.com

VGG Grafikergruppen
Assessorsgatan 16-18
118 57 Stockholm
+46 (0)8 751 14 02
(Contact: Ingela Jondell Asplund)
ingela.jondell@telia.com
www.vgg.se

Association of printmakers with workshop
for metal graphics and collagraphs, as well
as experimenting with new materials.

Visby Grafikgruppen
Ryska Grand 18
621 56 Visby
+46 (0) 498 144 34
(Contact: Anne Nilsson)
arsgotlandica@telia.com

Vanersborgs Konstgrafiska Verkstad
Edgastan 5
462 34 Vänersborg
+46 (0)33 13 96 51
(Contact: Bernt Russberg)
argun.tangne@telia.com
www.konstgrafiska.se

Collective workshop established in 1982
with facilities for etching, stone lithography
and screenprint. Occasional courses run.

See also:

Grafik I Vast
(Graphics in the West)
Storgatan 20
411 38 Göteborg
+46 (0)31 711 38 39
giv@ramverk.se
www.ramverk.se

Large printmakers' association organising
national and international exhibitions.

Grafikskolan i Stockholm
Virkesvägen 6
120 30 Stockholm
+46 (0)8 39 24 50
info@grafikskolan.se
www.grafikskolan.se

College of Printmaking Arts in Sweden, with
excellent facilities.

www.grafiktorget.com
Swedish printmakers' forum.

ISRAEL

Art & Etching Studio
11 Hayarmuch St
Jerusalem 93704
(Contact: Daphna Guttman)

The Artists' House
9 Alcharizi St
Tel Aviv
(no website)

Courses and open-studio facilities.

The Gottesman Etching Center
Kibbutz Cabri 25120
+972 (0)4 995 2713
(Contact: Ofra Raif, Director)
info@cabriprints.com
www.cabriprints.com
ofra@cabriprints.com

The etching workshop at Kibbutz Cabri was founded in 1993, and is located in a distinctive Western Galilee landscape overlooking mountains and sea. It is a venue for artists from Israel and abroad to produce etchings, assisted by experienced etching printers. The workshop contains the largest press in Israel, with a maximum size of 130 x 230 cm (51 x 90 in.) plus an extra aquatint box, large etching baths and photo-etching facilities. Artists who produce prints in the Cabri workshop may stay at the artists' residence in the kibbutz for as long as the work requires.

Classes in etching on various levels available to the public, plus masterclasses with well-known artists (such as Jim Dine in 2000). Various joint projects with museums, including the Israel Museum and the Tel Aviv Museum. The workshop welcomes visitors interested in observing the etching process at first hand and in viewing a large variety of prints, artist's books and portfolios published by Cabri Prints.

Jerusalem Print Workshop
Bernard and Barbro Art Center
38 Shivtei Israel St
Jerusalem 95105
(tel./fax) +972 (0)2 628 8614
(Contact: Arik Kilemnik, Director)
jprint@netvision.net.il
www.jerusalemprintworkshop.org

The largest and most important print workshop in the country, based in a spacious 19th-century Ottoman building in the heart of Jerusalem. Very well-equipped workshop plus gallery housing largest print and book-arts collection in the country. Invited artists work with skilled master printers in lithography, etching, woodcut and screenprinting. Open access for etching also available. Beginners to advanced

courses available in various techniques. The workshop is currently planning a major expansion onto an extra floor.

See also:

Har-El Printers & Publishers
www.harelart.com
Publishers of prints and artist's books based in Haifa, working with artists such as Jannis Kounellis and Edouardo Chillida.

The following universities also have printmaking departments within the context of fine art:

The Bezalel Academy of Art and Design, Jerusalem
Department of Fine Arts
Swig Building (sixth floor)
Mount Scopus
PO Box 24046
Jerusalem 91240
+972 (0)2 589 3317
art@bezalel.ac.il
www.bezalel.ac.il

Haifa University
Mount Carmel
Haifa 31905
+ 972(0)4 824 0111
www.haifa.ac.il

Tel Hai Academic College
www.telhai.ac.il/english

North America

NORTH AMERICA (USA
UNLESS OTHERWISE STATED)

NORTH AMERICA (USA UNLESS OTHERWISE STATED)

PRINT ASSOCIATIONS OF AMERICA

American Print Alliance
302 Larkspur Turn
Peachtree City
GA 30269-2210
director@printalliance.org
www.printalliance.org

This is a non-profit consortium of Print Councils in the USA and Canada. The Alliance publishes Contemporary Impressions, a quarterly journal of printmaking. It also supports and promotes printmaking through exhibitions and competitions, and provides advocacy for print organisations. The Alliance also publishes a Guide to Print Workshops in Canada and the United States, and have an online resource for classes and workshops.

Baren Woodcut Forum
Email via website:
www.barenforum.org

An online forum for everything related to woodblock printmaking, including forums, exchanges, exhibitions and supplies.

Boston Printmakers
c/o Emmanuel College
400 The Fenway
Boston
MA 02115
info@bostonprintmakers.org
www.bostonprintmakers.org

Established in 1947, the Boston Printmakers organise the North American Print Biennial, plus other exhibitions such as the Arches Student Print Exhibition. They also publish a seasonal newsletter.

The California Society of Printmakers
PO Box 99499
Emeryville
CA 94662
http://users.lmi.net/~jeaneger/csp.html

Formed in 1968 by a merger of the California Society of Etchers, founded in 1913, and the Bay Printmakers' Society, founded in 1958, the CSP is dedicated to enlarging understanding of contemporary printmaking among artists and the public, locally and nationally. CSP members offer free programmes in schools and universities to advance awareness of the purposes and techniques of printmaking. CSP Brown Bag programmes offer its members a unique chance to expand their printmaking knowledge. Exchange shows between California printmakers and artists occur nationally and also internationally in such countries as Japan, England and Denmark. The Society also presents an annual members' exhibition.

Florida Printmakers
The University of Miami
Department of Art & Art History
1540 Levante Avenue
Coral Gables
FL 33416
www.as.miami.edu

Los Angeles Printmaking Society
Contact via website:
www.laprintmakers.com

LAPS is a 'national non-profit organisation dedicated to the encouragement of printmaking, educating the public and promoting the interests of printmaking as an art form. We encourage students exploring printmaking media with student exhibitions and the LAPS Foundation grants. LAPS publishes a quarterly journal, Interleaf, as well as catalogs and posters in support of our biennial exhibition, The National.'

Maryland Printmakers
PO Box 540
Savage
MD 20763
info@marylandprintmakers.org
www.marylandprintmakers.org

Established in 1989, the objective of the organisation is to promote printmaking to the general public and artists working in the media through sponsorship of the following: juried, non-juried and travelling exhibits, a slide registry, a newsletter, charitable and educational lectures, demonstrations and programmes. Membership is open to any individual committed to the promotion of printmaking. Maryland Printmakers currently has more than 250 members worldwide. Visit their site to find out more about the benefits of becoming a member.

Mid America Print Council
www.midamericaprintcouncil.org

The Mid America Print Council is a non-profit organisation of artist printmakers and educators.

Monotype Guild of New England
PO Box 134
Sharon
MA 02067

(Contact: Susan Denniston, President)
dennistons@aol.com
www.mgne.org

Dedicated to the art of the unique print, the Guild's aim is to foster understanding and appreciation of monotypes and monoprints. To this end, it sponsors exhibitions, workshops, demonstrations and other special programmes for its members and the public.

New York Society of Etchers
120 West 86th Street

Suite 7A
New York
NY 10024
info@nysetchers.org
www.nysetchers.org

First conceived in 1998 as a platform for providing exhibition opportunities to intaglio printmaking specialists in New York City. Today the Society is an internationally recognised artist-run print organisation with dozens of major exhibitions to their credit. The Society is organised in the spirit of a predecessor group known as the New York Etchers' Club, founded in the 1877. Their published mission statement defines the group as that of an exhibiting society, which is equally dedicated to documenting a large body of contemporary print work with photographic reproductions of exhibited works.

Print Arts Northwest
416 NW 12th Avenue
Portland
OR 97209
+1 503 525 9259
http://www.PrintArtsNW.org
PAN@printartsnw.org

'We sponsor educational programs for artists and non-artists with lectures, demonstrations, classes and workshops. PAN also offers various outreach programs in the public and private school system providing opportunities for students to learn printmaking.'

Printmakers of Cape Cod
Box 999
East Falmouth
MA 02536
info@printmakersofcapecod.org
www.printmakersofcapecod.org

Exhibitions and workshops/demonstrations plus an annual scholarship to Cape Cod students.

The Print Club of Rochester
+1 585 475 4977
(Contact: Zerbe Sodervick, Membership Secretary)

Email via website:
www.roc-printclub.com

An organisation devoted to fine-art printmaking, the Club has been in existence since 1934, and has an unbroken string of commissioned prints and successful shows. 'Many of the artists we commission are of international stature. We also have educational demonstrations, and lectures given by visiting artists'.

Print Council of America
Department of Drawings and Prints
The Metropolitan Museum of Art
1000 Fifth Avenue
New York
NY 10028-0198
www.printcouncil.org

A non-profit-making organisation dedicated to the study of prints, comprised mainly of museum representatives and curators.

Seattle Print Arts
1122 East Pike Street
#1444
Seattle
WA 98122-3934
info@seattleprintarts.org
www.seattleprintarts.org

'Our mission is to foster intellectual and artistic dialogue, serve as a resource for news in the field of printmaking, forge links between artists, and serve as a base for a variety of activities that focus on the print arts. Since its formation in January 2000, Seattle Print Arts has organised symposia, lectures, print exchanges, demonstrations and several print exhibits, including two international exchange exhibitions. Seattle Print Arts also sponsors a printmaking scholarship at Seattle's Pratt Fine Arts Center.

Society of American Graphic Artists
32 Union Square
Room 1214
New York
NY 10003
http://saga.monmouth.edu

Evolved from Brooklyn Society of Etchers, founded in 1915, SAGA is a service organisation and has sponsored national and international exhibitions since 1922. Other activities include demonstrations and service events, such as a symposium on health hazards in the arts. SAGA travelling exhibitions have been shown in many museums and universities.

Southern Graphics Council
Visual Arts Building
Athens G.A. 30602
USA
www.southerngraphics.org and
www.sgcarchives.org

A non-profit membership organisation that advances the professionla standing of artists who make prints, drawings, books and hand-made paper. An annual conference also draws participants from the USA and increasingly attracts international participation.

Washington Print Club
www.washingtonprintclub.org

Founded in 1964 and open to all who are interested in fine-art prints and the graphic arts: collectors, connoisseurs, artists, and just plain folks who enjoy prints as an art form. The Club organises tours of important print-related exhibitions in the Washington, DC area, visits to significant private collections and to artists' studios, panel discussions and lectures. There is also a biennial show of prints from members' collections at an area museum.

PRINT WORKSHOPS

Abington Art Center
515 Meetinghouse Road
Jenkintown
PA 19046
+1 215 887 4882
www.abingtonartcenter.org
(Contact: Jeanne Pond)

Non-profit studio offers classes and studio hire, with intaglio and relief facilities.

Academy of Arts College
79 New Montgomery Street
San Francisco
CA 94105
+1 415 274 2200

Offers classes in printmaking,
papermaking, book arts, etc.

Ah Haa School for the Arts
PO Box 1590
300 Townsend Avenue
Telluride
CO 81435
+1 907 728 3886
staff@ahhaa.org
www.ahhaa.org

Community Arts Centre incorporates
American Academy of Bookbinding, offers
courses in papermaking, bookbinding and
conservation.

Anchor Graphics
119 West Hubbard Street
5W
Chicago
IL 60610
+1 312 369 6864
(Contact: David Jones, Director)
print@anchorgraphics.org
www.anchorgraphics.org

Ferric etching, screenprint and
lithography. Anchor Graphics at Columbia
College Chicago is a not-for-profit fine-art
print shop which, under professional
guidance, brings together a diverse
community of youth, emerging and
established artists with the public to
advance the fine art of printmaking.
Courses, lectures, demonstrations and
internships on offer. Open studio on
Thursday evenings and Saturday
afternoons.

Alpha Bet Editions and Penny Press
Lincoln College Centre for Book Arts
300 Keokuk Street
Lincoln
IL 62656
+1 217 732 3155
(Contact: Andrew Jumonville)

Offers classes in intaglio, relief, letterpress,
papermaking and bookbinding and book
arts.

Anderson Ranch Arts Centre
PO Box 5598
5263 Owl Creek Road
Snowmass Village
CO 81615
+1 970 923 3181
(Contact: Matt Christie, Director)
www.artranch@rof.net
www.andersonranch.org

Large arts centre established in 1966.
Offers classes in intaglio, relief, book arts,
photographic and computer equipment.
Also offers Anderson Ranch Editions fine art
print publishing. Residency scheme also
available.

Arrowmont School of Arts and Crafts
PO Box 567
556 Parkway
Gatlinburg
TN 37738
+1 865 436 5860
info@arrowmont.org
www.arrowmont.org

Offers classes in printmaking, papermaking
and book arts, and also screenprinted
enamelling.

Art Centre/South Florida Print Workshop
924 Lincoln Road
Miami Beach
FL 33139
+1 305 674 8278
(Contact: Terry Pearl)
www.artcntr@icanect.net

Non-profit-making organisation offering
classes, gallery, studio rental. Facilities for
intaglio, lithography, relief, screenprinting
and photography.

Art Lab Inc
Snug Harbor Cultural Center
1000 Richmond Terrace
Staten Island
NY 10301
+1 718 447 8667

info@snug-harbor.org
www.snug-harbor.org
(see also www.artlab.info)

Non-profit art school est. in 1975. Open
access plus classes and gallery. Has intaglio,
relief and photographic facilities.

Art & Art Education Teachers' College
Columbia University
444 Macy Hall
525 West 120th Street
New York
NY 10027
+1 216 678 3360
(Contact: Mahbobe Ghods/John
Baldacchino)
burton@exchange.tc.columbia.edu
www.tc.columbia.edu/a&h/ArtEd/courses.a
sp?course

Offers studio hire and classes with facilities
for intaglio, lithography, relief, water-based
screenprinting and photography.

Art Students' League of Denver
200 Grant Street
Denver
CO 80203
+1 303 778 6990
programming@asld.org
www.asld.org

Independent art school/artists' community
running printmaking classes in woodcuts,
collagraph, screenprints, intaglio,
lithographs, monotypes, etc. Print studio
open labs are offered outside of classes.
Also classes in book art, ceramics, etc.

Atelier Intaglio
PO Box 1181
Tarpon Springs
FL 34688
(Contact: Lin Carte)
atelierintaglio@earthlink.net
http://serenewoman.com

Monotype, etchings, engravings, photo-etch.

Atlanta Printmakers' Studio
675 Metropolitan Parkway SW
#6026
Atlanta
GA 30310

info@atlantaprintmakersstudio.org
www.atlantaprintmakersstudio.org

Founded in 2005 to promote the fine art of
printmaking. The well-equipped studio
provides capabilities for intaglio,
monotype, woodcut, linocut, letterpress,
screenprint, papermaking, book arts and
various mixed-media techniques. Ongoing
rotation of classes and workshops, covering
a variety of printmaking topics, plus
outreach, residencies and scholarships.

Aurobora Press
147 Natoma Street
San Francisco
CA 94105
+1 415 546 7880
(Contact: Michael Liener, Director)
monotype@aurobora.com
www.aurobora.com

An invitational fine-art press based in an old
fire station; 'dedicated to the monotype
medium'. Offers three-day, five-day and
weekend courses. Gallery also available.
Facilities for intaglio, relief, book arts,
papermaking and photography, as well as
computer equipment.

Avocet/Art Awareness
Route 42
Lexington
NY 12452
Postal address:
PO Box 37
NY 10013

(Contact: Andrea Callard)
anrea.callard@verizon.net
www.avocetportfolio.com

Collaborative printer/publisher runs summer
classes in relief and screenprinting

Below the Surface Printmakers' Atelier
27 North 4th Street
#301
Minneapolis
MN 55401

+1 612 340 1001
scotto63@tc.umn.edu
(Contacts: Denese Sanders or Patricia
Scott.)

Printmakers' studio, primarily for intaglio,
but including relief and monotype. Full
etching facilities based on monthly
membership, situated in the gallery area of
the city.

Bieler Press
4216-1/4 Glencoe Avenue
Marina del Rey
CA 90292
+1 310 821 8269
(Contact: Gerald Lang)

Facilities for letterpress and photography
and digital equipment. Runs classes and
publishes.

**Black Hills Print Symposium and
Papermaking Workshop**
Ox Yoke Ranch
Nemo
SD 57759 (summer)
(For the rest of the year, contact Frogman's
Press – see below.)

Offers intaglio, lithography, relief,
papermaking and computer facilities in
association with Frogman's Press.

Boxcar Press
501 W. Fayette Street
Studio 222
Syracuse
NY 13204
http://www.boxcarpress.com
Eco-etch plates and photogravure plates.

Bozeman Pass Printmakers
803 North Wallace Street
#404
Bozeman
MT 59715
+1 406 586 1272
bzprmk@gomontana.com

Runs classes in intaglio and relief printing

**Brodsky Center for Innovative
Print & Paper**
Mason Gross School of the Arts
33 Livingston Avenue
PO Box 270
New Brunswick
NJ 18925
+1 732 932 2222
(Contact: Kathleen Goncharov)
rcipp@rci.rutgers.edu
www.brodskycenter.org

Formerly the Rutgers Center, the Brodsky
Center invites artists to be in residence to
collaborate with the printers and
papermakers. There are three specific
programmes under which artists are invited:
a National Printmaking Fellowship Program,
the New Jersey Printmaking Fellowship
Program, and an International Fellowship
Program. From time to time, other artists are
also in residence, either by invitation or
contract. Studio facilities for intaglio,
lithography, relief, letterpress,
screenprinting, papermaking, bookbinding
and photography, plus computer equipment.

Brookfield Craft Centre
PO Box 122
Route 25
286 Whisconier Road
Brookfield
CT 06804
+1 203 775 4526
info@brookfieldcraftcenter.org
www.brookfieldcraftcenter.org

Offers classes in papermaking and book
arts.

Brandywine Workshop
730-32 South Broad Street
Philadelphia
PA 19146
+1 215 546 3657
prints@brandywineworkshop.com
www.brandywineworkshop.com

Enabling artists and students of diverse
backgrounds and experience to learn and
train in a setting that is collaborative,
experimental and practises high standards.
Visiting artists' fellowship, joint projects

and contract printing. Exhibitions held in the Printed Image Gallery.

Intaglio, offset lithography, relief, screen, photographic and computer facilities

C.R.A.T.E. Workshop
730 29th Street
#209
Oakland
CA 94609
+1 510 839 5930
(Contact: Mark Zaffron)
mzaffron@lxnetcom.com

Intaglio.

CSK Ink.
1673 Wazee Street
Suite A
Denver
CO 80202
+1 303 436 9236
(Contact: K. Kent Shira)

Offers publishing, classes, rental and exhibitions. Facilities include intaglio and lithography.

Carriage House Paper
245 Kent Avenue
Brooklyn
NY 11211
(tel/fax) +1 718 599 PULP (7857)
info@carriagehousepaper.com
www.carriagehousepaper.com

Workshops are offered on all aspects of papermaking and paper arts. Also supplier of materials and papermaking equipment.

The Center for Book Arts
28 West 27th Street
3rd Floor
New York
NY 10001
+1 212 482 0295
(Contact: Peter Smith)
info@centerforbookarts.org
www.centerforbookarts.org

Offers classes for varying levels of skill in letterpress, papermaking and bookbinding, paper marbling, typography and related fields, with a modest publication schedule for established and emerging artists

Center for Contemporary Prints
Matthews Park
299 West Avenue
Norwalk
CT 06850
+1 203 899 7999
info@contemprints.org
www.contemprints.org
(Contact: Anthony Kirk, Artistic Director & Master Printer)

Non-profit-making workshop and gallery (originally Connecticut Graphic Arts Center, est. 1995). The entire spectrum of printmaking arts is explored through workshops, collaborations with master printers, exhibitions, community programmes and an artist-in-residence scheme, (including accommodation). Also runs Monothon, a monotype marathon, and an international miniprint competition.

Centre for Works on Paper of the Samuel S. Fleisher Art Memorial
705 Christian Street
Philadelphia
PA 19147
(Contact: James Mundie, Registrar)
jmundie@fleisher.org
http://www.fleisher.org

The USA's oldest tuition-free art school. Offers a range of disciplines including printmaking for adults and children.

Chalk Circle
PO Box 116
35 Bloom Street
Gilbertsville
NY 13776
+1 (607) 783 2917

Limited-edition artist's books. Groups & private classes.

Cheltenham Printmakers' Guild
Cheltenham Art Centre
439 Ashbourne Road
Cheltenham

PA 19012
+1 215-379-4660
www.cheltenhamarts.org
info@cheltenhamarts.org

Established in 1969. Workshops and
demonstrations, critiques and instruction in
a variety of printmaking media: collagraph,
monoprint, monotype, silkscreen, drypoint
etching, linocuts and woodcuts – all with
water-based inks. Also paper lithography
and book-making.

Chicago Printmakers' Collaborative
4642 N. Western Avenue
Chicago
IL 60625
+1 773 293 2070
(Contact: Deborah Maris Lader)
http://www.chicagoprintmakers.com
ink1101@aol.com

Well-equipped for etching, aquatint,
lithography, screenprinting and
photographic facilities. Runs classes for all
levels. Workshop time and individual tuition
available by arrangement.

Circle B Press
500 Means Street
Atlanta
GA 30318
+1 404 222 9096
(Contact: Robin Bernet)

Facilities for intaglio, relief and bookbinding
available for classes and private hire.

Citadel Print Center
199 Martha Street
#23
San Jose
CA 95112
+1 408 289 9316
(Contact: Glen Rogers Perrotto)

Offers publishing, classes and gallery.
Facilities for intaglio, lithography, relief,
letterpress, photographic.

Clary Lake Farm Studio
PO Box 240
Whitefield

ME 04353-0240
+1 207 549-7087
(Contact: Francis Hodsdon)

Offers contract, rental and classes with
facilities for intaglio and lithography.

Contemporary Artists' Centre
Berkshire School of Contemporary Art
189 Beaver Street
North Adams
MA 01247-2873
+1 413 663 9555
(Contact: Suzanne Brandon Graving)
cacart@together.net

A non-profit-making organisation offering
classes and a gallery. Has facilities for
intaglio, relief, screenprinting,
papermaking and photography. Looking to
convert Notre Dame Church into major
arts centre (see
www.berkshireartstart.org).

Corvidae Press
Building 205
Fort Worden
Port Townsend
WA

Postal address:
Corvidae Press
PO Box # 2092
Port Townsend
WA 98368
(Contact: Bill Curtsinger, President)
billcurtsinger@gmail.com
www.corvidaepress.com

Corvidae Press is an association of artists
who share an interest in printmaking with
facilities for non-toxic etching, monotype
and relief printing.

Creative Arts Workshop, Inc.
80 Audubon Street
New Haven
CT 06510
+1 203 562 4927
(Contact: Kate Parantou, Programme
Director)
kparantou@creativeartsworkshop.org
www.creativeartsworkshop.org

Non-profit regional centre for education with facilities for intaglio, relief, screenprint and letterpress. A range of beginners' and advanced courses plus monitored sessions for experienced independent printmakers.

Crow's Shadow Institute
4800 St Andrew's Road
Pendleton
OR 97801
+1 541 276 3954
(Contact: Frank Janzen, Master Printer)
fjanzen@crowsshadow.org
www.crowsshadow.org

Non-profit arts organisation for technology, instruction and cultural exchange on Umatilla Indian Reservation. The institute houses a large print studio, computer-graphics lab and darkroom.

Dancing Paper Studio
Glen Echo Park
7300 MacArthur Boulevard
Glen Echo
MD 20812
+1 301 634 2330
info@glenechopark.org
www.glenechopark.org

Non-profit-making arts and culture centre, part of the National Park Service. Offers classes in papermaking, book arts and printing without a press. Plus pottery, glass, etc.

David Krut Print Workshop
526 West 26th Street
#816
NY 10001
+1 212 255 3094
(Contact: Kate McCrickard, Director)
info@dkrut.com
www.dkrut.com

Professional facility est. in 2002 (formerly Galamander Press) for collaborations between South African artists and international printmakers. Facilities for intaglio, relief, letterpress, screenprinting and photogravure.

Dayton Printmakers' Co-op
Postal address:
Dayton Visual Arts Center
40 West Fourth Street
Dayton
OH 45402
Studio:
913 Keowee Street
+1 937 277 4022
(Contact: David Sweeney)
dsweeney1@fuse.net

Offers classes and studio hire with intaglio, relief, lithography (plate and stone), screenprinting and letterpress facilities.

Dieu Donne Papermill
315 West 36th Street
Manhattan
New York
NY 10018
+1 212 226 0573
paul@dieudonne.org
www.dieudonne.org
(Contact: Paul Wong)

Non-profit-making studio dedicated to the creation, promotion and preservation of contemporary art in hand papermaking, founded in 1976. Gallery and 650 sq. m (7000 sq. ft) paper studio. Residencies and collaborative projects.

Discover Graphics Atelier
Torpedo Factory Art Center
#308
105 N. Union Street
Alexandria
VA 22314
+1 703 548 0186
penny@discovergraphics.org
www.discovergraphics.org
(Contact: Penny Barringer)

Courses in lithography, etching/intaglio, monoprint and collagraphy. Facilities also for hire to experienced printmakers.

Dobbin Mill
50-52 Dobbin Street
Brooklyn
NY 11222
+1 718 388 9631

(Contact: Robbin Ami Silverberg)
dobbinmill@earthlink.net

Dobbin Mill/Dobbin Books is a hand-papermaking mill and collaborative artist's book studio in Greenpoint, Brooklyn. Its facilities are comprised of a fully-equipped papermaking studio, a large bookbindery, a printmaking area and a papermaker's garden. An outdoor courtyard area is available for larger work.

Domino Press
1229 McDonough Street
South Plainfield
NJ 07080
+1 908 561 7795
(Contact: Pat Feeney-Murrell)

Classes and studio hire with a master printer. Facilities for lithography and relief printing.

Drexel Press
3030 Northern Boulevard
Long Island City
NY 11101
+1 718 361 1900
(Contact: George Drexel)
gdexel@ix.netcom.com

Offers classes and studio to rent with screenprinting, photographic facilities and computer equipment.

Drive By Press
+1 608 217 8804/615 456 6183
(Contact: Gregory Nannery & Joseph Velasquez)
drivebypress@yahoo.com
www.drivebypress.org

A print workshop in a van! Drive By Press is a 'self-funded endeavor' which travels across America giving demonstrations and workshops to universities, colleges and schools, (over 100,000 miles covered so far), and was created to educate and share the contemporary practice of printmaking with students and art audiences across America. Joseph and Greg offer PowerPoint demonstrations on the history of printmaking and host Q&A sessions.

East Side Art Center
26 Rochambeau Avenue
Providence
RI 02906
+1 401 331 2021
(Contact: Carolyn and Donald Simon)
eastsideartcenter@msn.com
www.eastsideartcenter.com

Classes in monotype and intaglio printing including polyester plate lithography.

Encaustic Monotypes in Sante Fe
523 Cortez Street
Sante Fe
NM 87510
(Contact: Paula Roland)
EncausticSantaFe@yahoo.com
www.paularoland.com

Workshops in encaustic techniques through printmaking, drawing, collage and painting.

Evil Prints
info@evilprints.com
www.evilprints.com

'Disgusting the masses since 1995!' Based in St Louis and run by artist Tom Huck, Evil Prints specialises in relief and screenprinting with a heavy-metal slant (posters, billboards and gig art for Motorhead, etc.). Tom has also lectured across the US. The workshop is in a large warehouse workshop space. Having moved into larger premises in 2008, the workshop now offers evening classes in relief printing and screenprinting.

Experimental Etching Studio/EES Arts Inc.
65 Sprague Street East
Hyde Park
MA 02146
+1 617 364 8462
(Contact: Deborah Cornell)
info@eesarts.com
www.eesarts.com

Printmaking cooperative founded in 1983 with large spacious workshop offering lithography and intaglio. Three-month guest membership available. Courses and masterclasses offered plus collaborative projects.

Expressions Graphics Ltd
149 Harrison Street
Oak Park
IL 60304
+1 708 386 3552
(Contact: Carol Friedl/Janet Schill/Kathy Kelly)
info@expressionsgraphics.org
www.expressionsgraphics.org

Non-profit-making Coop that offers membership, classes and gallery. Facilities for intaglio, lithography and relief printing, etc. Committed to safe and eco-friendly methods.

The Fabric Workshop and Museum
1214 Arch Street
Philadelphia
PA 19107
+1 215 568 1111
info@fabricworkshopandmuseum.org
www.fabricworkshop.org

Renowned innovative workshop 1160 sq. m (12,500 sq. ft), including gallery, fully equipped photo/video lab, a pigment/dye room and a darkroom. Artist-in-residence places and collaborations with major artists.

Fabrile Studio
216 D Paseo del Pueblo Norte
Taos
NM 87571
+1 505 751 0306
(Contact: Coralie Silvey Jones)

Offers classes and studio hire. Studio facilities for offset lithography, letterpress, papermaking and bookbinding.

Farmington Valley Arts Centre
25 Arts Centre Lane
Avon
CT 06001
+1 860 678 1867
info@fvac.net
www.fvac.net
(Contact: John Cusano)

Offers classes for all abilities in large arts centre with 23 studios and two galleries.

Facilities for printmaking, papermaking, bookbinding and photography. Short courses and summer camps.

Five Points Press
Little Five Points Community Center #7
1083 Austin Avenue
PO Box 5564
Atlanta
GA 31107
+1 404 633 2172
www.l5p.com

Community group/centre runs classes for all abilities. Studio has facilities for relief, letterpress and book arts.

Flying Fish Press
490 Colusa Avenue
Berkeley
CA 94707
+1 510 526 5204 Jchen@flyingfishpress.com
www.flyingfishpress.com
(Contact: Julie Chen)

Letterpress, bookbinding and book-arts courses mainly now run at other organisations (see website for details).

Frogman's Press
105 North 3rd Street
Box 142
Beresford
SD 57004
+1 605 763 5082
info@frogmans.net
http://www.frogmans.net
(Contact: Lloyd Menard)

Offers studio hire and classes in intaglio, lithography, monotype, mezzotint, letterpress and relief. Runs summer courses at the Warren M. Lee Center for Fine Arts, South Dakota University.

Garrison Art Centre
23 Garrison's Landing
PO Box 4
Garrison
NY 10524
+1 845 424 3960
dir@garrisonartcenter.org
www.garrisonartcenter.org

Est. in 1966. Offers studio hire, classes and gallery. Facilities for intaglio, silkscreen, relief printing and papermaking, plus ceramics, crafts and painting, etc.

Glassel School of Art
Museum of Fine Arts
5101 Montrose Boulevard
Houston
TX 77006
+1 713 639 7500
www.mfah.org

Educational wing of Houston Museum of Fine Art. Offers classes in printmaking, papermaking and book arts.

Graphic Arts Workshop
2565 Third Street
#305
San Francisco
CA 94107
+1 415 285 5660
(Contact: Sarah Newton/Leslie Lowinger)
leslow@hotmail.com
www.zpub.com/gaw

Est. in 1952 from California Labor School, a non-profit-making cooperative of artists working in traditional printmaking techniques. Classes are run for all abilities. Membership by application for 24-hour access as part of cooperative group. Facilities for etching, aquatint, letterpress and lithography.

The Graphic Workshop
Woodstock School of Art
4270 Route 212
PO Box 338P
Woodstock
NY 12498
+1 914 679 2388
(Contact: Paula Nelson)
wsart@earthlink.net
www.woodstockschoolofart.org

The Woodstock School of Art 'offers the most complete graphic shop facilities in the region'. In addition to classes in etching, block printing, and lithography, workspace may be rented at nominal fees.

Guild Studio School
100 Main Street
Northampton
MA 01060
+1 413 584 3299
(Contact: Julie Held)

Studio for hire, and also runs classes in intaglio and relief printing (see also www.binderyinabox.com for book-making and binding workshops).

Hannaher's Inc. Print Studio
Plains Art Museum
704 First Avenue North
Fargo
ND 58102
+1 701 293 1082
(Contact: Mark Franchino, Rusty Freeman)
museum@plainsart.org
www.plainsart.org/education/print_studio.php

Est. in 1997 as a facility attached to Plains Art Museum, and now a collaboration with Minnesota State University offering studies in fully working workshop and allowing public access.

Hawaii Art Centre
26 Manulele Street
Hilo
HI 96720
+1 808 961 3959
(Contact: Gretchen Grove)

Classes in printmaking and papermaking.

Haystack Mountain School of Craft
PO Box 518
Deer Isle
ME 04627
+1 207 348 2306
(Contact: Stuart Kestenbaum)

Runs courses with intaglio, lithography, relief, screenprint, papermaking and bookbinding facilities.

Henning Workshop
New York Institute of Technology
Wheatly Road
Old Westbury

NY 11568
+1 516 686 7611
(Contact: Roni Henning)
Offers classes in screenprint and pochoir
(water-based).

Highpoint Centre for Printmaking
912 W.Lake Street
Minneapolis
MN 55408
+1 612 871 1326
(Contact: Carla McGrath, Cole Rogers)
info@highpointprintmaking.org
http://highpointprintmaking.org

Large state-of-the-art workshop with
facilities for etching, relief, lithography
and screenprinting. Own gallery and
editioning 'professional shop'. Currently
campaigning for future move to
permanent purpose-built centre. Jerome
Emerging Printmakers' residency scheme
available.

Hill Country Arts Foundation
120 Point Theatre Road South
Ingram
TX 78025
+1 830 367 5120
(Contact: Krispen Spencer, Director)
krispen@hcaf.com
www.hcaf.com

Offers classes in monotype, relief and
water-based screenprinting, alongside
painting and ceramics courses, etc.

Hillside Press
39 Kingston Avenue
San Francisco
CA 94110

+1 415 826 7797
(Contact: Eric Holub)
Lithography, letterpress.

**Historic Rittenhouse Town Papermaking
Workshops**
206 Lincoln Drive
Philadelphia
PA 19144
+1 215 843 2228
(Contact: Andrew Zellers-Frederick)

Offers classes in screenprinting,
papermaking, bookbinding and book arts.

Honolulu Print Workshop
Honolulu Printmakers
Academy Art Centre
1111 Victoria Street
Honolulu
HI 96814
+1 808 536 5507
(Contact: Laura Smith)
laura@honoluluprintakers.com
www.honoluluprintakers.com

Non-profit-making workshop for
experienced artists, having merged with
Honolulu Printmakers, which was founded
in 1928. Facilities for relief, etching,
aquatint, gravure, monotype and
lithography. Electric and manual presses.
Exchange exhibitions, portfolios and
limited-edition prints.

Hui No'eau Visual Arts Centre
2841 Baldwin Avenue
Makawao
HI 96768
+1 808 572 6560
(Contact: Paul Mullowney)
www.huinoeau.com
info@huinoeau.com

Runs classes for all ages and abilities in a
range of art disciplines including
printmaking. Facilities for basic relief,
monotype, etching, lithography,
screenprinting and water-based
techniques. Open studio for past and
present students on Tuesdays and
Saturdays.

Hunterdon Art Centre
7 Lower Center Street
Clinton
NJ 08809-1303
+1 908 735 8415
Email via website:
www.hunterdonartmuseum.org

Printmaking and papermaking classes.
Has also run an open-juried print
exhibition for over 50 years.

Inkling Studio
3508 SW Corbett Avenue
Portland
OR 97239
+1 503 224 2540

Cooperative workshop since 1981. Has intaglio, relief, letterpress and photographic facilities.

The Ink People
411 Twelfth Street
Eureka
CA 95501
+1 707 442 8413
(Contact: Libby Maynard, Executive Director)
inkers@inkpeople.org
www.inkpeople.org

Non-profit-making, founded in 1979. Runs classes, exhibitions, workshops, films, etc. Facilities for intaglio, lithography, relief, screenprinting, photographic facilities and computer equipment.

The Ink Shop Printmaking Center & Olive Branch
2nd floor
CSMA Building
33 East State Street
Ithaca
NY 14850
+1 607 277 3884
artists@ink-shop.org
www.ink-shop.org

Not-for-profit printmakers' centre, fine-art press and gallery which offers professional facilities for the making of fine-art prints. Facilities include etching, lithography, proofing and letterpresses, a small darkroom and computer-imaging equipment. The Olive Branch Press prints editions and handmade books. Collaborative projects, group and exchange exhibitions organised, plus slide registry for collectors and curators.

Institute for Paper, Books and Prints
University of the Arts
320 South Broad Street
Philadelphia
PA 19102
+1 215 717 6490
(Contact: Mary Phelan)
mphelan@uarts.edu
www.uarts.edu/

Offers classes in printmaking, letterpress, papermaking and book arts as part of continuing education & weekend workshops.

John C. Campbell Folk School
Route 1
Box 14A
1 Folk School Road
Brass Town
NC 28902-9603
+1 828 837 8637
Email via website:
www.folkschool.org

Offers classes in etching, photopolymer, marbling and lithography, papermaking and bookbinding, and book arts. Also enamelling, glasswork, etc.

Josephine Press
2928 Santa Monica Boulevard
Santa Monica
CA 90404
+1 310 453 1691
(Contact: John Greco)
josephinepress@earthlink.net
www.josephinepress.com

Daily rental, custom-edition printing/collaboration and regular workshops in intaglio, lithography, paper lithography, etc.

K. Caraccio Printing Studio
315 West 39th Street
Room 806
New York
NY 10018
+1 212 594 9662
(Contact: Kathy Caraccio)
kathy@kcaraccio.com
www.kcaraccio.com

Offers classes, publishing and studio hire with a master printer. Facilities for intaglio and relief printing.

Kala Institute
1060 Heinz Avenue
Berkeley
CA 94710
+1 510 549 2977
(Contact: Archana Horsting, Executive
Director)
http://www.kala@kala.org
www.kala.org

Print studio and electronic media centre
over two floors. 740 sq. m
(8000 sq. ft) print studio includes resources
for intaglio, lithography, relief, letterpress,
photographic and custom
printing/editioning room. Also print archive
and 130 sq. m (1400 sq ft) exhibition
gallery. Impressive range of courses, from
stone lithography to photogravure, etc.
Artist-in-residence scheme, fellowships and
artist-in-schools schemes.

King Library Press
Special Collection and Archives
University of Kentucky
Lexington
KY 40506-0039
+1 859 257 8812
(Contact: Paul Evan Holbrook)
peholbr@post.harvard.edu
www.harvard.edu/arts

Devoted to the tradition of fine printing, the
Press produces books and broadsides.
Typesetting, printing, and binding are all
done here. Seminars and workshops, plus
Hammer Biennial invited lectures.

Lower East Side Printshop, Inc.
306 West 37th Street
6th Floor
New York
NY10018
+1 212 673 5390
(Contact: Dusica Kirjakovic, Executive
Director)
info@printshop.org or
dusica@printshop.org
www.printshop.org

Established in 1968. The Printshop is the
largest openly accessible print studio in
New York. It offers residencies for artists,

contract printing services for small and
large publishers, and educational
opportunities in all aspects of the print field
and at all levels of expertise, etc. The
Printshop supports innovation and
experimentation with the medium, and
promotes non-toxic materials and
processes. Excellently equipped spacious
facilities (two studios and two workrooms)
for etching, screenprinting, photopolymer,
darkroom and book-making.

Manhattan Graphics Centre
481 Washington Street
New York
NY 10013
+1 212 219 8783
(Contact: M. Mayer, J. Mensch and J.
Silberstang)
manhattangraphicscenter@verizon.net
www.manhattangraphicscenter.org

Non-profit-making cooperative fine-art
printmaking studio for experienced
printmakers. The centre's facilities include
etching presses, acid room, rosin box,
lithography presses, silkscreen area, a
complete darkroom and exposing room.
Semester-long courses in all aspects of
printmaking including paper litho and glass
print.

Mendocino Arts Centre
45200 Little Lake Street
PO Box 765
Mendocino
CA 95460
+1 707 937 5818
mendoart@mcn.org
www.mendocinoartcenter.org

Founded in 1959, runs classes in
screenprinting, papermaking and book arts
as well as open studios.

**Minneapolis College of Art and Design
(Out of Hand Press)**
2502 Stevens Avenue South
Minneapolis
MN 55404
+1 612 874 3700
continuing_studies@mcad.edu
www.mcad.edu

Studio runs classes and is available for hire. Facilities for intaglio, lithography, relief, letterpress, screen, book art and photography. Print paper and book making are part of continuing education evening, weekend and dinner-time courses.

Minnesota Center for Book Arts
The Open Book Building
1011 Washington Avenue South
Suite 100
Minneapolis
MN 55415
+1 612 215 2520
(Contact: Jeff Rathermel, Artistic Director)
mcba@mnbookarts.org
www.mnbookarts.org

'The largest and most comprehensive center of its kind in the nation.' Offers studios for 'masters and novices in letterpress, papermaking, woodcut, bookbinding, photography and polymer platemaking for letterpress. Also, courses, exhibitions, artist-in-residence places and book-art fairs.

Mixit Print Studio
32 Clifton Street
Somerville
MA 02144
+1 617 629 2568
(Contact: Jane Goldman & Catherine Kernan, Co-owners)
janegoldman@earthlink.net
www.mixitprint.com

A professional monoprint/intaglio studio established in 1987 as a direct outgrowth of Artist's Proof print cooperative. Workshops approximately four times a year in monoprint, woodcut and/or intaglio.

Montpelier Cultural Arts Centre
Print Studio
9652 Muirpark Road
Laurel
MD 20708
+1 301 377 7800
(Contact: Richard Zandler)
montpelier.arts@pgparks.com
www.pgparks.com/places/artsfac/
mac.html

Arts centre based in Montpelier Mansion in Prince George's County parkland. Offers classes and gallery. Has shared facilities for intaglio, lithography, relief, screenprinting, papermaking and photography. Applications in May, with selection by jury.

Muskat Studios
193 Cedar Street
Somerville
MA 02145
lithoqueen@muskatstudios,com
www.muskatstudios.com

Lithography studio/master printer. Courses in lithography and pronto- plate, etc. Upon completion of a workshop, artists have the option of working independently in the studio at their own pace.

New Grounds Print Workshop & Gallery
3812 Central Avenue SE
#100B
Albuquerque
NM 87108
+1 505 268 8952
(Contact: Regina Held, Director and Founder)
director@newgroundsprintworkshop.com
www.newgroundsprintworkshop.com

Opened in 1996, this was one of the first completely non-toxic print open-access workshops in America. It is fully equipped for etching, photogravure, monotype and relief printing. Classes and private instruction are available, and there are monthly exhibitions in the gallery.

New Jersey Center for Visual Arts
68 Elm Street
Summit
NJ 07901
+1 908 273 9121
(Contact: Danielle Mick, Director of Education)
deemick@artcenternj.org
http://artcenternj.org

Non-profit-making arts centre offering classes in intaglio, relief printing, monotype, papermaking and book arts. 'Printmaking lab' offers untutored sessions for experienced printmakers.

New Orleans School of Glassworks and Printmaking Studio
727 Magazine Street
New Orleans
+1 504 529 7279
(Contact: Ms Martin)
neworleansglassworks@gmail.com
www.neworleansglassworks.org

Established in 1990, a non-profit organisation offering studio hire with master printer, courses and gallery. Has facilities for intaglio (including glass plates), copper etching, screenprinting, papermaking and bookbinding.

North Shore Art League Print Studio
620 Lincoln Avenue
Winnetka
IL 60093
+1 847 446 2870
(Contact: Giedre Zumbakis)
nsal@sbcglobal.net
www.northshoreartleague.org

Offers daytime and evening classes. Facilities for intaglio, relief and screenprinting.

Oblation Papers
516 Northwest Avenue
Portland
OR 97209
+1 503 223 1093
info@oblationpapers.com
www.oblationpapers.com

Basically a commercial-wedding and special paper and stationery retail, with another outlet in Bridgeport Village, Portland, they also offer letterpress, bookbinding and papermaking courses 'for novices and experts alike'.

Oregon College of Art and Craft
8245 SW Barnes Road
Portland
OR 97225
+1 503 297 5544
admissions@ocac.edu
www.ocac.edu

Studio school classes and professional workshops in letterpress, papermaking and book arts, alongside ceramics, metal work, photography, etc. The college also offers an artist-in-residence programme.

Parker Press
1800 West Cornelia
#115
Chicago
IL 60657
+1 773 880 5854
(Contact: Teresa Parker/Phillip Turner)

Offers publishing, rental, classes and gallery. Facilities for intaglio, lithography, relief, letterpress, papermaking and bookbinding

Pat Merrill Fine Art Prints
8926 Benson Avenue
#H
Montclair
CA 91764
+1 909 949 1863
(Contact: Patrick Merrill)
pemerrill@csumona.edu

Offers publishing and rental with a master printer and classes in intaglio and relief.

Penland School of Crafts
PO Box 37
67 Dora's Trail
Penland
NC 28765-0037
+1 828 765 2359
(Contact: Kenneth Botnock)
info@poenland.org
www.penland.org

Based in the Blue Ridge Mountains, this arts centre runs classes in intaglio, lithography, relief, letterpress, papermaking and book arts. Short residencies and fellowships offered.

Pequeño Press and Waterleaf Mill & Bindery
5 Moon Canyon Avenue
PO Box 1711
Bisbee
AZ 85603
+1 520 432 5924
(Contact: Patrice Baldwin)

patbooks2@lycos.com
www.mindspring.com/~patbooks

Papermaking, bookbinding and marbling.
Runs classes and apprenticeships.

Peregrine Press
The Bakery Studios
61 Portland Street
Portland
Maine
ME 04101
+1 207 761 8226
(Contact: Liz Prescott, Secretary)
lprescott@gwi.net
www.peregrinepress.com

Established in 1991, this non-profit-making
cooperative has a maximum membership
currently set at 30. Etching, monotype,
relief printing, photopolymer, photo-intaglio
and photolitho available. Workshops and
lectures offered.

Perkins Centre for the Arts
395 Kings Highway
Moorestown
NJ 08057
+1 856 235 6488
create@perkinscenter.org
www.perkinscenter.org

Occasional classes in papermaking and
printing without a press.

Peters Valley Craft Education Centre
19 Kuhn Road
Layton
NJ 07851
+1 973 948 5200
(Contact: Kenneth Jones)
info@petersvalley.org
www.petersvalley.org

Photography department offers classes in
gum bichromate printing, gum cyanotype,
platinum prints and even mercury
daguerrotypes. Also screen textiles and
papermaking.

Philbrook Museum of Art
2727 South Rockford Road
PO Box 52510

Tulsa
OK 74152
+1 918 749 7941
AdultPrograms@philbrook.org
www.philbrook.org

Offers classes and studio hire with
screenprinting, intaglio, relief, book arts
and photographic facilities.

Phoenix Rising Printmaking Co-operative
938 Parsons Avenue
Columbus
OH 43206
+1 614 444 2473
(Contact: Anne Cushman)
phoenixrisingco-op@sbcglobal.net
www.phoenixrisingprintmaking.com

Non-profit-making cooperative founded in
1998, offering studio hire with intaglio,
relief, solar-plate, book-arts and letterpress
facilities, plus courses throughout the year.

Philagrafika
728 South Broad Street
Philadelphia
PA 19146
+1 215 557 8433
info@philagrafika.org
www.philagrafika.org

Formerly Philadelphia Print Collaborative,
this is a print organisation whose mission is
'To promote and sustain printmaking as a
vital and valued art form' and to establish
Philadelphia as an international centre for
printmaking.

Exhibitions include Quadrennial of the
Printed Image (scheduled for 2010) and the
Philadelphia Invitational Portfolio.

Pittsburgh Print Group
Pittsburgh Center for the Arts
6300 Fifth Avenue
Pittsburgh
PA 15232
+1 412 361 0873
www.pittsburghprintgroup.com

An artists' guild affiliated with the
Pittsburgh Center for the Arts. Founded in

1972, the Group's purpose is to support artists who are printmakers through exhibits, educational projects and other promotional activities. Open-studio sessions plus courses in etching, relief printing and book arts.

Pratt Fine Arts Center
1902 South Main Street
Seattle
WA 98144-2206
+1 206 328 2200
info@pratt.org
www.pratt.org

Daily/monthly workshop hire in well-equipped studio. Courses covering basic techniques for intaglio, relief printing and monotype are always offered. Other classes have included Vitreography, Printmaking Without the Press, Artist's Books, and Paper Sculpture.

The Printmakers' Studio Workshop of Central Pennsylvania
603 East Boal Avenue
Boalsburg
PA 16827-1502
+1 814 466 3049
(Contact: Kathleen Frank, Mary Lou Pepe)

Memberships, rental and classes with intaglio, relief, screenprint (paper and fabric) and photographic facilities.

Printmakers' Workshop
7814 Glenbrook Road
Bethesda
MD 20814
+1 301 656 9749
(Contact: Ann Zahn)
www.annzahn.com

Run by Ann Zahn since 1977, the studio offers rental and classes with intaglio, relief and lithography facilities.

The Printmaking Center
1600 St Michael's Drive
Santa Fe
NM 87505-7615
+1 800 456 2673 (ext. 6564)
(Contact: Don Messec)

tpc@csf.edu
www.csf.edu

Part of the college of Santa Fe, offering classes and studio hire with facilities for intaglio, relief and photography.

Printmaking Council of New Jersey
440 River Road
Somerville
Branchburg
NJ 08876
+1 908 725 2110
(Contact: Linda Helm Krapf, Executive Director)
director@printnj.org
www.printnj.org

Non-profit-making organisation founded in 1973, offering studio hire and classes with facilities for intaglio, lithography, letterpress, bookbinding, papermaking and photography. Two in-house galleries plus offsite print exhibitions and an outreach programme (The Roving Press), as well as teacher training and professional development. Adolf Konrad artist-in-residence programme offered.

Pyramid Atlantic
8230 Georgia Avenue
Silver Spring
MD 20910
+1 301 608 9101
(Contact: Jose Dominguez, Executive Director)
info@pyramid-atlantic.org
www.pyramidatlanticartcenter.org

Non-profit-making organisation founded in 1981, offering publishing, rental, classes and new contemporary art gallery. Has facilities for intaglio, letterpress, relief, lithography (plate and offset), papermaking, bookbinding and digital printing. Includes papermill, printshop, letterpress studio and bindery. Also organises the Pyramid Atlantic Book Arts Fair and Conference.

Redux Contemporary Art
136 St Philip Street
Charleston

SC 29403
+1 843 722 0697
info@reduxstudios.org
www.reduxstudios.org

Full print studio (formerly Print Studio South) based in large art centre with 550 sq. m (6000 sq. ft) of warehouse space for contemporary art. Print studio includes screenprint, letterpress, relief and intaglio.

RISD Print Editions
Rhode Island School of Design
Two College Street
Providence
RI 02903
+1 401 454 6200
(Ask for Continuing Education)
cemail@risd.edu
www.risd.edu

Has intaglio, lithography, relief, screenprint, digital and photographic facilities. Continuing education offers weekend and evening courses in screenprint, pochoir, etc.

RIT Non-Toxic Contemporary Printmaking
Rochester Institute of Technology
73 Lomb Memorial Drive
Rochester
NY 14623
(Contact: Keith Howard)
howard@mail.rit.edu
www.cias.rit.edu/art

Offers graduate certificate in non-toxic printmaking for teachers and professionals, run by Keith Howard, who developed and promotes 'non-toxic' methods.

Ringling School of Art and Design
Wildacres Art Workshops Continuing and Professional Education
2700 North Tamiami Trail
Sarasota
FL 34234-5895
+1 941 955 8866
www.ringling.edu/ContinuingStudies
cssp@ringling.edu

Runs printmaking on campus in Sarasota and at Wildacres in the Blue Ridge Mountains.

The Robert Blackburn Printmaking Workshop
Elizabeth Foundation for the Arts
323 West 39th Street
11th Floor
New York
NY 10018
+1 212 563 5855
rbpmw@efa1.org
www.efa1.org

Large well-equipped studio in midtown Manhattan, built on a programme of cultural diversity from the legacy of Robert Blackburn, a pre-eminent African-American printmaker who died in 2003. Lithography (plate and stone), intaglio, relief and digital media.

Round the Top Centre for the Arts
PO Box 1316
Damariscotta
ME 04543
+1 207 563 1507
www.maineprintproject.org/roundtop.html

Courses in printmaking offered.

Ruth Leaf Studio
711 Boccaccio Avenue
Venice
CA 90291-4810
+1 310 822 1895
(Contact: Ruth Leaf)

Available for rent. Facilities for intaglio and relief, and photographic facilities for non-toxic plates.

Saltgrass Printmakers
2126 S 1000 East
Salt Lake City
UT 84106
+1 801 467 1080
(Contact: Sandy Brunvand)
sandy@saltgrassprintmakers.org
www.saltgrassprintmakers.org

Non-profit-making workshop with facilities for screenprint, etching, relief printing, mezzotint, etc. Full course programme with guest printmakers running specialist masterclasses.

St Jives Intaglio Workshop
254 Hampton Drive
Venice
CA 90291-2623
+1 301 399 3987
(Contact: Annette Bird)
itsabird@ucla.edu

Rental facilities including intaglio and relief.

Seastone Papers
Box 331
West Tisbury
Martha's Vineyard
MA 02575
+1 508 693 5786
(Contact: Sandy Bernat)
Email via website:
www.seastonepapers.com

Hand papermaking and teaching studio offering classes in papermaking, surface design and book arts. Facilities set in woodland on the island of Martha's Vineyard, off Cape Cod.

Self-Help Graphics and Art Inc.
3802 East Cesar E. Chavez Avenue
Los Angeles
CA 90063
+1 323 881 6444
(Contact: Sister Karen Boccalero)
info@selfhelpgraphics.com
www.selfhelpgraphics.com

Non-profit organisation founded in 1982 running 'free and affordable' classes, exhibitions for the local community – adults and children.

Sev Shoon Arts Centre
2862 NW Market Street
Seattle
WA 98107
+1 206 782 2415
(Contact: Dionne Haroutunian)
sevshoon@sevshoon.com
http://www.sevshoon.com

'The Printmaking Center for Aspiring and Experienced Artists'. Facilities for etching, slikscreen, monotype, etc. in well-equipped studio. Fall and winter course programmes,

plus international artist-in-residence programme.

Silvermine Guild
1037 Silvermine Road
New Canaan
CT 06840
+1 203 966 6668
(Contact: Anne Connell)
Email via website:
www.silvermineart.org

Runs classes and gallery. Facilities for intaglio, lithography, photographic and computer equipment.

Sierra Nevada College
999 Tahoe Boulevard
Incline Village
NV 89450
+1 775 881 7588
(Contact: Sheri Leigh O'Connor)
sleigh@sierranevada.edu
www.sierranevada.edu

Offers printmaking and papermaking in summer school alongside glass, ceramics, photography, etc.

Sitka Center for Ecology and Art
PO Box 65
Otis
OR 97368
+1 541 994 5485
info@sitkacenter.org
www.sitkacenter.org

Offers classes in papermaking and book arts.

Slugfest Printmaking Workshop & Gallery
1906 Miriam Avenue
Austin
TX 78722
+1 512 477 7204
(Contact: Margaret Simpson, Tom Druecker)
http://www.slugfestprints.com
info@slugfestprints.com

Collaborative workshop producing museum-quality limited editions of original prints by both established and emerging artists. The workshop is also open to artists who wish to create or edition prints independently or with the assistance of Slugfest's printers. Introductory workshops are offered in lithography, relief printing, monotype, collagraph, book arts and letterpress.

Soho Graphic Arts Workshop
433 West Broadway
New York 10012
+1 212 966 7292
(Contact: Xavier Rivera)

Offers publishing, co-publishing, studio hire with a master printer, classes and gallery. Facilities for intaglio, lithography, relief, screenprinting and photography.

Solarplate
(formerly Hampton Editions)
PO Box 520
Sag Harbor
NY 11963-0024
+1 631 725 3990
(Contact: Dan Welden)
solarplate4@aol.com
www.solarplate.com

Dan Welden developed solarplate in the 70s and now offers workshops in the technique, plus occasionally other techniques. He is the co-author, with Pauline Muir, of Printmaking in the Sun.

Southwest School of Art & Craft/Print Studio
300 Augusta
San Antonio
TX 78205-1296
+1 210 224 1048
(Contact: Margaret Craig)
info@swschool.org
www.swschool.org

Printmaking classes including open studios for those enrolled in classes. Facilities for non-toxic printmaking: relief, monotype, collagraph and etching. Also papermaking and book arts in Picante Paper Studio.

Submarine Paperworks
PO Box 1295
Gualala

CA 95445
+1 707 884 4564
+1 415 822 7647
(Contact: Joan Rhine)
subpaper@mcn.org
www.studio-tours.com/site2005/SubmarinePaperworks.html

Offers occasional papermaking classes.

Sweetwater Print Co-operative Inc.
117 South Main Street
Gainesville
FL 32601
+1 352 375 0790
(Contact: Sue Jester)
chatmanej@cityofgainesville.org.
www.gvlculturalaffairs.org/website/faciliti es/facilities.html

Studio available for classes and rental. Facilities for intaglio, lithography, screenprinting, papermaking, book arts and photography.

Stonemetal Press
1420 S. Alamo
#104
San Antonio
TX 78210
+1 210 227 0312
info@stonemetalpress.com
www.stonemetal-press.com

A non-profit-making studio offering classes, gallery and studio hire with intaglio, relief, screenprinting, solarplate, papermaking and book arts.

Tamarind Institute
108-110 Cornell Drive SE
Albuquerque
NM 87106
(Contact: Marjorie Devon, Director, or Nancy Trevisco, Coordinator)
tamarind@unm.edu
http://tamarind.unm.edu

Affiliated with the University of New Mexico, College of Fine Art Tamarind is an internationally renowned training centre for lithography. Facilities for lithography (plate and offset), relief and photography.

Offers publishing/co-publishing and gallery.

Tiger Lily Press
Dunham Recreation Center
1945 Dunham Way
Cincinnati
OH 45238-3053
+1 513 591 0817
mullenem@ucmail.uc.edu
www.tigerlilypress.org
(Contact: Elaine Zumeta)

Non-profit-making organisation established in 1978. Offers studio hire and classes in intaglio, lithography and relief.

University of Iowa Centre for the Book
216 North Hall
Iowa City
IA 52242
+1 319 335 0447
(Contact: Kim Merker)
center-for-the-book@uiowa.edu
www.uiowa.edu/~ctrbook

Major research facility for book arts plus separate facility for papermaking. Classes for all abilities in letterpress, papermaking, and book arts.

USF Graphic Studio
University of South Florida/Printmaking
College of Fine Arts
3702 Spectrum Boulevard
Suite 100
Tampa
FL 33620-9498
+1 813 974 3503
(Contact: Margaret Miller, Director)
gsoffice@arts.usf.edu
www.graphicstudio.usf.edu

University-based atelier with international reputation, having worked with major artists and developed such techniques as heliorelief. Facilities for intaglio, lithography, relief and photography. Offers an array of educational programmes and opportunities for art students, arts professionals and the public, including lectures, workshops and internships.

Vermon P. Hearn Printmaker's Workshop in the Museum of Printing History
1324 West Clay
Houston
TX 77019
+1 713 522 4652
(Contact: Ann Stool-Kasman, Executive Director)
info@printingmuseum.org
www.printingmuseum.org

The museum features printmaking and letterpress workshops, a papermaking shop and a bookbindery. Courses in letterpress, marbling, papermaking, book arts, lithography, silkscreen, monotype, etc. The Houston Book Arts Group meet monthly at the museum.

Visual Studies Workshop
31 Prince Street
Rochester
NY 14607
+1 585 442 8676
(Contact: Kirsten Merola, Artists' Programmes)
info@vsw.org
www.vsw.org/education

One of the country's largest non-profit-making centres. Summer workshops, weekend and evening classes in book arts alongside photography, digital media and film. Residencies available. Also runs an in-house MFA in association with the State University of New York College.

Woman's Studio Workshop
Binnewater Arts Center
PO Box 489
Rosendale
NY 12472
+1 845 658 9133
(Contact: Carrie Scanga)
info@wsworkshop.org
www.wsworkshop.org

Non-profit studio founded in 1974 along feminist lines, offering classes, summer courses, residencies, studio rental and a gallery. WSW houses fully equipped studios for etching, papermaking, screenprinting, clay, letterpress and photography.

Yama Prints
140 West 30th Street
#4E
New York 10001-4005
+1 212 222-3992
(Contact: Betty Winkler)
yamaprints@juno.com
www.yamaprints.com

Editioner and-or proofing for artists.
Classes offered in carborundum and
etching.

Zea Mays Printmaking
221 Pine Street
Studio 320
Florence
MA 01062
+1 413 584 1783
(Contact: Liz Chalfin, Director)
liz@zeamaysprintmaking.com
www.zeamaysprintmaking.com

Studio, workshop, educational facility and
research centre dedicated to new
approaches in printmaking and alternatives
to toxic printmaking. Large (185 sq. m/2000
sq. ft) workshop with facilities for etching,
photopolymer, and relief printing. Contract
printing undertaken. Also own gallery and
archives.

Zygote Press
1410 E 30th Street
Cleveland
OH 44114
+1 216 621 2900
(Contact: Wendy Sorin)
www.zygotepress.com

A non-profit-making studio offering classes,
gallery and studio hire with intaglio, relief
and letterpress, lithography (including
waterless), screenprinting and computer
equipment.

See also:

Hatch Show Print
316 Broadway
Nashville
TN 37201
+1 615 256 2805

hatchshowprint@bellsouth.net
www.hatchshowprint.com

Original letterpress poster company with
big reputation for gig posters, especially for
country & western music.

International Print Center New York
www.ipcny.org

A major non-profit institution devoted to
the exhibition and understanding of fine-art
prints. Excellent website.

Maine Print Project
www.maineprintproject.org

A collaborative organisation comprising
Maine institutions and museums
celebrating 200 years of printmaking with
exhibitions and educational programmes.

The Print Center, Philadelphia
www.printcenter.org

Contemporary Print Gallery since 1915.

Print Research Institute of North Texas
PO Box 305100
Denton
TX 76203-5100
+1 940 369 7575
(Contact: Catherine Chauvin, Master
Printer; Natalie O'Brien, Programme
Coordinator)
obrien@unt.edu
http://www.art.unt.edu/print/

Invitational collaborative press within the
University of North Texas.

Tugboat Printshop
298 Main Street
Pittsburgh
PA 15201
+1 412 621 0663
(Contact: Paul Roden & Valerie Lueth)
tugboatprintshop@gmail.com

Private workshop which also undertakes
commissions.

ARGENTINA

Prcyecto'Ace
Conesa 667
altos
C1426AQM
Buenos Aires
(phone/fax) + 54 (11) 4551 3218
(Contact: Alicia Candiani, Founder and
Director)
info@proyectoace.com.ar
www.proyectoace.com.ar

Established in 2003, and having moved to
refurbished premises in 2005, this
contemporary art workshop has
interdisciplinary facilities including a non-
toxic printmaking workshop, photography
lab/darkroom, a reading room
specialising in contemporary art and print
media, and computer-graphics resources.
Its mission is 'to promote the print as a
major medium of experimentation by
exploring its relationships and
hybridisations with other artistic fields ...
to be an inspiring place for creativity that
seeks to unite artists around the world
and to reduce the distance between old
and new technologies and artistic genres'.
In this way Proyecto'ace has became a
unique cultural resource, respected by
those interested in cutting-edge
approaches to print media.

Ace runs an artist-in-residence
programme, offering two to four-week
artist residencies all year round for
professional artists and art professors as
well as emerging artists through the
SUB30 programme. The residency includes
access to equipment, an exhibition in the
Políglota Gallery and assistance in the
creation of the work by providing
interdisciplinary print-research facilities,
exhibition space, materials and lodging in
the guesthouse. Each year two
international projects are opened to artists
and students seeking 'an unforgettable
intense art-making experience combined
with a cultural overview of the attractive
city of Buenos Aires, as well as the
opportunity to learn Spanish and even
some Tango'!

Centro de Edición Litografias
Bordabhere 3574
Sáenz Peña
Buenos Aires
+54 11 4757 1787
(Contact: Natalie Giacchetta, Director)
centroedicion@gmail.com

'Dedicated to the promotion, exchange,
stimulation and support of printmaking
and editioning of lithography as a means
of artistic expression.' The centre also
promotes printmaking through exhibitions
and fairs and offers the occasional
talk/demonstration.

See also:

Mirta Kupferminc
Castillo 357
Capital (c.p. 1414)
+54 11 4821 6969
mirta@mirtakupferminc.net
www.mirtakupferminc.net

Private studio. Special groups by
arrangement, plus specialist assistance.
Mirta travels away a lot and exhibits and
teaches around the world.

BRAZIL

Atelie Espaco Coringa
Rua Fradique Coutinho
934-Casa 2
Pinheiros
São Paulo
+55 (11) 3813 87 41
www.espacocoringa.com.br

Collective located in Vila Madalena,
on the west of São Paulo, with facilities
for woodcut, etching, metal, painting,
drawing, photography and video. The
group also publish works, and work on
projects including public interventions
and agitprop events. Workshops and
residency programme available.

Atelie Aberto
Rua Santos Dumont
323 Cj 02

Cambui
Campinas
São Paulo
CEP 13024-020
+55 (19) 3251 79 37
contato@atelieaberto.art.br
www.atelieaberto.art.br

Atelier Inventio
Rua Antonio Cezarino
387 Bosque
Campinas
São Paulo
CEP 13015-000
contato@atelierinventio.art.br
www.atelierinventio.art.br

Workshop equipped for silkscreen, etching, aquatint, monotypes and more. Courses available. The workshop also supports study groups who discuss contemporary practice and critical texts.

Atelier Piratininga
Rua Fradique Coutinho
934 Vila Madalena
São Paulo
+55 (11) 3816 68 91
atelierpiratininga@gmail.com
(Contact: Ernesto Bonato)
www.atelierpiratininga.com.br
atelierpiratininga.blogspot.com

The first studio to adopt non-toxic printmaking in Brazil. The studio is equipped to offer a professional work environment for etching and relief printing. Workshops, courses, projects, exchanges and symposia organised through the workshop.

Graphias – Casa de Gravura
Rua Joaquim Távora
1605 Vila Mariana
São Paolo
CEP 04015-003

+55 (11) 5539 18 58
graphias@terra.com.br
www.graphias.com.br
Gallery with workshop for artists to work in etching, relief printing, screenprint and lithography. Editioning, including book arts.

See also:

www.cantogravura.com.br
Website of Gravura Brasiliera based in São Paolo.

CANADA

Maritime and Atlantic Printmakers Society (MAAPS)
PO Box 20053
Spryfield RPO
349 Herring Road
Halifax
Nova Scotia
B3R 2K9
+1 902 477 4394
peter.mac@ns.sympatico.ca
www.maaps.ca

Established in 2006, a regional federation of printmaking in Atlantic Canada, incorporating the Nova Scotia Printmakers' Alliance and the Printmakers' Council of Prince Edward Island. In 2007 the Society set up the MAAPS International Print Exhibition, a biennial invitational international exhibition. The Society's principal aim is to be a voice for printmaking, promoting international links.

ARPRIM – Regroupement pour le promotion de l'art imprimé
(Formerly Conseil Québécois de L'Estampe)
372 Ste Catherine Street West
#426
Montreal
Quebec
H3B 1A2
+1 514 525 2621
info@arprim.org
www.arprim.org

Association with 200 members dedicated to the promotion of printmaking. Publishes print-media resource directory of Canada. Website lists courses and events.

Alberta Printmakers' Society
PO Box 6821

Station D
Calgary
Alberta
T2P 2E7
+1 403 287 1056
alberta.printmakers@yahoo.ca
www.albertaprintmakers.ca

Etching, silkscreen, lithography, relief,
collagraph and monoprint.

Atelier Circulaire
5445 Avenue de Gaspe Espace,
503 Montreal
Quebec
H2T 3B2
+1 514 272 8874
info@atelier-circulaire.qc.ca
www.atelier-circulaire.qc.ca

Intaglio, lithography, relief, letterpress and
photographic facilities.

Atelier Dupont
30 Main Street
Frelighsburg
Quebec
J0J 1C0
+1 450 298 5504
info@atelierdupont.com
www.atelierdupont.qc.ca

Intaglio & papermaking. Private studio of
Michael Dupont, offering two-day courses
in non-toxic printmaking.

Atelier du Scarabée
3224 Rue du Pin
CP 375
Val-David
Quebec
Canada
J0T 2N0
+1 819 322 5068

Atelier d'Estampe Sagamie
50 Rue St Joseph
CP 93
Alma
Quebec
Canada
G8B 5VX
+1 418 662 7280

sagamie@cgocable.ca
www.sagamie.com

Has evolved to specialise exclusively in
contemporary digital prints.

Atelier de l'Ile Inc.
1289 Rue Dufresne
Val-David
Quebec
J0Z 2N0
+1 819 322 6359
art@atelier.qc.ca
www.atelier.qc.ca

Established in 1978, the studio is set in the
mountains north of Montreal. Intaglio,
relief, screen, lithography, papermaking,
computer, photographic & video facilities.
Residencies and exchanges undertaken.

Ateliers Graff
963 Rue Rachel Est
Montreal
Quebec
H2J 2J4
+1 514 526 9851
cdesjardins@graff.ca
www.graff.ca

Established in 1966, and 'dedicated to the
development and the promotion of
contemporary printmaking practices, the
centre offers printmaking studios for
serigraphy, digital printmaking, etching,
woodcut and lithography. It also offers
specialised training courses, private
introductory and proficiency courses,
artists' talks given by both national and
international figures, and facilitates
collaborations between artists and
printmakers.' Each year Graff invites artists
from disciplines other than printmaking to
produce an edition under the supervision of
an expert printmaker.

Atelier Les Milles Feuilles Inc.
25 Avenue Principale
3ième étage
CP 64
Rouyn-Noranda
J9X 5C1
+1 819 764 5555 poste 5

mfeuilles@sympatico.com or
xylomag@hotmail.com
www.lesmillefeuilles.qc.ca

Non-profit-making workshop. Intaglio,
relief, screen & lithography. The association
organises exhibitions, conferences and
cultural trips.

Atelier Presse Papier
73 Rue St Antoine
Trois Rivières
Quebec
G9A 2J2
+1 819 373 1980
presse.papier.atelier@tr.ggocable.ca
sites.rapidus.net/atelier.presse.papier

Major print workshop with international
reputation founded in 1979. Intaglio, relief,
screenprinting, lithography, computer and
photographic facilities. Print bursaries and
awards offered. (See also Trois Rivières
International biennial in the open print
section.)

Atelier Saidye Bronfman
L'Atelier de Gravure
5170 Côte Ste Catherine
Quebec
Montreal
H1V 2AX
+1 514 739 2301

Intaglio, lithography, screen and
photographic facilities.

Atelier West
38 Elizabeth Avenue
Deer Lake
Newfoundland
A8A 1H5
+1 709 635 3604
info@atelierwest.ca
www.atelierwest.ca
Contact: Audrey Feltham

Intaglio, collagraph, relief and waterless
lithography. Instructional days Monday to
Friday. Edition printing and print
consultation undertaken.

Banff Centre for the Arts
Printmaking Department
(aka Velvet Antler Print Studio)

107 Tunnel Mountain Drive
Box 1020
Station 28
Banff
Alberta
ToL OCo
+1 403 762 6402
wendy_tokaryk@banffcentre.ca
www.banffcentre.ca

Well-equipped studio in large arts centre.
Facilities for etching, screen,
letterpress/book arts, relief, lithography,
textile printing and dyeing, photography
and digital image-making. Proposals for
projects are by application, with 24-hour
access offered.

Dundarave Printshop
1640 Johnston Street
Granville Island
Vancouver
British Columbia
V6H 3S2
+1 604 689 1650
info@dundaraveprintworkshop.ca
www.dundaraveprintworkshop.ca

Non-profit society set up in 1971 dedicated
to contemporary fine-art printmaking.
Custom-built workshop with adjacent
gallery. Intaglio, relief, collagraph and
monotype plus new non-toxic techniques.
Courses held throughout the year on
Tuesday evenings.

Engramme
501 Rue St Vallier Est
Montreal
Quebec
G1K 3P9
+1 418 529 0972
(Contact: Louise Sanfacon, Director)
engramme@meduse.org
www.meduse.org/engramme

Artist-run workshop set up in 1973. Etching,
relief, screen, lithography and digital
facilities, now established within the

Meduse Cooperative. National and international exchanges welcome.

Fairview College Printmaking Workshops
PO Box 3500
Peace River
Alberta
T8S 1V9
+1 403 243 7877

Ground Zero Printmakers' Society
420 Williams Street
Victoria
British Columbia
Canada
V9A 3Y9
+1 250 383 3689
Info@exchangesgallery.org
www.exchangesgallery.org/studios

Xchanges is a member-driven artists' cooperative operating a gallery and affordable studios for practising artists. They house eighteen individual and group studios, pottery, and cooperative printmaking and photography studios. Facilities for etching, intaglio, relief and small water-based screenprinting. Courses and training programmes run throughout the year. Xchange centre also has its own gallery available to rent.

Imago Inc.
140 Rue Botsford
#35
Moncton
New Brunswick
E1C 4X5
+1 506 388 1431
imago@nb.aibn.com
www.atelierimago.com

Etching, relief, lithography & bookbinding. Scholarships and residencies offered, as well as lectures, workshops and interdisciplinary projects.

Le Zocalo
L'Atelier d'art de Longueuil,
80 Rue St Jean
Longueuil
Quebec
J4H 2W9

+1 450 679 5341
info@zocaloweb.org
www.zocaloweb.org

Etching, collagraphs, carborundum, relief, letterpress and monotype in well-equipped workshop. Through residencies and exchanges with other workshops and multidisciplinary arts, the centre aims to create links both nationally and internationally. Extensive exhibition programme.

Malaspina Printmakers' Society
1555 Duranleau Street
Granville Island
Vancouver
British Columbia
V6H 3S3
+1 604 688 1827
(Contact: Bobbi Parker, Executive Director)
msprint@telus.net
www.malaspinaprintmakers.com

Charitable non-profit artist-run centre that supports the development of printmaking as a contemporary art form and promotes and preserves traditional print practice. Facilities include etching, lithography, photographic studio and digital lab. A dynamic exhibitions programme runs in the Society's own gallery, which includes curated and juried exhibitions, members' group shows, and a consignment sales portfolio. Scholarships and mentoring scheme offered to printmakers.

Martha Street Studio/Manitoba Printmakers' Association
11 Martha Street
Winnipeg
Manitoba
R3C OW7
Canada
+1 204 779 6253
(Contact: Sheila Spence, Executive Director)
printmakers@mts.net
http://www.printmakers.mb.ca

Large well-equipped studio for intaglio, silkscreen and lithography, including darkroom and digital facility. Courses in a wide range of techniques including letterpress and bookbinding, 3D silkscreen, cyanotype, etc. Also organises annual Steamroller Festival, printing large-scale relief prints.

Minutia Press
1716 Lee Avenue
Vancouver Island
Victoria
British Columbia
Canada
V8R 4WB
+1 250 598 1937

Intaglio.

New Leaf Editions
1370 Cartwright Street
Granville Island
Vancouver
British Columbia
V6H 3R8
+1 604 689 9918
info@newleafeditions.com
www.newleafeditions.com

A collaborative printmaking workshop established by Peter Braune in 1985 on Granville Island, it offers facilities for intaglio, relief, letterpress and photography. There is also a steel-facing facility.

Open Studio
468 King Street West
Toronto
Ontario
M5V 1L8
+1 416 504 8238
opstudio@interlog.com
www.openstudio.on.ca

One of the largest fine art printmaking centres in Canada. Intaglio, relief, lithography, screenprinting and photographic facilities. Extensive education programme in all print media; weekend and courses running for up to eight weeks. Residencies and scholarships offered. The Open Studio Gallery also has a large space and a print sales resource.

Riverside Studio
235 Chalmers Street
Box 925
Elora
Ontario
N0B 1S0
+1 519 846 0173
oxley@sympatico.ca
www.stuoxley.com

Etching and relief printing as well as photographic darkroom run by Master Printer Stu Oxley, offering one-to-one technical assistance. Accommodation and custom printing.

Sawai Atelier
662 Alexander Street
Vancouver
British Columbia
V6A 1C9
+1 604 255 9785

Intaglio & relief.

Squeeegeeville
3938 Island Highway
Royston
British Columbia
+1 250 334 2598
(Contact: Andy MacDougall)
andy@squeegeeville.com
www.squeegeevillec.om

Commercial screenprinting specialist offering courses and training, plus very good web resource and forum. Supplies POSjet products, prototyping and art-poster printing.

Society of Northern Alberta Print Artists (SNAP)
10309-97 Street
Edmonton
Alberta
T5J 0M1
+1 780 423 1492
snap@snapartists.com
www.snapartists.com
(Contact: Matthew Rangel & Mitch Mitchell, Workshop Directors)

Established in 1982. Large workshop and gallery with facilities for etching, screenprinting, lithography and photo-etching, as well as two darkrooms. Open access/daily rental plus a range of courses on offer. Also organises Edmonton Print International.

Station Studio
4008 16th Street SW
Calgary
Alberta
T2T 4H4
+1 403 243 7877

St Michael's Printshop
72 Harbour Drive
2nd Floor
PO Box 193
Station C
St John's
Newfoundland
A1C 5J2
+1 709 754 2931
stmichaelsprintshop@nfld.net
www.stmichaelsprintshop.com

Established in 1972. Intaglio, lithography and relief-printing facilities. Residence scholarship programme. Membership includes 24-hour access. Visiting artists' programme offers six one-month residencies.

Sunbury Shores Print Workshop
139 Water Street
St Andrews
New Brunswick
E5B 1A7
+1 506 529 3386
info@sunbury shores.org
www.sunburyshores.org
(Contact: Robert van der Peer)

Not-for-profit arts and nature centre on the shores of Passamaquoddy Bay, includes printmaking workshop alongside pottery studio, gallery and library. Courses, studio rental and editioning in intaglio and relief printing. Non-toxic and environmentally friendly methods used.

CUBA

Taller Experimental de Gráfica de la Habana
Callejón del Chorro
Habana Vieja
La Habana
tgrafica@cubarte.cult.cu
www.cnap.cult.cu

Founded in 1962, this workshop has been a centre of experimentation for generations of etchers in Cuba. It runs courses and has a gallery promoting printmaking.

See also:

La Fototeca de Cuba
Calle Mercaderes Nº 307
Plaza Vieja
10400 La Habana
(tel.) +53 7 862 2530/(fax) 204 2744
fototeca@cubarte.cult.cu
www.fcif.net

Photographic workshop/gallery offering courses and lectures.

The Havana Biennial
www.bienaldelahabana.cult.cu

An international event organised by the Centro de Arte Contemporáneo "Wifredo Lam", which promotes visual arts in Cuba.

MEXICO

Centro de las Artes de Guanajato
Av. Revolucion 204
esq. Vasco de Quiroga
Zona Centro
C.P. 36700
Salamanca
Gto
+52 (464) 641 6612
cenartgto_grafica@yahoo.com.mx
Center for the Arts of Guanajuato located in the former Convent of San Juan de Sahag. Opened in 2002, the centre is an academic institution supported through

the National Council for Culture and Arts.
It was conceived as an area of training
and experimentation/production, aimed
at improving the skills profiles of artists
and art teachers from the centre-west
region, and offers long-term academic
tutoring, residences and training.

Instituto de Artes Gráficas de Oaxaca
IAGO
Macedonio Alcalá No 507
Centro
Oaxaca
Oaxaca
CP 68000
+52 (951) 516 6980/516 2045
http://institutodeartesgraficasdeoaxaca.b
logspot.com

IAGO was founded by Francisco Toledo, an
important Mexican graphic artist who also
founded the Taller Papel Oaxaca, a paper
workshop/factory based at a former
(20th-century) textile factory overlooking
the Etla Valley, a beautiful cultural region
of Mexico.

Museograbado
Colón s/n esq. con 1a del Seminario
Zacatecas
Zacatecas
98600
+52 (492) 9243705
www.museograbado.com

A large workshop established in 1999,
dedicated to education and the promotion
of printmaking as a contemporary art
form, mixing materials and skills,
creativity and concepts for contemporary
artists who are assisted and supported in
all aspects of the creation of new work.
Research, exhibitions and an extensive
education programme, including non-toxic
printmaking for children, professional
training courses, seminars and
collaborative projects.

Nuevo León Art
Avenida Colon # 400
Oriente
CP 64000
Centro

Monterrey
Nuevo León
+52 (81) 8374 1226
www.artesvisualesnuevoleon.org

A very large arts centre inside the Parque
Fundidora in Monterrey, in industrial,
English-looking building, with facilities for
contemporary art including printmaking.
Involved in the exhibition/conference
Notóxico: Encuentro Internacional de
Grabado.

Taller Leñateros,
(The Woodlanders' Workshop)
Calle Flavio A. Paniagua 54
San Cristobal de las Casas
Chiapas
+ 52 (967) 678 5174
tallerlenateros@yahoo.com.mx
www.tallerlenateros.com

'Taller Leñateros is a cultural society, an
alliance of Mayan and mestizo women and
men, founded in 1975 by the Mexican poet
Ambar Past. Among its multiple objectives
are the documentation, praise and
dissemination of Amerindian and popular
cultural values: song, literature and
plastic arts. We have created a multi-
ethnic space for artists and emerging
artists. We foment artistic creation among
the most marginalised communities. The
Woodlanders invent, teach and exercise
the arts of handmade paper, binding,
solar silkscreen, woodcuts and natural
dyes. We benefit the environment by
recycling agricultural and industrial
wastes in order to create crafts and
objects of art. Taller Leñateros survives
thanks to the sale of artist's books,
postcards, posters and printed shirts.'

see also:

www.larutadelagrafica.blogspot.com
Blog site with print events and
information.

**La Siempre Habana – Obra Gráfica
Contemporánea**
Cerrada de Eucalipto No.3
Col. Tlaltenango

Cuernavaca
Morelos

+52 (777) 317 2770/(mobile) +52 (0)44 55
3988 7829
(Contact: Luis Miguel Valdes)

Contract printer/gallery that works with
international artists.

Rest of the World

AUSTRALIA

The Print Council of Australia Inc.
Office 5
5 Blackwood Street
North Melbourne
VIC 3051
+61 (0)3 9328 8991
adminpca@netspace.net.au
www.printcouncil.org.au

Established in 1966, The Print Council
of Australia Inc. is a not-for-profit
visual-arts organisation that promotes,
through IMPRINT magazine, all forms
of contemporary prints, artists' books
and paper art, and provides support
and advocacy for Australian
contemporary artists – in particular,
emerging artists.

ANU School of Art Print Workshop
Faculty of Art – Printmedia and Drawing
Workshop
The Australian National University
Canberra
ACT 0200
+61 (0)2 6125 5817
(Contact: Patsy Payne, Head of Workshop)
Patsy.Payne@anu.edu.au
www.anu.edu.au

Offers lithograph, offset, relief, intaglio
and silkscreen-printing for students.

Australian Print Workshop
210 Gertrude Street
Fitzroy
Melbourne
VIC 3065
+61 (0)3 9419 5466
(Contact: Anne Virgo)
auspw@bigpond.com
australianprintworkshop.com

Large open-access print workshop with
etching, lithography and relief-printing
facilities. Offers custom printing and
publishing, international projects and
gallery as well as an extensive exhibition
programme.

Baldessin Press – Printmaking Studio
90 Shaftesbury Avenue
St Andrews
Melbourne
VIC 3761
+61 (0)3 9710 1350
(Contact: Rob Hails)
baldessinpress.com
info@baldessinpress.com

Printmaking studio offering traditional and
contemporary etching with motorised
etching press, manual press, photogravure,
aquatint box, and artist's books. Open to
the public for hire on Sundays with a
technician. Courses and retreats run at the
bluestone cottage or the studio garret flat.

Buku-Larrngay Mulka Print Workshop
(also known as Yirrkala Arts)
Buku-Larrngay Mulka Centre
Yirrkala
NT 0880
+61 (0)8 8987 1701
prints@yirrkala.com
www.yirrkala.com/prints

Aboriginal arts centre (formally established
in 1975). Lino, screen and etching print
workshops with artists from this
community, Yirrkala, and the homelands of
the Miwatj region.

Centrehouse
178 Longueville Road
Lane Cove
New South Wales

NSW 2206
+61 (0)2 9428 4898
centrehouse@bigpond.com
www.centrehouse.org.au

Etching, relief and screen available. Rental to groups and individuals. Non-toxic approach adopted. Courses also run.

Cooroy Butter Factory
(CBF) PO Box 467
Maple Street
Cooroy
QLD 4563

Open-access print workshop in community arts and environment centre.

CPM (Community Printmakers Murwillumbah Inc.)
33-35 Kyogle Road
Bray Park via Murwillumbah
NSW 2484
+61(0)2 6672 8276
(Contact: Anne Stadler, Workshop/Gallery Coordinator)
Email via website:
www.cpmprintstudio.com

CPM has facilities for etching, lithography, relief printing and screenprinting. Exhibition space for members open to the public. While CPM is not a teaching institution its members are generous, so beginners can learn by observing and asking questions.

Darwin Visual Arts Association
56 Woods Street
(PO Box 1618)
Darwin
NT 0801
+61 (0)8 8981 9351
(Contact: Haley West, Marina Baker)
info@dvaa.net.au
www.dvaa.net.au

An artist-run initiative, DVAA provides facilities including a darkroom, a printmaking studio, artists' studio spaces plus the Woods Street Gallery.

Fire Station Print Workshop
2 Willis Street

Armadale
VIC 3143
+61 (0)2 9509 1782
firestat@firestationprintstudio.com.au
www.firestationstudio.com

Prevously Malvern Community Print Access Workshop, it offers gallery, workshop space, a photographic darkroom and artists' studios. Supervised access and one-to-one tuition available for practising artists, and classes for all abilities. Printmaking courses include etching, sugar-lift, aquatint, drypoint, monoprint, linocuts, woodcuts (including a Japanese technique known as Mocovito).

Fremantle Arts Centre
1 Finnerty Street
Fremantle
Western Australia
Postal address:
PO Box 891
Fremantle
WA 6959
+61 8 9432 9555
fac@fremantle.wa.gov.au
www.fac.org.au

Large arts centre and contemporary art gallery running courses in screenprinting, relief printing, etc. Also offers Fremantle Print Award annually (now in its 33rd year).

Hunter Island Press Inc.
3 Heathorn Street
Sandy Bay
Hobart
TAS 7003
(Contact: Yvonne Rees-Pagh, President)
Email via website:
www.hunterislandpress.org.au

Established in 2004, the studio runs courses in relief, lithography, polyplate lithography, collagraphs, artist's books and digital media.

Impress Printmakers Studio, Brisbane
73 Warilda Street
Camp Hill
QLD 4152
(Contact: President, John Doyle)

info@impress.org.au
www.impress.org.au/

Established in 2004, it has facilities for etching, relief printing, screenprinting, artist's books and solar plate. Courses and residencies available. Collaborations with other print workshops are welcomed.

Julian Ashton Art School
The Rocks Campus
117 George Street
The Rocks
Sydney – City
Postal address:
PO Box N676
Grosvenor Place
NSW 1220
+61 (0)2 9241 1641
Email via website:
www.julianashtonartschool.com.au

Printmaking courses in lithography, etching, intaglio and solar plate.

KickArts Printmaking Studio
Centre of Contemporary Arts
96 Abbott Street
Cairns
QLD 4870
+61 07 4050 9494
info@kickarts.org.au
www.kickarts.org.au

New printmaking studio being set up in 2009, within large arts centre, looking to present a programme of workshops including training and instructing artists on printmaking techniques, as well as running custom printing/editioning.

Lancaster Press
14 Eames Avenue
Brooklyn
Melbourne
VIC 3025
+61 (03) 9314 3036
(Contact: Peter Lancaster)
www.lancasterpress.com.au

Printmaking studio offering specialised facilities in direct lithography for artists and printmakers. Informal night classes are offered, working on a pay-per-attendance basis. Class numbers are small to maximise personal attention.

Megalo Access Arts
Canberra Technology Park
49 Phillip Avenue
Watson
ACT 2602
+61 (0)2 6241 4844
megaloht@cyberone.com.au
www.megalo.org
Open from 9.30-5.00, Monday to Saturday,

Megalo was established in 1980 as a community-access screenprint workshop. In 2000 the printmaking equipment from the Studio One print workshop was incorporated to establish what is now a comprehensive printmaking facility. Facilities include screenprinting on fabric or paper, etching, relief, lithography and a digital studio. The Megalo Printmaker in Residence Program provides participating artists with a stipend (living allowance and materials) and six weeks' access. International artists can apply for a travel subsidy.

Megalo also undertakes editioning and large-scale art commissions, runs community projects and youth courses, and has its own gallery

Melbourne Printmakers Studio
Studio 4
64 Regent Street
Richmond
VIC 3142
+61 (0)3 9416 1606
(Contact: Yvonne Watson)
melbourneprintmakers@bigpond.com

Offers etching, linocuts, engraving and digital art works.

Newcastle Printmakers' Workshop
(PO Box 102)
27 Popran Road
Adamstown
Newcastle
NSW 2289
+61 (0)2 4944 8393

(Contact: Ardel Prout, Chairperson)
⟨····prout?····⟩protu@1dl.net.au

Access etching, relief, lithography and screenprinting workshop, exhibitions and classes. Newsletter available.

Northern Editions
Building Orange 9
Charles Darwin University
Casuarina Campus
Darwin
NT 0909
(Contact: Emma Fowler-Thomason)
emma.fowler-thomason@cdu.edu.au
www.northernedditions.com.au

Located on the campus of Charles Darwin University, this print publisher also runs workshops on campus and for the community, plus tours and workshop demonstrations and collaborative projects.

Open Bite Australia
West Australian School of Visual Arts
Edith Cowan University
2 Bradford Street
Mount Lawley
Perth
WA 6050
+61 (0)8 9370 6239
(Contact: Clive Barstow, Amanda Allerding)
c.barstow@ecu.edu.au
www.scca.ecu.edu.au/projects/openbite/o
babout.html

Run within the printmaking studio in The School of Communication and Contemporary Arts, Edith Cowan University, the workshop has been established to offer access and instruction at various levels to artists and members of the community wishing to engage in printmaking. Facilities for etching, collagraph, drypoint, silkscreen, lithography, relief, photography, digital.

Pine Street Creative Arts Centre
64 Pine Street
Chippendale
Sydney
NSW 2008
+61 (0)2 9245 1503
(Contact: Jane Hooper, Coordinator)

pinestreet@cityofsydney.nsw.gov.au
www.pinestreet.com.au

Printmaking in a wide range of fine-art printing techniques, from intaglio to relief, using non-toxic processes.

Portland Bay Press
21 Julia Street
Portland
VIC 3305
Contact:
Bronwyn Mibus, Convenor:
bronibus@hotmail.com
Therese Dolman, Secretary:
dolmanm@hotkey.net.au
Etching studio and gallery.

Primrose Park Arts Centre
PO Box 152
Cremorne
North Sydney
NSW 2090

paperarts@primrose-park.com.au
www.primrose-park.com.au

Paper arts, bookbinding, photography and calligraphy based in arts centre run on a voluntary basis.

Printmakers' Association of Western Australia Inc.
PO Box 78
Northbridge
WA 6865
+61 (0)8 9328 9449
printwa@iinet.net.au or
adelled@hotmail.com
(for E-bytes newsletter)
http://pmawa.iinet.net.au

Founded in 1974 with the intention of providing support for members as they pursue professional exposure in the artistic field of printmaking. The Association now extends this help by providing an equipped studio, exhibition space, workshops, professional assistance, exchanges, exhibition opportunities, a newsletter and online hosting facilities.

The Print Studio
PO Box
373 Hindmarsh
SA 5007
(Contact: Dianne Longley)
dianne@diannelongley.com.au
diannelongley.com.au

Open-access studio with etching, relief and photopolymer printmaking equipment as well as desktop publishing facilities. Provides workshops and editioning. Dianne is internationally renowned for her work in photopolymer.

Tapir Print Workshop
25 Weld Street
7004 South Hobart
Tasmania
+61 (0)3 6223 1402
(Contact: Nic Goodwolf)
info@tapirstudio.org
www.tapristudio.org

Offers facilities for etching, collagraphs and woodblock printing as well as the use of a large bookbinding press. Goodwolf Editions offers a limited-edition printing service from Tapir Studio. (Tapir has a sister studio in Berlin in Germany.)

Warringah Printmakers' Studio
48/343 Condamine Street
Manly Vale
NSW 2093

+1 (0)2 9949 2325
(Contact: Annie Day/Susan Baran)
anthea@printstudio.org.au
www.printstudio.org.au

Specialises in promoting safer printmaking techniques. Electric and manual presses, exposure system, fume cupboard, relief, intaglio, lithography, studio hire and classes, plus custom printing available on request.

Workshop Arts Centre
33 Laurel Street
Willoughby
Sydney
NSW 2068

Tel: 9958 6540
workshoparts@tsn.cc
www.workshoparts.com

Arts Centre founded in 1961 with facilities for etching, relief printing and lithography. Weekend, evening and summer-holiday workshops offered.

See also:

Basil Hall Editions
30 Buchanan Terrace
Nakara
NT 0810
+61 (0)8 8927 0605
basil_hall_editions@ozemail.com.au
www.basilhalleditions.com.au

Avaliable to artists and art centres who wish to collaborate with experienced printers. Equipped for etching, litho, silkscreen and relief.

Crown Street Press
154 Crown Street
East Sydney
NSW 2010
+61 (0)2 9331 5394 (Sydney)
(Contact: James Whitington)
info@crownstreetpress.com
crownstreetpress.com

Equipped to develop and print etchings, relief prints and monotypes. Have 1 x 2 m (39 x 79 in.) etching press and 2.5 m (98 in.) wide roller for large mono or relief prints. Available for plate preparation and editioning.

Bill Young Print Workshop
King Valley
Middle Park
Victoria
www.enjaypresses.com.au/index.html

Private press owned by Bill Young, who since 1993 has run Enjay etching presses.

Fern Tree Printmakers
150 Summerlease Road
Fern Tree
TAS 7054

+61 (0)3 6239 1518 (Veronica Steane) or
(0)3 6223 4872 (Sue Pickering)
sgbrown@netspace.net.au

Formed in 1994, Fern Tree Printmakers'
consists of former students from the
Tasmanian School of Art, Hobart, who
banded together to share the capital
costs of printmaking equipment and for
mutual support. As all the equipment is
privately owned, Fern Tree Printmakers is
not a community-access group. However,
they have participated in some print-
exchange projects with artists from
around Australia.

Griffith Street Studio
20 Hutchinson Street
Bardwell Park
Sydney
NSW 2207
www.pamelagriffith.com
mail@pamelagriffith.com
+61 (0)2 9502 1675

Personal etching studio welcomes group
visits for viewings and demonstrations.

Inkubations Printmaking Group
Cooloola-based printmaking group
+61 (0)7 5486 6285
(Contact: Beth Wilson)
(See also www.moskett.com)

Founded in 2000 by Mo Skett and Barb
Hart, and brings together printmakers who
meet every two months.

Noose Arts & Crafts
Wallace House
PO Box 320
Tewantin 4565
7 Wallace Drive
Noosaville 4566
+61 (0)7 5474 1211
wallacehouse@spiderweb.com.au
www.noosaartsandcrafts.org.au

Occasional printmaking and papermaking
courses.

Open Bite Inc.
www.openbiteprintmakers.com

Group of Sydney-based printmakers who
organise exhibitions/exchanges.
(Not to be confused with Open Bite
Australia print workshop in Perth.)

Printbank
meet at:
Mackay Fibre Arts Meeting Rooms
Pitkin House
Pitkin Street
Walkerston
QLD
+61 (0)7 4951 3296
geraldinemoylan@hotmail.com

Southern Highlands Printmakers
5 Spencer Street
Mittagong
NSW 2575
+61 (0)2 4871 3151
(Contact: Tony Deigan, President)

Printmakers' group established in 1993
which is open to anyone in the region who
wishes to join (up to 10% of members may
also reside outside the Southern
Highlands). Members meet as a group
four times per year and exhibit together
every two years.

Sydney Printmakers
The Sydney Printmakers' group was
established in 1961 as a forum for the
promotion and exhibition of prints, and
has advocated the vital place of
printmaking within art and contemporary
practice in particular. The group aims to
educate the public, demystify processes
and dispel popular misconceptions
about prints versus reproductions, and
to encourage people to collect prints.
Since 1961 over 70 exhibitions have
been held in which the prints of more
than 280 artists have been shown in
Sydney, regional New South Wales and
places overseas, including China, Chile
and Norway.

Tableland Printmakers' Assoc. Inc.
PO Box 1278
Atherton
QLD 4883

www.printsandprintmaking.gov.au
National Gallery of Australia's website; a bit slow, and not all links are there, but worth a browse.

HONG KONG

Open Printshop Hong Kong
L8-05 Jockey Club Creative Arts Centre
30 Pak Tin Street
Shep Kip Mei
Kowloon
Hong Kong
+853 2319 1660
contactus@open-printshop.org.hk
www.open-printshop.org.hk

Set in a large (some 10,200 sq. m/110,000 sq. ft) former factory opened in 2008, which houses three galleries, a theatre, cafes, shops, 120 artists' studios and communal studios/workshops.

INDIA

Chhaap Print Studio
D-8 Vrundavan Bungalows

Opp Mathura Nagari
Tandalja Road
Opp O.P. Road
Vadodara 390020
+91 98251 94208
(Contact: Kavita Shah)
info@chhaap.org
www.chhaap.org

Kanoria Centre for Arts
KL Campus
CEPT
Opp Gujarat University Building
Navrangpura
Ahmedabad 380009
+91 79 2630 8727/6391
kanoriaarts@vsnl.net

Founded in 1984 by Urmila Kanorai and her husband Kailash Kumar, the centre accepts year-round applications for their artist-residency programme, and offers open-studio facilities for artists who work in painting, sculpture and printmaking. Artists must provide their own finances for board and lodging.

Roopankar Museum of Fine Arts
Bharat Bhavan
J.Svvaminathan Marg
Shamla Hills
Bhopal- 462 OOB
Madhya Pradesh
+91 755 661398/660239

Bharat Bhavan is a multi-arts complex in the Shamla Hills, 'providing interactive proximity to the verbal, the visual and the performing arts'. It consists of Roopankar Museum of Fine Arts, a fully equipped lithography studio, a ceramic workshop, and a workshop and facilities for stone craft and metal casting. Since 1992, Bharat Bhavan has also organised the International Biennial of Print Art, India.

JAPAN

Aomori Contemporary Art Centre (printing studio)
152-6 Yamazaki Goshizawa
Aomori City
Aomori
+81 17 764 5200
acac-1@acac-aomori.jp
www.acac-aomori.jp

Beautiful modern contemporary print studio with two large etching presses in purpose-built art centre, designed by the world-renowned architect Ando Tadao. The site includes exhibition halls, theatre, woodwork workshop, computer suite and photographic facility. The construction was designed around the theme of 'invisible architecture', with the circular buildings buried deep inside the surrounding forest.

ACAC is intended to be a driving force behind a new artistic environment. Taking art and nature as our main theme, we plan to develop various programmes as an exporter or purveyor of an art culture, filled with 'internationality' and 'locality', in this rich natural environment of Aomori City. The main programme is the artist-in-residence programme, in which native and international artists are invited to actively participate through various exchange programmes such as projects and workshops.

Kyoto International Woodprint Association
KIWA
64-29 Matsunoki-cho
Shimogamo
Sakyo-ku
Kyoto
75 606-0816
(Contact: Richard Steiner)
rks-rks1@nifty.com
www.kiwa.net

Based in Steiner Print Workshop. 'The first solely contemporary woodblock print and international competition in Asia.' Formed in 1997 by Richard Steiner and the students of his Steiner Print Workshop in Kyoto for the purpose of exhibiting and running competitions, they also produce an annual newsletter and maintain an archive of prints.See www.richard-steiner.net

Nagasawa Art Park (NAP)
Japanese Woodblock Printmaking
Programme
Nagasawa
Awaji City
Hyogo
(contact: CPO Box 61, Tokyo, 3100-8691)
www.endeavor.or.jp/nap

Open to international artists, print teachers and printmakers who wish to learn the Japanese water-based printmaking technique. The artists not only enjoy a traditional Japanese lifestyle with the local people in Nagasawa village, but also have the opportunity to meet and work with other international artists during their residencies. Since 1997 over 70 artists from 28 countries have participated in the programme. NAP in Awaji City is now well-known as a self-development programme for international art leaders.

see also:

Atelier Naganuma
www.n-hanga.com

Aura Intaglio Print Studio
www2.odn.ne.jp/aura/con.html
aura-21@excite.co.jp

Center for Contemporary Graphic Art and Tyler Graphics Archive Collection
Miyata 1
Shiota
Sukagawa-shi
Fukushima
962-0711
Japan
+81 24 879 4811
www.dnp.co.jp

Machida City Museum of Graphic Arts
4-28-1 Haramachida
Machida-shi
Tokyo 194-0013
+81 42 726 2771

Located in Serigaya Park, this museum is dedicated to collecting and exhibiting prints from around the world from varying historical periods. Having steadily expanded its collection since the opening in 1987, it now has 17,000 prints. The museum not only presents different selections from the collection in its permanent and temporary exhibitions, it is also active in organising workshops and lectures.

Sannohe Print Art Studio
www.town.sannohe.aomori.jp/si/hanga

Zon Print Studio
m_02000312@yahoo.co.jp
www.zonprint.info

PAKISTAN

The National College of Art, Lahore
4-Shahrah-e-Qauid-e-Azam,
Lahore
+92 42 9210599/9210601
info@nca.edu.pk
ww.nca.edu.pk

The Cowasjee Printmaking Studio in the university is one of the best-equipped workshops in Pakistan. The degree course includes all intaglio, offset and direct lithography, relief printing, as well as silkscreen printing and calligraphy. Summer courses run June-August, and include open screenprinting. Artist-in-residence scheme also offers up to two months' work in shared space and access to a workshop and equipment.

Neeleebar Studios
122 Civil Lines
Sahiwal 57000
+92 300 9691822
neeleebar@yahoo.com

Etching, collagraphs, relief printing. Open access, short courses and training.

University of the Punjab
Allama Iqbal Campus
PO Box No. 54000
Lahore
Pakistan
registrar@pu.edu.pk
www.pu.edu.pk

Offers an MFA in Graphic Arts.

SOUTH AFRICA

Artists' Proof Studio
The Bus Factory
3 President Street
West Entrance
Newtown Cultural Precinct
Newtown
postal address:
PO Box 664
Newtown 2113
Gauteng
Johannesburg
(Contact: Cara Walters, Studio Manager)
+27 (0)82 330 9859
artistsp@mweb.co.za
www.artistproofstudio.org.za

APS was conceived and founded in 1991 by well-known South African artists Kim Berman and Nhlanhla Xaba. With its state-of-the-art equipment and expert staff, APS offers intensive training programmes in printmaking and organises exchange programmes with local and international printmakers. APS also coordinates art-related poverty relief and AIDS-awareness projects throughout South Africa. The mission of the studio is to provide an environment of excellence for artists to develop printmaking as a democratic and accessible medium of expression. State-of-the-art facilities are equipped for etching, lithography and other techniques. Training and professional development courses, plus design foundation course in printmaking, outreach programmes and collaborative print projects. The studio also has its own gallery.

ArtprintSA.com
PO Box 1236
White River 1240
Mpumalanga Province
+27 13 751 3225
(mobile) +27 (0)83 676 3229
mark@artprintsa.co.za
www.artprintsa.com/www.artists-press.net

Printer/editioner whose aim is to introduce global audiences to South African printmaking, to introduce visual artists to print techniques, and to provide artists with the opportunity to collaborate with master printers. The studio offers facilities for lithography, letterpress, intaglio monoprinting and relief printing. They also undertake a small number of outreach projects working to positively engage with the community. Self-catering guesthouse available for guest artists. In 2008 ArtprintSA held its first monoprint class.

David Krut Print Workshop
PO Box 892
Houghton
2041 Johannesburg
+27 (0)11 880 4242
(Contact: Jill Ross, Workshop Manager)
dkrut@icon.co.za

DKW was established in 2002. The aim of the workshop is to provide a professional facility for collaborations between South

African artists and local and international printmakers. Emerging and established artists are regularly invited to create limited-edition intaglio prints and monotypes at DKW. With a business in New York, DKW work with some major artists – among them, Cy Twombly, Jasper Johns, Christo and David Hockney – and at the other end of the scale they work in community projects such as Body Maps, a collaboration with Cape Town University to create works by people with HIV.

See also:

www.impact2003.uct.ac.za
The website of the 2003 Impact Print Conference looked at the impact of prints in a social, political and cultural context.

www.phumanipaper.org
Indigenous South African hand made paper and products. plus papermaking research and development unit based within University of Johannesburg.

Printers and Publishers

To many printmakers the idea of a 'master printer' editioning their work is an alien concept; a luxury afforded only to the 'big names'. However, there are print studios that are approachable and open to new artists looking to create a series or portfolio of work, with the guidance and assistance of an experienced printmaker. As a printmaker, I find it interesting and revealing to see where the 'big names' actually get their work printed; whilst some print workshops are 'closed shop', some are more approachable than you would think. Moreover, open-access workshops such as Edinburgh Print Workshop have an established reputation as printer-publishers, while other print workshops are also seeing a business opportunity in being able to offer a bespoke printing service to individual artists.

So what is a master printer? Well, first of all, it is worth stating that some printers do not like to refer to themselves as master printers, preferring to be seen as collaborative printers working alongside the artist to create new bodies of work. Master printers are experienced printmakers who are much more than technicians; they are artists in their own right, who guide and support artists to bring out the best qualities in the printmaking process. They either work at or own printer-publishers or printer-editioners (sometimes referred to as contract printers). Galleries and agents may refer an artist (who may or may not know much about printmaking) to a printer to work with them. Some artists approach the printing houses directly, while sometimes the relationship is in reverse, with the printer inviting an artist to work with them. In each case the business deal is a mutual relationship. The artist has to be comfortable with the workshop, and vice versa. While one artist may need a working studio for an intense period of creativity, others may choose to have plates or stones prepared and then go away to work in their own time and in their own studios, before bringing the plates back to have them proofed and a BAT print produced (BAT stands for 'Bon à tirer', literally meaning 'good to print'). This BAT mark serves as the benchmark approved by the artist for an edition to be produced to the exact same standard.

In simplified terms a printer-publisher is a print studio that pays an artist to work with them to produce a portfolio of prints, with the printer-publisher owning the right to sell the works. There are still a good number of printer-publishers thriving in the UK, such as Paragon Press (the imprint of Charles Booth-Clibborn established in 1986), Thumbprint (formerly Hope Sufferance press), Paupers Publications, Coriander Studio and, of course, Curwen Press. Ever wondered where the likes of Damien Hirst, Tracey Emin, the Chapman Brothers, Paula Rego et al. have their work printed? You need look no further than these printer-publishers (and a handful of similar print houses abroad).

Also, for the sake of simplification and compartmentalisation I have used the term 'printer-editioner' to mean anywhere that an artist can go to get their work printed. These businesses are often small firms offering a service to print existing plates or produce new plates. In fact they are sometimes artists who offer a sideline in printing for others. An artist may like to create their own prints but may tire of printing a large edition, for example, or they may wish to produce an original print but do not have the equipment or knowledge to do this alone. They may even be a printmaker, but do not have the experience of, say, lithography. In this last case, studios like Oaks Editions, Hole Editions or Editions 19/20 are the ideal places to get a unique one-to-one service, and to learn hands on by working with experienced lithographers.

I have also listed publishers here (as opposed to printer-publishers). These businesses do not have print facilities themselves, but they do commission work from artists and they work with master printers. They can also act as middlemen to galleries, as well as selling direct to their own client list.

Of course, in simplifying and categorising there is a danger that some complexities are missed. In truth, there are many aspects and a fluid business model whereby printer/publishers negotiate each job on the basis of the size of edition, the type of work, the artist's experience with printmaking, the market value, etc. An artist approaching a printer will not find a simple price list, but must go with a clear idea of what they are looking to achieve. It must also be emphasised that this is an exclusive club, and printer-publishers have to maintain high standards in who they represent and work with in order to keep their reputation. But with open-access workshops and individual printmakers offering a service at the other end of the market, there really are more opportunities then ever before for artists and printmakers to have their work editioned and, moreover, to work with master printers to improve and develop their work.

PRINTERS, PUBLISHERS

Appledore Press (printer/editioner)
Flat 1
Ruberry House
9A St Mary's Terrace
Penzance
Cornwall
TR18 4DZ

+44 (0)1736 363161
www.appledorepress.com

Set up in 1976, and recently moved to new premises. Original hand-printing lithographers working in collaboration with artists (projects have included working with the late Ted Hughes.)

artHester (publishers)
78 Highsett
Cambridge
CB2 1NZ
+44 (0)7798 676954
(Contact: Richard Saltoun or Abigail Croydon)
arthester@easynet.co.uk
www.arthester.co.uk

'We publish editions by important, established figures and by younger, less well-known artists. We offer coherent groups of works, not single images. The editions are small, numbered editions of around thirty examples.' Specialists in postwar artists such as Patrick Caulfield, Richard Hamilton, Allen Jones, John Latham and Joe Tilson.

Artswipe Editions

07956 382 530
mark@artswipe.com
www.artswipe.com
Screenprint editioning for artists.

Artizan Editions (printer/publisher)
Ground Floor
East Wing
Industrial House
Conway Street
Hove
BN3 3LW
+44 (0)1273 773959
(Contact: Sally Gimson)
info@artizaneditions.co.uk
www.artizaneditions.co.uk

Established in 1994. 'One of only a few screenprint workshops working in direct collaboration with artists. We began by producing bespoke work for publishers and individual artists including Bridget Riley.

Saddened by the lack of knowledge around original prints, we decided to start publishing with artists.'

Bon à Tirer Editions (printer/editioner)
Top Floor
15 East Campbell Street
Glasgow
G1 1DG
+44 (0)141 946 2756
lambbo@compuserve.com

Boxwood Books & Prints (printer/publisher)
Ashbrook
Winsford
Minehead
Somerset
TA24 7HN
+44 (0)1643 851 588
(Contact: Peter Nicholls)
boxwood.books@virgin.net
www.boxwoodbooks.com

'We are now one of the leading British specialists in rare private press books, illustrated books – especially those illustrated with wood engravings – and books about the art of wood engraving. We also offer signed, limited-edition wood engravings, many of which were produced to illustrate books. While the focus is on the twenties and thirties of the last century, when British wood engraving attained prominence throughout the world and attracted many of the finest artists working in Britain, we also stock engravings by many contemporary artists.

Castle Editions (publisher)
The Orchards
London Road
Carlisle
Cumbria
CA1 3DZ
+44 (0)1228 516410
info@castle-editions.com
www.castle-editions.com

Publisher of prints and multiples by contemporary artists. Each edition is created in close collaboration with the artist. Castle work with renowned printers such as Thumbprint in London.

Claire Benson (editioner)
3 Coulsons Place
Penzance
Cornwall
TR18 4DY
+44 (0)7851 097368
clairebprintmaker@hotmail.co.uk

Available to all artist-printmakers. Service for printing intaglio plates to edition sizes of at least 100 on a Rochat housed in a private studio, which will print plates upwards of 70 x 80 cm (27 x 31 in.). Claire has three years' experience printing in professional studios for artists include Sir Anthony Frost, Gary Hume, John Hoyland and Sheila Oliner. Projects undertaken and accommodation available for consultations.

Clink Press (editioner)
23 Blue Anchor Lane
London
SE16 3UL
+44 (0)20 7232 1916
trevor@trevorprice.co.uk
www.trevorpricestudios.com

The Clink Press is a printmaking workshop and editioning studio. It primarily editions the etchings and drypoints of Trevor Price, but is also used by other artists including Mychael Barratt, Freya Payne, Bryan Poole, Anita Klein and Katherine Jones. Originally set up on Clink Street on the South Bank of the Thames, it has since moved to larger premises in a converted Victorian warehouse in Bermondsey, and is just a few minutes' walk from Tower Bridge. Editioning work undertaken.

Coriander Studio (printer/publisher)
www.corianderstudio.com

One of Europe's longest-established and most prolific producers of limited-edition prints for publication by international artists and publishers. They specialise in screen-printing and more recently are pioneers in the field of giclée digital printing (only working with artists who take a fundamental interest and involvement in making their digital prints and for whom the print will ultimately be a finished artwork in its own right). Founded in London in 1972 by painter Brad Faine, Coriander has achieved a reputation as one of the finest producers of such prints in the world.

As well as producing prints, Coriander also has a tradition of commissioning and publishing work from artists with whom they have developed a close working relationship. The first of these was Patrick Hughes in 1975, and since then artists such as Peter Blake, Damien Hirst, John Hoyland, Michael Craig Martin, Bruce McLean, Brendan Nieland, David Mach, Storm Thorgerson, Ivor Abrahams, Sandra Blow and Terry Frost have collaborated with the studio.

Coln Valley Press (printer/publisher)
Oerle Hall
Berriew
Powys
SY21 8QX
+44 (o)1686 650531
susankeen@colnvalleypress.co.uk
www.colnvalleypress.co.uk

Publisher exclusively of prominent artists in the field of wood engravings: Colin See-Paynton, Hilary Paynter, John Bryce, Simon Brett, Howard Phipps, Sarah van Niekerk and Trevor Hardrell.

Counter Publications (publisher/co-publisher)
44a Charlotte Road
London
EC2A 3PD
+44(0)20 7684 8888
info@countereditions.com
www.countereditions.com

Founded in 2000, 'Counter Editions commissions and produces prints and multiples by leading contemporary artists. The editions are exclusive to Counter Editions and each is created in close collaboration with the artist. They are produced by leading printers such as Thumbprint Press and Coriander Studios. We have worked with over twenty-five leading artists, including five Turner Prize winners. We have collaborated with major institutions, such as the Serpentine Gallery and the Hayward Gallery, and currently co-publish editions with the Tate Gallery, while the editions have been purchased by numerous international collections, including Museum of Modern Art, New York, Kunstmuseum, Zurich, the V&A, and the British Council.'

Curwen Press (printer/publisher)
Chilford Hall
Linton
Cambridge
CB1 6LE
(Contact: Jenny Roland)
info@thecurwenstudio.co.uk
www.thecurwenstudio.co.uk

Established in 1863, this was the first of its kind in the UK, based on the French atelier system to offer facilities for artists' original printmaking. 'We are not just printers, we are artist-printers.' Curwen have worked with some of the biggest names in British art including Barbara Hepworth, Graham Sutherland, Elizabeth Frink and John Piper, as well as less-established artists They currently work with the likes of Paula Rego. Experts in lithography, they have pioneered continuous-tone lithography (contone). Master printer and director until his recent retirement, Stanley Jones set up the Curwen Print Study Centre next door to Curwen Press to continue his 'vision of a central educational establishment to continue the varied methods of printmaking skills'. Jones also helped found the Printmakers' Council, and was president for many years, and is still an active artist and supporter of printmaking.

David T. Bowyer (artist-printmaker/editioner)
Studio 4 Frameworks
5-9 Creekside
London
SE8 4SA
+44 (0)20 8853 3962
bowyer@aol.com

Colour proofing/editioning. Hard and soft-ground etching and aquatint. Also antique plate restoration.

Hackleys (what do they do?)
C/o SNAP Studio
20/21 Lower Park Road
Bristol
BS1 5BN
+44 (0)7944 951124
(Contact: David Abbott)
studio@hackleys.com
www.hackleys.com

Based at SNAP Studio, this 'small but ambitious' Bristol firm design and print (digital and screen-printed) quirky and classic posters for events, gigs and exhibitions, plus work on other design projects.

Halfmoon Printmaker (printer-editioners)
Farland Studio
127A Half Moon Lane
London
SE24 9LP
+44 (0)20 7274 8836
Contact: Sonia Rolo & Martin Ridgwell)
info@halfmoonprintmakers.com
www.halfmoonprintmakers.com

Studio space in London shared by professional printmakers. Editioning undertaken.

Hippo Screenprinters (printer/editioner)
Unit A2
107 High Street
Stratford
London
E15 2QQ
+44 (0)20 8519 8550
lynne@hipposcreenprinters.co.uk
www.hipposcreenprinters.co.uk

Limited-edition, hand-pulled screenprints for artists. Water- or spirit-based inks used plus advice given on creating a screenprint from either a finished digital image or an original artwork.

Hoft Publishing (publisher)
+44 (0)20 8525 9665
portfolio@houseoffairytales.org
www.houseoffairytales.org

Established by the artists Deborah Curtis and Gavin Turk, a publishing arm of House of Fairy Tales, 'an arts-based education project which uses the vast narrative scope of fairy tales to provide creative, innovative and transformative learning experiences for children of all ages and their families'. Their first portfolio included 23 international artists who gave their artwork in exchange for a special edition of the portfolio.

Hole Editions (printer/publisher)
Unit 12
Mushroom Works
St Lawrence Road
Newcastle-upon-Tyne
NE6 1AR
+44 (0)191 224 3449
+44 (0)774 647 3216
(Contact: Lee Turner)
lee@holeeditions.co.uk
www.holeeditions.co.uk

A collaborative lithography workshop, working with artists as publisher or contract printer. Founded in Newcastle-upon-Tyne in 2005 by Lee Turner, trained as master printer at Tamarind Institute in Alberquerque. Monotype sessions are also available.

Jealous Prints
27 Park Road
London
N8 8TE
+44 ()20 8347 7688
info@jealousgallery.com
www.jealousprints.com

Screenprint editioning for artists and galleries by Master Printer Matthew Rich

Making Space (printer/editioner)
Primrose Cottages
Barton Estate
Whippingham
Isle of Wight
PO32 6NS
+44 (0)1983 884246
(Contact: Jonathan Ward)
makingspace@btinternet.com

Merivale Editions (publisher/agent)
14 Merivale Road
London

SW15 2NW
+44 (0)20 8785 9034
peter@merivaleeditions.com
www.merivaleeditions.com

Founder and owner: Peter Sampson.
Merivale Editions was founded in 1982 as
an exercise in making art collecting as easy
and accessible as book collecting.

'The Merivale Editions idea was simple: a
small family-run business, without the staff
and gallery overheads that inflate most art
sales, which could commission or source
prints from the best printmakers and sell
them affordably and easily by mail order or
personal appointment. We continue to
foster young talent and bring collections of
older work to the public.'

Noble Fine Art Artists and Printmakers (printer/editioner)
Unit 9
Home Farm Business Centre
East Titherley Road
Lockerley
Hampshire
SO51 OJT

info@noblefineart.co.uk
www.noblefineart.co.uk
A family business run by Julia and David
Noble, with a gallery selling their own
paintings and prints, and also running
workshops in printmaking and painting.
Specialist printing service predominantly
based in intaglio printing such as
copperplate etching and photogravure. 'We
are constantly expanding our facilities and
techniques to include many traditional
printing and alternative photographic
processes, many of which are enjoying a
resurgence as a counterpoint to the
ubiquitous digital print.'

Oaks Editions Lithography (printer/editioner)
The Old Stables
Oaks Park
Croydon Lane
Sutton
SM7 3BA
+44 (0)20 8542 4541 (no phone at studio)

simonburder@oaksfineart.co.uk
www.oaksfineart.co.uk

Collaborative printing service to suit the
individual artist. All projects are discussed
fully and an estimate made which can take
account of varying levels of involvement
with the production of editions. Simon
Burder has worked with many artists over
the last 20 years, and has a widely
respected reputation, with work in various
printmaking books. (See open-access
workshops section for more details.)

Other Criteria (publisher)
www.othercriteria.com

Other Criteria collaborates closely with
artists on high-end ambitious
multiples/publications including books,
prints, artist's editions, posters and
clothing; working with artists such as
Damien Hirst, Mat Collishaw and Jane
Simpson

Paragon Press (publisher)
6 Wetherby Gardens
London
SW5 0JN
+44 (0)20 7370 1200
www.paragonpress.co.uk

Paragon Press is the site of one of the
major global print publishers. Based in
London and founded by Charles Booth-
Clibborn, Paragon Press specialises in
producing original print series and
portfolios in limited editions by
contemporary artists in varying media such
as etching, woodcut, linocut, screenprint
and lithography.

Paupers Publications (printer/publisher)
Standpoint Studios
45 Coronet Street
London
N1 6HD
+44(0)20 7729 5272
(Contact: Mike Taylor & Simon Marsh)
pauper@talk21.com
www.pauperspublications.com
(Paupers Publications also run Tricorne
Publications)

Facilities for etching, lithography, silkscreen and relief printing. The Paupers Press has worked with many of the UK's leading contemporary artists. Recent artists include Paula Rego, Christopher le Brun, Jake & Dinos Chapman, Sue Webster & Tim Noble, and Andrejz Jackowski. They work in conjunction with other publishers & galleries such as Paragon Press, Marlborough Gallery, Flowers Graphics, Purdy Hicks and the Tate Gallery.

In 2002, Mike and Simon also initiated the Artists' International Print Project, a collaboration with the Scuola Internazionale di Grafica in Venice, Italy. The project invites artists to work within the school's printmaking studios in the Cannareggio area at the heart of Venice. Invited artists to date have included Hughie O'Donoghue, Christopher Le Brun and Tony Bevan.

Pratt Contemporary Art/Pratt Editions (printer/editioner)
The Gallery
Ightham
Sevenoaks
Kent
TN15 9HH
+44 (0)1732 882326
pca@prattcontemporaryart.co.uk
www.prattcontemporaryart.co.uk

Founded in 1977, the studios have facilities for screen, intaglio, relief and digital printing, as well as a further studio for producing sculpture. Since its inception the core activity has been printmaking and the development of new methods and materials, such as the digital process and the polymer intaglio plate process, and more recently for the making of fine artists' books. Artists include Kristian Krokfors, Antonio Poteiro and Ana Maria Pacheco.

Printmaker (printer/editioner)
14 Rowallan Close
Caversham
Reading
Berkshire
RG4 6QS
+44 (0)118 946 1964

enquiries@printmaker.co.uk
www.printmaker.co.uk

Specialists in screenprinting. 'We collaborate with artists and makers who want to produce multiples of their work, limited editions and other more unusual projects such as artists' books and installations. We also offer a photostencil making service to printmakers wishing to screenprint their own work. Computer-cut stencils, digital separations and giclée prints and proofs can also be prepared for artists working with digital imaging techniques.'

Printmaker also runs a website that has an extensive links page and regularly updated small ads and listings for print equipment, courses and opportunities.

The Print Studio, Cambridge (printer/publisher)
Building 10
The Michael Young Centre
Purbeck Road
Cambridge
CB2 2HN
+44 (0)1223 416415
(Contact: Kip Gresham)
printstudio@ukonline.co.uk
www.theprintstudio.co.uk

The Print Studio works with artists. It is an artists' workspace rather than a printing company. It supplies publishers and galleries from many parts of the world. Processes offered are screenprinting, etching, monoprinting, monotype, carborundum prints and relief printing. Artists they work with include Alan Davie, Michael Brick, Alan Grabham and Anthony Green. An online estimated quote can be given to artists wishing to work in the studio or with Kip Gresham. The studio publishes editioned prints, monoprints and sometimes portfolios each year.

Print (vb.n) (printer/editioner)
Original Print Gallery/Studio
8 Huguenot Place
Wandsworth

London
SE18 2EN
+44 (0)20 8874 9138
printvbn@btinternet.com
www.simonlawsonprints.com

Print (vb.n.) is a beautiful gallery set on
East Hill in Wandsworth, South London. It
is dedicated to contemporary printmaking
by artists of the highest quality. Works
include etchings and screenprints by
leading artists including Royal
Academicians. Simon Lawson, an artist
and Royal Academy Printmaking Tutor, is
always on hand to inform and advise on
purchasing a unique piece of art. Simon
has produced prints for studios including
Alecto Editions, Hope Sufferance Press
and Thumbprint Editions, and has now
established this gallery with his partner
Ann Hobson, to produce his own and
other contemporary artists' original prints.
The studio houses a 19th-century star-
wheel press, a Victorian press and an Art
Equipment press.

Simon Whittle (printer/editioner)
39 Tasman Road
London
SW9 9LZ
+44 (0)7789 818450
cyan18@yahoo.co.uk

**Stoneman Publications/Stoneman
Graphics (publisher)**
Orchard Flower Farm
Madron Hill
Penzance
Cornwall
TR20 8SR
+44 (0)1736 361756
linda@stonemangraphics.co.uk
danny@stonemangraphics.co.uk
www.stonemanpublications.co.uk

Run by Linda Stoneman and mainly selling
work produced in the studios of her late
husband, the master printer Hugh
Stoneman. Artists include Sir Terry Frost,
Grayson Perry, Ian McKeever, Eileen
Cooper, Christopher le Brun, Garty Hue,
Blek le Rat and many others.

**Tag Fine Art/Tag Inventory
(gallery/publisher)**
16 Elia Street
London
N1 8DE
(Contact: M.J. Hobby-Limon)
+44 (0)7968 099945
info@tagfinearts.com
www.tagfinearts.com

Tag Inventory specialises in contemporary
prints by established international artists
such as Damien Hirst, Banksy and Antony
Micallef. TAG provides an outlet for working
artists to exhibit and sell their work. Acting
as a support network for its stable, TAG
offers advice regarding commissions within
the trade; a hub, it proposes alternative
exhibiting opportunities and a forum for
broader critical discussion about
contemporary art. The selection criteria for
artists wishing to join TAG are based on the
proviso that they are working in a creative
capacity in an alternative arts environment,
that they take an integrated approach to
their work, crossing traditional boundaries
and engaging with other creative
disciplines, such as architecture, graphic
design and fashion.

Ceramic Transfer Printing
(Contact: Frea Buckler)
freabuckler@hotmail.com

Ceramic transfer-printing service for artists
and enamellers. 'We screenprint all
transfers by hand, ensuring rich, accurate
representations of drawings or
photographic imagery.'

Short Courses in the UK

Whilst every open-access print workshop offers a range of courses in printmaking and related media, they are not the only provider of short courses. The following places offer printmaking courses on a vocational level. From independent art schools to individual artists offering an experience in their own print studio, there are unique opportunities to find out more about printmaking techniques and learn first-hand from artists themselves. Again, this list does not pretend to be absolutely comprehensive – there must be many more artists and organisations offering similar services – but it does offer a glimpse of the variety available.

Before committing to a course it is really important to find out more about what is on offer and whether it suits your needs, either as a beginner or as an experienced printmaker. Each venue and tutor has their own style, and resources range from the small, personalised studio environment to more spacious facilities catering for larger groups. Always enquire or even go along first to see what is on offer.

Annette Rolston
The Art Factory
Hall Road
Norwich
+44 (0)1379 741406
www.annetterolston.co.uk

Courses in monoprinting, collagraph, drypoint, block printing and book art for individuals or schools, etc. With her mobile printing press Annette is able to teach a comprehensive range of techniques to all ages and abilities at a large variety of venues. Print facilities are also for hire to experienced printmakers. She also works with InPrint art and poetry group in and around Norfolk (see www.inprintarts andpoetry.co.uk).

Bracken Press
Byways
Low Street
Scalby, nr. Scarborough
YO13 0QW
+44 (0)1723 378278
mail@brackenpress.com
www.brackenpress.com

A private press run by Michael Atkin set up in 1974. Tailor-made courses for everyone from beginners to the experienced printmaker in intaglio, block printing and book-making in well-equipped studio.

Brenda Hartill
Pound House
Udimore
Rye
East Sussex
TN31 6BA
+44 (0)1424 882942
brenda.hartill@gmail.com
www.brendahartill.com

8-day intensive collagraph & etching courses plus 1-day lectures/demonstrations in Brenda's gallery studio in the glorious Sussex countryside. Occasional residencies for overseas professional printmakers. The workshop/studio is in the grounds of an ancient timbered house set in two acres of beautiful garden with stunning views.

Brignell Bookbinders
25 Gwydir Street
Cambridge
CB1 2LG
+44 (0)1223 321280
www.brignellbookbinders.com
brignell@ntlworld.com.

Specialist firm for bookbinding and book conservation, established in 1982. Courses in bookbinding, cloth repairs, boxes and slip cases, etc. one Saturday every month.

Sue Brown
8 Commercial Street
Cheltenham
GL50 2AU
sb.brown@talk21.com

www.hampenfactory.co.uk
Weekend courses in collagraph, non-toxic etching and gum-arabic transfer. Also 10-week collagraph courses for 2009. Contact Sue for full details and availability.

Cambridge Regional College
King's Hedges Road
Cambridge
CB4 2QT
+44 (0)1223 418200
enquiry@camre.ac.uk
www.camre.ac.uk

Long-term courses in printmaking and advanced printmaking in bright new print studio.

Castle Screenprint Workshop
(Contact: Martin Leedham)
martinleedham@me.com
www.martinleedham.com

Screenprint workshop and tuition available in Ashby de la Zouch, Leicestershire. Kippax hand bench, small textiles carousel and water-based inks. Beautiful quiet spot in Georgian former stable and dovecote. Experienced printmakers may be able to hire out workshop. Hoping to add an etching press in 2009.

Catseye Private Press
Home to Roost
Crowden Road
Eccles-on-Sea
Norfolk NR12 0SJ
+44 (0)1692 582292
(Contact: Graham Pressman, master printer, hot foiler and publisher)
graham@tractorbits.com
www.catseyepress.co.uk

'Print your own work on a 19th-century iron hand press.' Studio for hire on a daily rate with assistance where needed for letterpress. Selection of type for titling, headings and footers on Albion press and Cropper treadle platen. Local accommodation available.

City & Guilds of London Art School
124 Kennington Park Road
London
SE11 4DJ
+44 (0)20 7735 2306
info@cityandguildsartschool.ac.uk
www.cityandguildsartschool.ac.uk

Printmaking daytime and evening tutored sessions with Jason Hicklin and Chris Roantree. Pay per session.

Lesley Davy – Adventures in Printmaking
Weekend courses in collagraph in north London warehouse printmaking studio. Suitable for all levels.
Contact: Lesley Davy
+44 (0)7879 876007
lesley.davy@lineone.net
lesley.davy@lineone.net
http://axisweb.org

David Dodsworth
Etching studio to let in Whitechapel area of East London (in former Horn & Horseshoes pub), with an optional painting/drawing studio, plus accommodation. Studio fully equipped with 107 x 188 cm (42 x 74 in.) etching press.

info@studioliveworkineastlondon.co.uk
http://studioliveworkineastlondon.co.uk

Fermynwoods Contemporary Art
The Water Tower
Benefield Road
Brigstock
Kettering
NN14 3JA
+44 (0)1536 373469
gallery@fermynwoods.co.uk
www.fermynwoods.co.uk

Contemporary gallery in converted watermill amongst beautiful countryside with a print studio attached, equipped with large etching press and stone lithography. Printmaking and related courses run alongside excellent exhibition programme. Past workshops have included masterclasses with Stanley Jones, Marc Balakjian and Simon Marsh.

Hampstead School of Art
King's College Campus
19-21 Kidderpore Avenue
London
NW3 7ST
+44 (0)20 77941439
hsaNW3@aol.com
www.art-school-hampstead.co.uk

Courses in etching, drypoint, collagraph and monoprint run by Theresa Pateman and Emiko Aida, usually on Mondays (morning, afternoon and evening) and Saturdays. The independent art school, founded 40 years ago, was the inspiration of Henry Moore who, with other leading artists of the postwar period, decided to found a centre of artistic excellence in Hampstead.

The Institute
Hampstead Garden Suburb Institute
11 High Road
London
N2 8LL
+44 (0)20 8829 4141
(email via website)
www.hgsi.ac.uk

Day and evening courses for all levels, from 1 to 30 weeks long, including solar-plate etching, screenprint and drypoint, in new £6m arts centre.

Joanna Allen Stockport
7 Beech Avenue
Cale Green
Stockport
SK3 8HA
+44 (0)161 476 2153
+44 (0)7505 508573 (mob.)
joannaallen7@hotmail.co.uk
www.joannaallen.co.uk

Collagraph-printing workshops throughout

the year at Hallam Mill, Stockport, as well as workshops in schools and colleges.

Longden Gallery
2 Shaw Street
Macclesfield
Cheshire
SK11 6QY
+44 (0)1625 433953
info@longdengallery.co.uk
www.longdengallery.co.uk

Longden Gallery is part of Longden Arts Ltd, a group of professional artists who work collectively in shared print and ceramic studios. The gallery is open to submissions from printmakers. Membership is by invitation only. Currently, four printmakers use the workshop on a daily/regular basis. They also occasionally offer tuition in printmaking and ceramics.

Magenta Sky Printmaking
49B Castle Street
Salisbury
Wiltshire
SP1 3SP
+44 (0)1722 414300
info@magenta.sky.com
www.magenta-sky.com

'Distance-learning printmaking' from the self-proclaimed 'Printmaking Academy', plus workshops and classes in Salisbury Arts Centre. See website for details.

Minerva Art Courses
Stanhill House
2 Uley Road
Dursley
Gloucestershire
GL11 4PF
+44 (0)1453 548299
minart@hotmail.co.uk
www.minart.co.uk

Courses in monoprinting, collagraph and drypoint. Two to three-day courses in a congenial atmosphere. Small groups of four to eight people ensure individual attention.

The National Print Museum
Old Garrison Chapel

Beggars Bush
Haddington Road
Dublin 4
Ireland
+353 1 660 3770
(Contact: Mairead White)
npmuseum@iol.ie
www.nationalprintmuseum.ie

Founded in 1996 in a converted garrison chapel, the museum has an extensive educational programme for schools. Courses in printmaking, bookmaking, papermaking and letterpress as well as lectures and events throughout the year.

Nicola Slattery Art Courses
+44 (0)1986 788853
artpeople@btopenworld.com
www.nicolaslattery.com

Printmaking courses in drypoint and collagraph set in Earsham Hall near the border of Suffolk and Norfolk, run by an experienced and well-known artist/printmaker.

The Otter Bindery
42 Hare Hill
Addlestone
Surrey
KT15 1DT
+44 (0)1932 845976
(Contact: Marysa de Veer)
marysa@bookbinding.com
www.otterbookbinding.com

Bookbinding courses in 'relaxed cottage setting' on the first Saturday of every month. One-day individual tutoring by arrangement.

Proof Print
32 Hicks Close
Probus
Truro
Cornwall
TR2 4NE
+44 (0)1726 884239
oli@oliverwest.net
www.oliverwest.net

Proof Print Arts has been running printmaking and sketchbook holidays for 10 years. 'With the use of a mobile studio incorporating a 21-inch press, we offer holidays in Cornwall, Europe and South Africa. With friendly, one-to-one, professional tuition, along with small groups and flexible schedules.'

Pulp Paper Arts Workshop
Unit F
41 Purdon Street
Partick
Glasgow
G11 6AF
+44 (0)141 337 2842
alison@paperartsworkshop.co.uk
www.paperartsworkshop.co.uk

A hand-papermaking arts workshop which provides 'a range of services for experienced artists and makers as well as those just beginning to explore this versatile medium', including a variety of evening classes, weekend and day courses and summer schools in all aspects of papermaking, artist book-making and related media. There is also provision for undertaking commissions and collaborations, plus excellent facilities for hire and technical assistance in developing skills and personal artwork. The facilities include a 2.3 kg (5 lb) Hollander beater for professional processing of fibres, a 100-tonne hydraulic press, a variety of vats and traditional moulds and deckles. Depending on the scale and volume of work to be made, artists and makers can arrange to attend the workshop on an individual basis or opt to share with one or two friends or colleagues.

Roker Print
tony.redman@btinternet.com

Private studio run by Tony Redman. Outreach courses delivered to art groups, local authority, etc. with portable press.

Silkworm Studios
55-57 Tontine Street
Folkestone
Kent
www.silkwormstudios.com
(Contact: Sarah Massey)

Newly set up in December 2008, they run workshops in screenprinting plus tailored tutoring in screenprint on request. Also editioning for artists and foil blocking available.

Strule Arts Centre
Townhall Square
Omagh
Northern Ireland
BT78 1BL
+44 (0)28 8224 5321 (ext. 400)
jean.brennan@omagh.gov.uk
www.struleartscentre.co.uk
(Contact: Jean Brennan, Arts Manager)

A new print studio set up in 2008 in a state-of-the-art purpose-built arts centre in the heart of Omagh. The centre encompasses a theatre, cinema, dance studio, recording studio, ceramics studio, photographic studio and print workshop. There are plans for access for printmakers run by a lead artist. Courses run in screenprinting throughout the year, plus a broader print programme being rolled out.

Studio Five
1st floor
The Mews
46-52 Church Road
Barnes
London
SW13 0DQ
+44 (0)20 8563 2158
studio5bookarts@aol.co.uk
www.studio5bookbindingarts.blogspot.com
www.markcockrambooks.co.uk

Founded in 2003 by Mark Cockram, who specialises in contemporary bookbinding and book arts. A variety of courses on offer, including introductory and intermediate (two and four days), there is also the opportunity to work in 'open studio' on specific projects with Mark's guidance and tutelage. Wed to Sun, 10am-6pm. The studio is fully equipped, with workspace for three students at any one time.

Studio 74
Four Seasons
Battenhall Avenue
Worcester
WR5 2HW
+44 (0)1905 357563
haywardpowis@hotmail.com
www.powishayward.co.uk

Paul Powis and Sara Hayward run creative painting and printmaking weekend courses from their rural Worcester studio. Students benefit from small group sizes, a relaxing location and expert tuition.

West Cork Art School
Factory Lane
Bandon
Cork
Ireland
(021) 4776847 (023) 42973 087
2671897◁···what's going on here?···▷
(Contact: Ken Parker/Rosita Kingston)
info@westcorkartschool.com
www.westcorkartschool.com

Located in the heart of Bandon town, 30 minutes from Cork City with printmaking facilities including a Griffin etching press and a screenprint vacuum bed. Regular courses in printmaking.

See also:

Sue Corr
www.suecorr.com
The Studio Space
Royal Oak Stables Courtyard
Betws-y-Coed
Conway
LL24 0AH
01690 710028
suecorr@btinternet.com
www.suecorr.com

Courses in acrylic resist etching collagraphs and solar plate.

LETTERPRESS COURSES

Alembic Press
Hyde Farm House
Marcham
Abingdon

Oxford
OX13 6NX
+44 (0)1865 391391
(Contact : Claire M. Bolton)
AlembicPrs@aol.com
http://members.aol.com/alembicprs/index.htm

Five-day and weekend courses in printing and binding, etc. Sunday afternoon open workshops on casting type from monotype composition and supercasters are held approximately once a month.

Anchor Press Museum Project
4 Elwin Road
Tiptree
Colchester
Essex
CO5 0HL
United Kingdom
info@anchorpress.org.uk
www.anchorpress.org.uk

Demonstrations and educational exhibitions are given at county fares and heritage events across Essex whilst funding is sought for developing the educational facility at Anchor Press.

Incline Press
36 Bow Street
Oldham
OL1 1SJ
+44 (0)161 6271966
books.inclinepress@virgin.net
www.inclinepress.com

Letterpress courses tailored to suit individuals' needs, delivered by Graham Moss and Kathy Whelan.

Richard Lawrence
Widcombe Studios
Comfortable Place
Upper Bristol Rd
Bath
BA1 3AJ
+44 (0)1225 313494/+44 (0)781 2094781
zrlawrence@aol.com
www.glassimpression.myzen.co.uk

Letterpress tuition and classes available

from printer with 30+ years of experience.

Graham Pressman
Rosemound
Cart Gap Road
Happisburgh
Norwich
Norfolk
NR12 0QL
+44 (0)1692 582 292
graham@tractorbits.com
www.retail.tractorbits.com

Print your work on 19th-century iron hand presses. Floor-standing Albion and a tabletop Imperial, as well as a Cropper treadle platen for small, high-speed work. A selection of type for titling, headings and footers. Overnight accommodation can often be arranged at the local country pub of an owner-operated B&B in the village. All near beach, countryside walks and Norfolk Broads.

See also:

Central St Martins College of Art & Design
www.csm.arts.ac.uk
(click on courses – short courses – letterpress)

London College of Communication
www.lcc.arts.ac.uk/courses/printing/letterpress.htm

The National Print Museum
www.nationalprintmuseum.ie

The Type Museum
100 Hackford Road
Stockwell
London
SW9 0QU
www.thetypemuseum.org

Museum established in 1992; currently under development.

Universities

PRINTMAKING IN FURTHER AND HIGHER EDUCATION

Once in many respects the third grace of the fine-art department next to painting and sculpture, changing times and a broader spectrum of subjects and techniques offered has meant that some universities have sidelined, downsized or even abolished printmaking altogether. However, universities such as UWE, Bristol, The Royal College of Art, London and the University of Brighton, along with a few others, have stood fast and even strengthened their printmaking. The following is a list of all universities where printmaking is offered. I have avoided going into detail, as the courses offered have many different aspects to them and can change from year to year (and, quite frankly, there isn't room in this directory). Depending on what the aspiring student of printmaking is looking for, there is a course available, but as with any degree it is highly advisable to speak to each printmaking department and to visit a few before committing.

UNIVERSITIES THAT RUN PRINTMAKING DEGREES AND POSTGRADUATE COURSES

Anglia Ruskin University, Cambridge
www.anglia.ac.uk
MA

Bournemouth (Arts Institute)
www.aib.ac.uk
FD (Foundation degree)

Bradford College
www.bradford.ac.uk
PG.Cert., PG.Dip., MA

Brighton (University of)
www.brighton.ac.uk
BA, MA

Bristol, University of the West of England
www.uwe.ac.uk
MA

Buckinghamshire Chilterns University College
www.bcuc.ac.uk
MA
* Camberwell College of Arts
www.camberwell.arts.ac.uk
MA

* Central Lancashire (University of)
www.uclan.ac.uk
MA

Chester (University of)
www.chester.ac.uk
Research

Dublin, National College of Art & Design
www.ncad.ie
BA, MFA

Edinburgh College of Art
www.eca.ac.uk
MA, MFA, M.Phil., Ph.D.

Glasgow School of Art
www.gsa.ac.uk
BA, MA

Grays School of Art, Aberdeen
www.rgu.ac.uk
BA, MA

Limerick School of Art & Design
www.lit.ie
BA

London College of Communication
www.lcc.ac.uk
Grad.Cert./ Grad.Dip.

London Print Studio (University of Brighton)
www.londonprintstudio.org.uk
MA/PG.Dip.

Maidstone, Kent (University College for the Creative Arts)
www.ucreative.ac.uk
BA

Royal College of Art
www.rca.ac.uk
MA

Wimbledon School of Art
www.wimbledon.arts.ac.uk
BA, MA
Winchester School of Art
www.wsa.soton.ac.uk
BA, MA

UNIVERSITIES THAT RUN FINE-ART COURSES WITH PRINTMAKING DEPARTMENTS

Aberystwyth (University of Wales)
www.aber.ac.uk
BA, MA

Bath Spa University
www.bathspa.ac.uk
BA, MA

Bedfordshire (University of)
www.beds.ac.uk
BA, MA

Birmingham City University
www.bcu.ac.uk
BA, PG.Cert., PG.Dip., MA

Bolton (University of)
www.bolton.ac.uk
BA

* Canterbury (University College for the Creative Arts)
www.ucreative.ac.uk

BA, MA

Central Saintt Martins College of Art & Design
www.csm.arts.ac.uk
BA, MA

Coventry University
www.coventry.ac.uk
BA, MA

Chichester (University of)
www.chiuni.ac.uk
BA, MA

Cork Institute of Technology
www.cit.ie
BA

* Cumbria (University of)
www.cumbria.ac.uk
BA, MA

De Montfort University, Leicester
www.dmu.ac.uk
BA, MA

* Derby (University of)
www.derby.ac.uk
BA

Dublin Institute of Technology
www.dit.ie
BA

Duncan of Jordanstone (University of Dundee)
wwwdundee.ac.uk
BA, MFA

East London (University of)
www.uel.ac.uk
BA, MA

Falmouth (University College)
www.falmouth.ac.uk
BA, MA

Farnham (University College for the Creative Arts)
www.ucreative.ac.uk
BA, MA

Goldsmiths (University of London)
www.goldsmiths.ac.uk
BA, MFA, M. Phil., Ph.D.

Greenwich (University of)
www.gre.ac.uk
BA

* Hertfordshire (University of)
www.herts.ac.uk
BA, MA

Kingston (University of)
www.kingston.ac.uk
BA

Leeds Metropolitan University
www.leedsmet.ac.uk
BA, MA

Lincoln (University of)
www.lincoln.ac.uk
BA MA

Liverpool Hope University
www.hope.ac.uk
BA

Liverpool John Moores University
www.ljmu.ac.uk
BA

Loughborough College of Art & Design
www.lusad.ac.uk
BA

* Manchester Metropolitan University
www.mmu.ac.uk
BA, MA

Middlesex University
www.mdx.ac.uk
BA

* Newcastle (University of)
www.ncl.ac.uk
BA

Newport (University of Wales)
www.newport.ac.uk
BA

Northampton (University College)
www.northampton.ac.uk
BA, MA

Northumbria University
www.northumbria.ac.uk
BA, MA

North Wales School of Art & Design, Wrexham
www.newi.ac.uk
BA, MA

* Norwich School of Art
www.nsad.ac.uk
MA, MA, M.Phil., Ph.D.

Oxford Brookes University
www.brookes.ac.uk
BA

Plymouth (University of)
www.plymouth.ac.uk
BA, MA

Salford (University of)
www.salford.ac.uk
BA, MA, PG.Dip.

Sheffield Hallam (University of)
www.shu.ac.uk
BA, MA

Slade School of Fine Art, London
www.ucl.ac.uk/slade
BA, MA, MFA

Sligo (Institute of Technology)
www.itsligo.ie
BA

Staffordshire University, Stoke-on-Trent
www.staffs.ac.uk
BA, MA

* Suffolk School of Art & Design
www.suffolk.ac.uk
BA

Sunderland (University of)
www.sunderland.ac.uk
BA, MA

Teesside (University of), Middlesborough
www.tees.ac.uk
BA

**UHI Millennium Institute
(Scottish Highlands and Islands)**
www.uhi.ac.uk
BA

**Ulster (University of), School of
Art & Design,**
Belfastwww.arts.ulster.ac.uk
BA

Westminster University
www.wmin.ac.uk
BA

* Wolverhampton (University of)
www.wlv.ac.uk
BA, MA

* Worcester (University College)
www.worc.ac.uk
BA

* AA2A (Artists' Access to Art Colleges)
AA2A is a project providing visual artists
and designer-makers with the opportunity
to undertake a period of research or to
realise a project using workshop and
supporting facilities in the fine-art and
design departments of higher and further
education institutions. This gives
participating artists and makers the
opportunity to use equipment which
otherwise might not be available to them.

There are currently 22 universities and
colleges in England hosting AA2A. The 11
universities marked above with an asterisk
are offering printmaking as part of the
scheme. There are other colleges in the
scheme listing access to print, but it is best
to check that their print facilities meet your
own needs; some are quite limited. Each
participating institution offers places to
four artists or makers. Each artist/maker
has up to 100 hours' access, which they can
use over a period of at least 17 weeks
between October and April.

Printmaking Suppliers

GENERAL PRINTMAKING SUPPLIERS

L. Cornelissen & Son
105 Great Russell Street
London
WC1B 3RY
+44 (0)20 7636 1045
info@cornelissen.com
www.cornelissen.com

Specialist printmaking and painting suppliers.

Daler Rowney Ltd
PO Box 10
Bracknell
Berkshire
RG12 8ST
+44 (0)1344 424621
www.daler-rowney.com

General art suppliers.

Graphic Chemical and Ink Co.
732 North Yale Avenue
Villa Park
Illinois
60181
USA
+1 630 832 6004
sales@graphicchemical.com
www.graphicchemical.com

Great Art
Normandy House
1 Nether Street
Alton
Hants.
GU34 1EA
+44 (0)1420 593332
welcome@greatart.co.uk
www.greatart.co.uk

General art & craft supplier (good, cheap rollers).

Hawthorn Printmaker Supplies
Hawthorn House
Appleton Roebuck
York
YO23 7DA
+44 (0)7855 621841
www.hawthornprintmaker.co.uk
Specialist printmaking supplies plus etching presses.

Intaglio Printmaker
62 Southwark Bridge Road
9 Playhouse Court
London
SE1 0AT
+44 (0)20 7928 2633
info@intaglioprintmaker.com
www.intaglioprintmaker.com

Specialist printmaking suppliers.

McClains Print Supplies
15685 SW 116th Avenue
PMB 202
King City
Oregan
97224-2695
USA
+1 503 641 3555
mail@mcclains.com
www.mcclains.com

Pegasus Art
Griffin Mill
London Road
Stroud
GL5 2AZ
+44 (0)1453 886560
info@pegasusart.co.uk
www.pegasusart.co.uk

Art suppliers. Print Co-op with good range of print supplies for mail order.

Rollaco Engineering
72 Thornfield Road
Middlesborough
TS5 5BY
+44 (0)1642 813785
sales@rollaco.co.uk
www.rollaco.co.uk

Etching supplies and good-quality rollers, as well as etching presses.

Specialist Crafts Ltd
Unit 2B
Wanlip Road Industrial Estate
Syston
Leicester
LE7 1PD
+44 (0)116 2697711
post@speccrafts.co.uk
www.speccrafts.co.uk
(see also www.homecrafts.co.uk)

General arts suppliers.

T.N. Lawrence & Son Ltd
208 Portland Road
Hove
BN3 5QT
+44 (0)1273 260260
artbox@lawrence.co.uk
www.lawrence.co.uk

Specialist printmaking and painting suppliers.

See also:

www.artdiscount.co.uk
for lino, lino tools, rollers, system 3 acrylic, etc.

www.jacksonsart.co.uk
for Lukas water-based lino ink, lino, rollers, system 3 and speedball.

See also educational suppliers such as:

ESPO: www.espo.org.uk
NES Arnold: www.nesarnold.co.uk

Plus
www.danielsmall.com
www.printmaking-materials.com

ETCHING PRESS MANUFACTURERS

Artichoke Print Workshop
Unit S1
Bizspace
245A Coldharbour Lane
London
SW9 8RR
+44 (0)20 7924 0600
www.printbin.co.uk

Suppliers of KB etching presses and etching blankets.

Beevers Engineering
64 Darlinghurst Grove
Leigh-on-Sea
Essex
SS9 3LF
+44 (0)1702 712219
enquiries@beeverspress.co.uk
www.beeverspress.co.uk

Hydraulic press engineers (for relief, etching and lithography).

Bewick Presses
Riverside Dimensions
35 Harwood Court
Riverside Park Ind. Est.
Middlesborough
Cleveland
TS2 1PU
+44 (0)1642 805777

Etching presses (formerly Bewick & Wilson).

Gunning Arts Ltd
28 Church Hill
Ironbridge
Shropshire
TF8 7PZ
+44 (0)1952 433816
davegunning@gunningarts.co.uk
www.gunningarts.co.uk

Etching presses and hotplates.

Harry F. Rochat Ltd
15A Moxon Street
Barnet
Hertfordshire
EN5 5TS
+44 (0)20 8449 0023
info@harryrochat.com
www.harryrochat.com

New, refurbished and restored etching presses plus servicing, rollers, blankets, inks, levigators and relief litho and nipping presses also available.

Hawthorn Printmaker Supplies
Hawthorn House
Appleton Roebuck
York
Yo23 7DA
+44 (0)7855 621841
www.hawthornprintmaker.co.uk

Now also manufacturing etching presses.

Hunter Penrose
32 Southwark Street
London
SE1 1TU
+44 (0)207 407 5051
sales@hunterpenrose.co.uk
www.hunterpenrose.co.uk

Etching presses, hotplates, sinks and aquatint booths.

John Pears
5 Whitton Drive
Spennymoor
County Durham
DL16 6LU
+44 (0)1388 818004
john@rolllacopresses.co.uk
www.rollacopresses.co.uk

Etching presses (not to be confused with Rollaco Engineering; similar press specs, but different products by brothers with two separate firms).

Practical Etching Presses
344 Henley Road
Ilford
Essex

IG1 2TJ
+44 (0)20 8478 6420

Rollaco Engineering
72 Thornfield Road
Middlesborough
Cleveland
TS5 5BY
+44 (0)1642 813785
sales@rollaco.co.uk
www.rollaco.co.uk

Etching presses as well as supplies and good-quality rollers.

Specialist Crafts Ltd
Unit 2B
Wanlip Road Industrial Estate
Syston
Leicester
LE7 1PD
+44 (0)116 2697711
post@speccrafts.co.uk
www.speccrafts.co.uk
(see also www.homecrafts.co.uk)

William Horwood & Sons Ltd
Flint Cottage
19 The Village
Clifton-upon-Teme
Worcestershire
WR6 6EN
+44 (0)1886 812495
martin.horwood@ukgateway.net
www.williamhorwood.com

Portable etching presses.

Interwood
Allwood Machinery
Unit 3 Galliford Road
The Causeway
Maldon, Essex
CM9 4XD
+44 (0)1621 859477
info@allwood.co.uk
www.interwood.co.uk

Medium to large-scale hydraulic veneer presses for relief and etching work, etc.

ETCHING PRESSES AROUND THE WORLD

American French Tool Company
Rhode Island
USA
www.americanfrenchtool.com

Bendini Etching Presses
Bologna
Italy
tel.: +34 72 51 60 28

Conrad Machine Company
Michigan
USA
www.conradmachine.com

Ettan Press
California
USA
www.ettanpress.com

HALE-presses
Anjanankoski
Finland
www.halepress.com

Polymetaal
Leiden
The Netherlands
www.polymetaal.nl

Praga Industries
Ontario
Canada
www.praga.com

Takach Press Corporation
Albuquerque
USA
www.takachpress.com

Thomas Fine Art Presses
British Columbia
Canada
www.thomaspresses.com

SCREENPRINT EQUIPMENT

Adelco Screen Process Ltd
Highview
High Street
Bordon
Hants.
GU35 0AX
+44 (0)1420 488388
sales@adelco.co.uk
www.adelco.co.uk
Hand-print tables plus other industrial units.

Cirgraphics Ltd
Victoria Road
Rushden
Northants.
NN10 0AS
+44 (0)1933 315005
joncrisp@cirgraphics.com
www.cirgraphics.com

Exposure units and sinks, etc.
(also run Art Equipment——is that a company with this name?——).

Creative Printers of London
Unit B6
Bernard Road
Danes Road Industrial Estate
Romford
Essex
RM7 0HX
+44 (0)1708 731294
creativeprinters@btconnect.com
www.creative-printers.co.uk

Exposure units, carousels, etc.

H.G. Kippax & Sons
Upper Bankfield Mills
Almondbury Bank
Huddersfield
HD5 8HF
+44 (0)1484 426789
www.hgkippax.co.uk

Screen beds, exposure units and all machinery.

Mascoprint
Stags End Cottage Barn
Gaddesden Row
Hemel Hempstead
Hertfordshire
HP2 6HN
+44 (0)1582 791190

info@mascoprint.co.uk
www.mascoprint.co.uk

Suppliers of Natgraph machinery plus own-make light box, and supplies.

Micro Screen Printing Supplies Ltd
98 Englefield Road
London
N1 3LG
+44 (0)20 7354 1431

Multiprint Machinery
Unit 1
Park Court
Park Lane Business Park
Kirby-in-Ashfield
Nottingham
NG17 9LB
+44 (0)1623 487554 (Chris Hopper: sales)
sales@multiprintmachinery.com
www.multiprintmachinery.com

Screen beds, UV light boxes, etc.

Natgraph Ltd
Dabell Avenue
Blenheim Industrial Estate
Nottingham
NG6 8WA
+44 (0)115 979 5800
alan.shaw@natgraph.co.uk
www.natgraph.co.uk

Screen beds, UV light boxes, drying cabinets and alall machinery.

Parker Graphics Ltd
Progress House
Erskine Road
London
E17 6RT
+44 (0)1992 618006
sales@mmparker.com
www.parkergraphics.co.uk

New and reconditioned machinery. Specialists in exposure units and lamps for screen, litho and flexography.

Peter Potter Ltd
Water Lane
Storrington

Pulborough
RH20 3EA
West Sussex
+44 (0)1903 743397
peter.potter@btconnect.com
www.peterpotter.co.uk

Screen beds and fabric printing tables.

Richards of Hull
Unit 1
Acorn Estate
Bontoft Avenue
Hull
HU5 4HF
+44 (0)1482 442422
sales@richards.uk.com
www.richards.uk.com

Sinks, tanks, wash-out booths, and extraction units.

Trumax Ltd
Tower Road North
Warmley
Bristol
BS30 8XP
+44 (0)117 9353320

Screen beds, exposure units, etc.

SCREENPRINTING MATERIALS

AP Fitzpatrick Fine Art Materials
142 Cambridge Heath Road
London
E1 5QJ
+44 (0)20 7790 0884
info@apfitzpatrick.co.uk
www.apfitzpatrick.co.uk

Screen inks and general art supplies.

Cadisch Precision Meshes
Unit 1
Finchley Industrial Centre
879 High Road
Finchley
London
N12 8QA
+44 (0)20 8492 0444
info@cadisch.com

www.cadisch.com

Screen stretching, meshes and Kiwo stencil-making products.

Colenso
Unit 2/3
Fairoak Court
Whitehouse
Runcorn
Cheshire
WA7 3DX
+44 (0)1928 701356
www.colenso.co.uk
sales@colenso.co.uk

Screen emulsions, chemicals, mesh and solvent-based inks.

Folex
18/19 Monkspath Business Park
Shirley
Solihull
West Midlands
B90 4NY
+44 (0)121-7333833
www.folex.co.uk

Screen coatings and films

London Graphic Centre
Covent Garden Flagship
16-18 Shelton Street
Covent Garden
London
WC2H 2JL
+44 (0)20 7759 4500
www.londongraphics.co.uk

Suppliers of screen and relief products plus spray paints and airbrushes.

Screen Colour Systems Ltd
Waterfall Cottages
Waterfall Road
London
SW19 2AG
+44 (0)20 8997 1694
sales@screencoloursystems.co.uk
www.screencoloursystems.co.uk

Screen inks and screens manufactured.

Screen Sense Ltd
45 Cherry Tree Road
Chinnor
Oxon
OX39 4QZ
+44 (0)7957 358250
info@screen-sense.com
www.screen-sense.com

Screens manufactured and stretched.

Screenstretch
Unit F
Prestwich Industrial Estate
Coal Pit Lane
Atherton
Manchester
M46 0RL
keith@screenstretch.co.uk
www.screenstretch.co.uk

Screen manufacturers, screen stretching and sundries.

Small Products
20 St Andrews Way
off Devons Road
Bow
London
E3 3PA
+44 (0) 207 537 4222
sales@smallproducts.co.uk

www.smallproducts.co.uk
Suppliers of Aquagraphic inks.

Steve Wood
Unit 14
Centre Park
Marsden Business Park
Rudgate
Todwith
York
YO26 7QY
+44 (0)1423 358 988
www.steve-wood.co.uk
screen@steve-wood.co.uk

Screenprinting inks and sundries.

Tick Tack Ltd
The Old Chapel
125 High Street

Marshfield
Chippenham
Wiltshire
SN14 8LU
+44 (0)1225 891055

Screens manufactured and stretched

WHERE ELSE TO LOOK
There are also many local commercial
screenprint suppliers to the printing
industry. I recommend finding a local
supplier through local directories such as
Yellow Pages and Thomson as well as on
the internet. They are often approachable
for individuals, and can supply bespoke
screens, etc. to order.

LARGER COMMERCIAL INKS AND CHEMICALS SUPPLIERS

Arets Graphics
www.arets.com

Inks & More Ltd
www.inksandmore.co.uk

Sericol (UK Sales)
www.sericol.co.uk
Sun Chemical Gibbon
www.sunchemical.co.uk

Coates
www.coates.com

MISCELLANEOUS SUPPLIES

ACE Safety
Longworth Limited
Leltex House
Longley Lane
Sharston
Manchester
M22 4SY
+44 (0)161 945 1333
webservices@longworth.co.uk
www.acesafetydirect.co.uk

Safety goggles, respiratory equipment and
cleaning products.

Bay Plastics Ltd
Unit H1
High Flatworth
Tyne Tunnel Trading Estate
North Shields
Tyne and Wear
+44(0)191 258 0777
enquiries@bayplastics.co.uk
www.bayplastics.co.uk

Drypoint Perspex.

Business Textile Services Ltd
Units 7 & 8
Springmill Industrial Estate
Avening Road
Nailsworth
Gloucestershire
Gl6 0BS
+44 (0)1453 832266
enquiries@bustex.co.uk
www.bustex.co.uk

Recycled rags.

Chronos UK Ltd
www.chronos.td.uk

Cheap scribes plus number and letter
punches for book-making, etc.

Dantex Graphics Ltd
Danon House
5 Kings Road
Bradford
BD2 1EY
+44 (0)1274 777 777
Info@dantex.com
www.dantex.com

Supplier of solar plates.

Chris Daunt
1 Monkridge Gardens
Dunston
Gateshead
Tyne and Wear
NE11 9XE
+44 (0)191 420 8975
info@chrisdaunt.com
www.chrisdaunt.com

Supplier of good-quality end-grain wood-engraving blocks, burnishers and sandbags. Endorsed by the Society of Wood Engravers.

ETCHING/PHOTO-ETCHING SUNDRIES

Dustraction
PO Box 75
Manderville Road
Oadby
Leicestershire
LE2 5ND
+44 (0)1162 713212
sales@dustraction.co.uk
www.dustraction.co.uk

Dust extraction including spray booths.

Industrial Wiper Co.
Imperial House
St Nicolas Circle
Leicester
LE1 4LF
01162 624411
mail@I-w-c.co.uk

Supplier of recycled rags.

Andrew Purches
6 Hyde Lane
Upper Beeding
Steyning
West Sussex
BN44 3WJ
+44 (0)1903 814331
andrew@lenticular-europe.com

Press sales, removals and rebuilds, lithoplate graining, stone-litho workshop in West Sussex for course work and commissioned press work.

Timstar Laboratory Supplies Ltd
Marshfield Bank Industrial Estate
Middlewich Road
Crewe
CW2 6UY

Chemical suppliers who can supply acid.

See also www.3mselect.co.uk for safety goggles and first aid, as well as Scotch Tape, etc.

Biz Engineering
Edison Road
off Millmarsh Lane
Brimsdown
Enfield
Middlesex
EN3 7QA
+44 (0)208 216 6260
www.bizengineering.com

Suppliers of polished zinc, mild steel and aluminium.

Sally Dyas
Rocquette Villa
Rocquettes Lane
St Peter Port
Guernsey
GY1 1XT
+44 (0)1481 711130
s_dyas@hotmail.com
www.sallydyas.com

Supplier of photopolymer film.

Lazertran Ltd
8 Alban Square
Ceredigion
SA46 0AD
+44 (0)1545 571 149
(contact: Mick Kelly)
mic@lazertran.com
www.lazertran.com

Decal waterslide transfer papers, for phototransfer, photo-etching, etc.

Martin Maywood
The Old School
81 High Street
Owstan Ferry
North Lincolnshire
DN9 1RL
+44 (0) 1427 728 175
info@mezzotint.co.uk
www.mezzotint.co.uk

Supplier of quality pre-rocked copper mezzotint plates.

Mati Basis
13 Cranbourne Road
London
N10 2BT
+44 (0)20 8444 7833

Metal merchants.

Smiths Metal Centres
www.smithmetal.com
Centres in 11 locations across the UK:
Biggleswade, Birmingham, Bristol,
Chelmsford, Ferndown, Gateshead,
Horsham, Leeds, London, Norwich and
Nottingham.

Suppliers of aluminium, copper, steel and
plastics.

W & S Allely Ltd
PO Box 58
Alma Street
Smethwick
West Midlands
B66 2RP
+44 (0)121 558 3301
www.allely.co.uk

Site locations also in the North-east, North,
South-west & South-east.
Suppliers of aluminium and copper sheet.

PAPER MERCHANTS

Compton Marbling
Solveig Stone
Lower Lawn Barns
Tisbury
Salisbury
Wilts.
SP3 6SG
+44 (0)1747 871147
solveig@comptonmarbling.co.uk
www.comptonmarbling.co.uk

Handmade marbled papers for
bookbinders, conservationists, paper
specialists and furniture restorers around
the world.

John Purcell Paper (JPP)
15 Rumsey Road

London
SW9 0TR
+44 (0)20 7737 5199
jpp@johnpurcell.net
www.johnpurcell.net

Fine-art/printmaking paper specialists

JvO Papers
6 Mill Row
Millgate
Aylsham
Norfolk
NR11 6HZ
+44 (0)1263 731099
john@jvopapers.com
www.jvopapers.com

Fine-art/printmaking paper specialists

Khadi Papers
Chilgrove
Chichester
PO18 9HU
+44 (0)1243 535 314
paper@khadi.com
www.khadi.com

Specialists in Indian papers, rag papers and
papermaking equipment.

Nautilus Press & Paper Mill
77 Southern Row
London
W10 5AL
+44 (0)208 9687302

R.K. Burt
57 Union Street
London
SE1 1SG
+44 (0)1207 407 6474
sales@rkburt.co.uk
ww.rkburt.co.uk

Fine-art/printmaking paper specialists

Shephards Bookbinders Ltd.
76 Southampton Row
London
WC1B 4AR
+44 (0)207 8311151
www.falkiners.com

Fine-art/printmaking paper specialists. plus bookbinding suppliers – formaly Falkners Fine Papers.

Two Rivers Paper Company
Pitt Mill
Roadwater
Watchett
Somerset
TA23 0QS
tworiverspaper@googlemail.com
www.tworiverspaper.co.uk

handmade fine-art/printmaking paper specialists

Wookey Hole Handmade Paper
Wells
Somerset
BA5 1BB
+44 (0)1749 672243
paper@wookey.co.uk
www.wookeypaper.co.uk

Handmade paper mill still in operation making specialist papers, and open to visitors as a working museum.

See also:

www.paperchase.co.uk
Stores that supply craft papers and some printmaking papers.

www.thepapeterie.com
The supply shop of Arjo Wiggins Paper mill (formerly Stoneywood Mill) in Aberdeen; also for craft papers, etc.

LETTERPRESS AND BOOKBINDING SUPPLIERS

Alpha Engraving Co.
Unit F1 Southway
Bounds Green Industrial Estate
Bounds Green Road
London
N11 2UL
+44 (0)20 8368 1674
alphablocks@btconnect.com

For flexoplates, letterpress plates, etc.

Caslon Limited
Caslon House
Lyon Way
St Albans
Herts.
AL4 0LB
+44 (0)1727 852211
sales@caslon.co.uk
www.caslon.co.uk

Suppliers of Adana presses, accessories, type fonts and foil blocking machines.

F.J. Ratchford Ltd.
Kennedy Way
Green Lane
Stockport
Cheshire
Sk4 2JX
+44 (0) 161 480 8484
info@fjratchford.co.uk
www.fjratchford.co.uk

Suppliers of moving materials, tools, papers and sundries.

Hubbard Type Foundry
Unit 21 Cornish Way
Lyngate Industrial Estate
North Walsham
Norfolk
NR28 0AW
+44 (0)1692 405479
(contact: Brian Hubbard)
hubbardtypefoundry@btopenworld.com
www.hubbardtypefoundry.com

A massive range of hot-metal typefaces are available. If not 'on the shelf', they can be cast to order, generally within four days. Brian also teaches monotype and typesetting on a one-to-one basis.

J Hewit and Sons Ltd.
Kinould Leather Works
Currie
Edinburgh
EH14 5RS
+44 (0)131 449 2206
sales@hewitt.com
www.hewitt.com

Suppliers of equipment, tools, materials

and sundries for all craft bookbinding requirements.

Joyce & Co. Ltd
14 Little End Road
Eaton Socon
St Neots
Cambs.
PE19 8JH
+44 (0)1480 405290
www.joyce-pm.com

Print packaging and finishing company; supplier of bookmaking screws second-hand quoins.

Preston Mouldtype
Leyland Lane
Leyland
Preston
PR25 1UT
+44 (0)1772 425026

Supertype
Send SAE to:
Supertype
The Wheatleys
Dewsbury Rd Gomersal
W. Yorks.
BD19 4LH

For small founts of type.

The Type Museum
100 Hackford Road London
SW9 0QU
+44 (0)20 7735 0055
enquiries@typemuseum.org
www.typemuseum.org

The museum's trading arm Monotype Hot metal has a matrix-making service and spare parts for monotype casters etc.

Linecasting Machinery Ltd
Unit 34
John Wilson Business Park
Chestfield
Whitstable
Kent
CT5 3QY
+44 (0)1227 770665
linecasting@btconnect.com
www.linecasting.com

Specialist engineers to the printing industry, including hot-metal typecasting machines and lines of type to order.

The following websites are by far the best places to find the current suppliers, courses in letterpress and active letterpress printers:

www.letterpressalive.co.uk
Run by Alembic Press with links to everything connected with letterpress and private presses.

www.britishletterpress.co.uk
Run by Benjamin Brundell, this site has information on letterpress history, how-to-guides, suppliers and much more.

Open Print

EXHIBITIONS/EXCHANGES

Printmaking has a great advantage over other art forms both for exchange and for open exhibitions or competitions because of the possibility of editioning and the comparable (compared to painting and sculpture) ease of postage for prints. There is a plethora of print opens which now operate though universities, galleries and print workshops. The use of internet and emailing has increased the opportunity to bring such information to the attention of artists. More and more print workshops and universities are realising the potential for open-print competitions, with mini-print exhibitions in particular being a strong model to follow, because small prints are easy and cheap to post and are also more likely to sell.

The following is a list of just some of the international opportunities available to the printmaker today in the UK. Whilst this section lists every regular open, I have excluded those which limit themselves only to artists from their own region and those which do not have a definite future date. Of course there are also many book arts fairs and general art opens which include printmaking; too many to list here. There will undoubtedly also be fairs or exchanges I have overlooked; by no means should you take this to be a fully comprehensive list.

UK AND IRELAND

British International Mini-Print Exhibition
Run by the Printmakers' Council (formerly held at the Gracefield Arts Centre in Dumfries, and originally held at Off-Centre Gallery, Bristol). Maximum image size 70 sq. cm (10_ sq. in.). Paper size preferably no larger than A4. Approx. 200 prints are selected. The exhibition tours venues nationally for up to two years.

contact: Printmakers' Council,
Ground Floor Unit,
23 Blue Anchor Lane,
London,
SE16 3UL.
tel.: +44 (0)20 7237 6789
(Wednesdays 2-6 pm)
email: www.7thminiprint.com/_contact.cfm
website: www.7thminiprint.com

Leeds Imprint
C/o Paul Hudson,
88 Ash Road,
Leeds,
LS6 3HD.
email: paul.e.hudson@talktalk.net
website: www.leedsimprint.org.uk

Annual exhibition open to printmakers living or working in the Leeds and Bradford area, established in 2004 and held across various venues throughout June. (Paul is also planning to open a print workshop in Leeds. Anyone interested should contact him.)

Norwich Print Fair
Annual exhibition for two weeks every September in the deconsecrated St Margaret's Church in Norwich, which has been refurbished as an exhibition space. Martin Mitchell started the Norwich Print Fair in 1995. As a professional printmaker working in Norwich, he had the idea of creating an annual exhibition that could showcase the versatility and scope of contemporary printmaking in the East Anglian region; now with approximately 30 artists showing each year.

contact: Martin Mitchell
website: www.norwichprintfair.co.uk

Originals

Annual print open organised by the Federation of British Artists and based at The Mall Galleries in London, this exhibition is supported with many prizes and accompanying workshops in printmaking run by Artichoke Printmaking. Open to all printmaking techniques, with collection points around the UK.

contact: Federation of British Artists,
17 Carlton Terrace,
London,
SW1Y 5BD.
email: info@mallgalleries.com
website: www.mallgalleries.org.uk

Printfest

Established in 2001 by artists Judy Evans and Ronkey Bullard, this annual 'festival of printmaking' takes place in Coronation Hall in Ulverston, Cumbria, and invites submissions from printmakers to apply for a stand as a 'unique selling opportunity set in the beautiful setting in the Lake District'.

contact: Tina Balmer,
Artistic Director,
6 Benson Street,
Ulverston,
Cumbria,
LA12 7AG.
email: thebalmers@ticali.co.uk
website: www.printfest.org.uk

RBSA Print Open

Annual open at RBSA's own gallery in Birmingham, on two floors of gallery space. All traditional printmaking techniques accepted.

contact: The Honorary Secretary,
Royal Birmingham Society of Artists,
4 Brook Street,
Birmingham,
B3 1SA.
tel.: +44 (0)121 236 4353
email: secretary@rbsa.org.uk
website: www.rbsa.org.uk

Wrexham Print International

Biennial exhibition established in 2001 and run by Yale College and Wrexham Arts Centre. Any artist from anywhere in the world may apply. Send up to six images. The panel will be looking for innovation in all techniques of printmaking. The exhibition takes place in the Memorial Gallery, Wrexham plus touring venues. The next exhibition is in April 2011, with submissions in late 2010/Jan 2011.

contact: Tracy Simpson,
Wrexham Arts Centre,
Rhosddu Road,
Wrexham,
Wales.
LL12 7AA.
tel.: +44 (0)1978 292093
email: gallery@yale-wrexham.ac.uk
website: www.wrexham.gov.uk/arts

See also

IMPACT Print Conference

www.uwe.ac.uk/amd/cfpr

It is also important here to refer to IMPACT Print Conference, which was established by the Centre for Fine Print Research at the University of the West of England in 1996, and has subsequently grown into a major event in the international printmaking calendar. Having been held in South Africa, Poland/Germany and Estonia, it arrives back in the UK in September 2009, and features exhibitions, masterclasses and demonstrations run alongside major debates. Its reputation will undoubtedly increase as it moves to a different global venue every two years.

INTERNATIONAL PRINT OPENS/EXCHANGES

Reputedly the first biennial of its kind, the Ljubljana Biennial of Graphic Arts in Slovenia, which began in 1955, became the model for similar exhibitions such as those in Tokyo, Grenchen in Switzerland, Germany, Krakow, Florence and Bradford. There are now many well-established print opens and exchanges around the world, which offer an international stage for printmakers and printmaking, in the form of opportunities to extend your CV, to get into exhibition catalogues and to show alongside other work of international standing.

Acqui Terme International Biennial of Engraving

Established in 1990. Etchings no larger than 50 x 70 cm (19½ x 27½ in.). Each artist should send no more than one print. Works after the exhibition will be included in the collection of the Museum of Engraving, Castello Paleologi, Acqui Terme. The next event is in 2010, with submissions in September 2009.

contact: Giuseppe Avignolo,
President,
Rotary Club,
Aqcui Terme,
Ovada,
2030 District,
Piazza Italia,
N.9- 15011
Aqui Terme,
Italy.
tel.: +39 (0)144 57937
email: info@acquiprint.it
website: www.acquiprint.it

Americas Biennial Exhibition & Archive

As of late 2007 this is an amalgamation of Iowa Biennial and Texas Biennial, and 'represents the continents of the Americas and prints from around the world'. With an inaugural exhibition in the University of Iowa it then becomes an international travelling exhibition. The maximum print size allowable is 9 x 9 cm (3½ x 3½ in.), and the next deadline for submission is mid-2010.

email: information@americasbiennial.org
website: www.americasbiennial.org

Aomori Print Triennial

Open to all printmaking techniques except digital. Artists may submit as many as three works, up to a maximum size of 150 x 150 cm (59 x 59 in.). No submission fee for artists living outside of Japan. The next exhibition is in 2010, with applications to arrive by July 2009, and prints to be mailed in August.

contact: Aomori Print Triennial Committee,
c/o Aomori Contemporary Art Centre,
152-6 Yamakazi.
Goshizawa,
Aomori,
Japan.
tel.: +81 (0)17 764 5200
email: triennial@acac-aomori.jp
website: www.acac-aomori.jp/trienniale

Bharat Bhavan International Biennial of Print

Established in 1989. All print techniques accepted from any country in the world. Send up to three prints, unmounted, in a mailing tube. Selection is by international jury. There are invited artists and an open section.

contact: J. Swarninathan Marg,
Shamla Hill,
Bhopal 462002,
M.P., India.
tel.: +91 (0)755 2661398

BIMPE Biennial Miniature Print Exhibition

Established in 2000, and organised by Dundarave Print Workshop and New Leaf Editions in Vancouver, this exhibition is open to up to three works per artist in any print media, with a maximum size restriction of 15 x 10 cm (6 x 4 in.).

contact: Peter Braune,
Katie Dey,
New Leaf Editions,
1370 Cartwright Street,
Vancouver,
BC V6H 3R8,
Canada.
tel.: +1 604 689 9918
email: info@bimpe.com
website: www.bimpe.com

Bitola International Graphic Triennial

A themed triennial, the next open is in 2012. All techniques except monotype are accepted. Open to artists from all over the world, there is a size limit on each submission of 100 x 70 cm (39½ x 27½ in.).

contact: Vlado Goreski,
Project Manager & Art Director,
Institute and Museum,
Binolta,
7000 Republic of Macedonia.
tel.: +38 970 207 037
email: grafik@freemail.org.mk

Cadaqués Mini-Print International
Established in 1981, this well-known annual exchange attracts entrants from all over the world. Any image submitted must be no larger that 10 x 10 cm (4 x 4 in.), with paper no larger than 18 x 18 cm (7 x 7 in.).

contact:
Mercedes Barbera,
President of Adogi,
Ap. de Correos 9319,
08080 Barcelona,
Spain.
email: adogi@miniprint.org
website: www.miniprint.org

Caixanova International Engraving Biennial
A maximum of two original prints per artist, and works no larger than 170 x 100 cm (67 x 39½ in.), nor any smaller on one side than 50 cm (19½ in.). Mechanical printing techniques of any kind will be rejected. No entry fees. The next exhibition is in 2010.

contact: International Engraving Biennial,
Caixanova,
Area Sociocultural,
Avenida de Pontevedra,
9, 32005,
Ourense,
Spain.
tel.: +34 988 392389
email: ourense@centrosocialcixanova.com
website: www.caixanova.es

Carbunari International Small Engraving Salon
Open submission and invited artists. Each artist should send five works, with the longest side no longer than 17 cm (6_ in.).

Works become the property of the Florean Museum.

contact: Bochnis Mircea,
Florean Museum,
PO Box 1 of Postal 9, 430510,
Baia Mare,
Maramures,
Romania.
email: mirceabochnis@sintec.ro

Cascade International Print Exchange
Annual exchange established in 2005. Send an edition of 15 identical hand-pulled original prints. 13 randomly selected prints from other artists mailed to each participant 12.7 x 17.8 cm (5 x 7 in.) paper size.

contact: Cascade Print Exchange,
Department of Art,
106 Fairbanks Hall,
Oregon State University,
Corvallis,
OR 97331-3702, USA.
email: cellerik@onid.orst,edu
website: www.cascadeprint.org

Cluj International Mini-Print Biennial
Maximum paper dimensions: 22 x 30 cm (8⅝ x 11¾ in.). All printmaking techniques accepted. Entry is free.

contact: Ovidiu Petca,
C.P. 1132 O.P. 1 400750,
Cluj-Napoca,
Romania.

Contemprints International Miniature Print Exhibition
Max print size 26 sq. cm (4 sq. in.). Organised by the Center for Contemporary Printmaking, Norwalk Connecticut, America, this biennial exhibition has given rise to and now alternates annually with Footprint (see entry below). The next submissions are in 2011.

contact: Center for Contemporary Printmaking,
Matthews Park,
299 West Avenue, Norwalk,
Connecticut 06850.

email: info@contemprints.org
website: www.contemprints.org

Estampe.Be
International bookmarks exchange
established in 1999. Participants should
submit 11 identical original prints 5 x 20 cm
(2 x 8 in.), the size of a bookmark.
Participants will receive 10 bookmarks in
return. The submission deadline for the
2010 exchange is December 2009.

contact: Hugues Pryzsiuda,
Rue Tourette,
128, 6000 Charleroi,
Belgium.
email: bookmarks2009@estampe.be
website: www.estampe.be/exchange

European Biennial Competition
for Graphic Art
Established in 1985. Themed print open for
any resident of a member state of the
European Union. Any print method
acceptable except pure photography.
Preselection by photo, and a maximum of
three images per artist. Next submission
deadline is April 2011.

contact: Rotariale VZW,
P/A Crowne Plaza, Burg 10, B-8000,
Brugge,
Belgium
tel.: +32 59 51 00 32
email: eric.wieme@pandora.be
website: www.graphicartes.be

Egyptian International Print Triennial
Triennial established in 1990. All
traditional prints accepted. The size of
each work to be no larger than 100 x 70
cm (39$\frac{1}{2}$ x 27$\frac{1}{2}$ in.). Work selected by
international jury. The governmental
Sector of Fine Arts organises an
international symposium in parallel with
the Triennial to discuss issues and the
development of printmaking. Next
exhibition 2012; submissions usually by
31st December of previous year.

contact: Farouk Sheheta,
The Egyptian International Print Triennial,
Ministry of Culture,

Sector of Fine Arts,
Egypt, 1 Kafour Street,
Orman,
PO Box Orman Giza.
tel.: 202/7482156
email: printtrienniale@yahoo.com
website: www.fineart.gov.eg

Edmonton Print International
Organised by the Society of Northern
Alberta Print Artists (SNAP), Canada, this
open-juried print exhibition is a major
event that has evolved from the example
of other major print exhibitions run by
SNAP in recent years. It is aimed to be
held every four years. Original work in all
traditional printmaking techniques is
eligible, including intaglio, relief,
lithography and screenprinting as well as
digital and 3D print-based work and print
installations. There are no size limits.
Each artist may submit up to five images.
Next submission deadline for exhibition in
2012 will be April 2012.

contact: EPI 2012,
Society of Northern Alberta Print-Artists,
10309-97 Street,
Edmonton,
Alberta,
T5 0M1,
Canada.
tel.: +1 780 423 1492
email: epi@snapartists.com
website:
www.edmontonprintinternational.com

Fête de la Gravure
Established in 1995, this biennial event
'aims to propose a vision of etching as
practised today. It is part of the engraving
festival organised across Liège. The next
exchange is in 2011, with submissions
deadline likely to be in June 2010.

contact: Madame Regine Remon,
Cabinet des Etampes et Dessins de la Ville
de Liège,
Parc de la Boverie,
3 B-4020 Liège, Belgium.
email: cabinetdesestampes@skynet.be
website: www.cabinetdesestampes.be

Footprint International Print Competition
Biennial established in 2008. Prints must be 30.5 x 30.5 cm (12 x 12 in.). Organised by the Center for Contemporary Printmaking, who also established a miniprint biennial in 2007. The next exhibition is in March 2010, with submission in January or February of that year.

contact: Center for Contemporary Printmaking,
Mathews Park,
299 West Avenue,
Norwalk,
CT 06850,
USA.
email: info@contemprints.org
website: www.contemprints.org

German International Exhibition of Graphic Art
Triennial open to all artists born after 1965. All printmaking techniques, three-dimensional works and monoprints accepted. Maximum paper size 90 x 120 cm (35½ x 47¼ in.). The next exhibition is in 2011, with preselection in January and submission at the end of March of that year.

contact: Sabine Müller,
c/o Kunstverein Zu Frechen E.V.,
Kolpingplatz 1, (Stadsaal),
50226 Frechen,
Germany.
tel.: +49 (0)2234 16967
email: info@kunstverein-frechen.de
website: www.kunstverein-frechen.de/grafik-triennale_e.html

Grafinnova International Exhibition of Prints and Drawings by Young Artists
Ostrobothnian Museum, Vaasa, Finland.
contact: c/o post address – PO Box 3,
65101 Vaasa,
Finland.

tel: +358 (0)6 325 3800
email: museoinfo@vaasa

Graphica Creativa
The oldest print international in the Nordic countries, set up in 1975. (Thanks to

Graphica Jyväskylä has become a centre for printmaking.) Past exhibitions have included chains of printmakers whereby artists are invited to propose four international partner printmakers, and the July 2009 exhibition is based on the theme of Co-op, whereby projects and collaborations are invited from all artists with a description of the idea and process and the names and CVs of each artist. The next exhibition after that is in 2012.

contact: Graphica Creativa Society,
Jyväskylä Art Museum,
PO Box 165,
40101 Jyväskylä,
Finland.
tel.: +35 850 4622 695
email: jukka.partanen@jkl.fi
website: www.3.jkl.fi/taidemuseo

Guanlan International Print Biennial, China
There is no limit to print variety and skills, but prints should be no bigger than 100 x 100 cm (39½ x 39½ in.) and no smaller than 30 x 30 cm (12 x 12 in.). The next exhibition is in 2011, with submissions by February 2011.

contact: Ji Donmei,
Yan Min,
Guanlan Culture and Art Center,
Bao'an District,
Shezhen,
China,
518110.
tel.: +86 755 2802 3942
email: cnglbanhua@126.com
website: www.guanlanprints.cn

Ibizagrafic Print Biennial
Exhibition open to all artists. Traditional as well as digital print techniques accepted. Maximum size 100 x 100 cm (39½ x 39½ in.). Next exhibition in 2010.

contact: Pere Mari, Ibizagrafic,
Museu d'Art Contemporani d'Eivissa,
Ronda Narcis Puget,
s/n 07800 Eivissa.
Ibiza
tel.: +34 971 302723

email: coordinador@eivissa.org/
mac@eivissa.org
website: www.eivissaweb.com/news/

Ingráfica International Contemporary Art Print Festival
Established in 2008. The aim of INGRÁFICA is to establish an important, non-commercial event for the world of graphic and serialised art in Spain. Works of any size in etching, lithography, screenprinting, additive processes, electrographic and digital works, etc. Application is open to artists of any nationality. There is no age limit.

contact: INGRÁFICA C/Atocha, 91 – 1º dcha. 28012 – Madrid, Spain.
tel./fax: +34 91 308 00 49
email: info@ingrafica.org
website: www.ingrafica.org

Imoga International Print Biennial
Established 2008. Subject matter open. Three works (with two copies each). All traditional techniques accepted except digital. Printed surface not to exceed 70 x 100 cm (27½ x 39½ in.). Next exhibition in September 2010, with submission in June of that year.

contact: Eda Tekcan Tomba, Istanbul Grafik Sanatlar Musezi, Unalan Mah, Barajyola Sok no.14, Uskudar TR-34700 Istanbul, Turkey.
tel.: +90 216 470 9292
email: info@imoga.org
website: www.imoga.org

Kochi International Print Triennial
Established in 1984. Original prints on paper only, paper size not to exceed 100 x 100 cm (39½ x 39½ in.). Several prizes.

contact: 287-4 Hakawa Ino-Cho Agawa-Gun Kochi-ken 781-2128 Japan.
email: tosawasi@basil.ocn.ne.jp
website: www.tosawashi.or.jp

Krakow International Print Triennial
One of the oldest international print exhibitions in Europe, established in 1966. The website is extensive and includes symposia and print forums. The next exhibition is in 2010.

contact: Prof. Witold Skulicz, Krakow International Print Triennial, Dunajewskiego 2/6, 31-133 Krakow, Poland.
email: smtg@triennial.cracow.pl
website: www.triennial.cracow.pl

L'Arte e il Torchio (Art & the Printing Press), International Biennial of Small Engraving
Established in 1997. A limit of two works per artist, each no larger than 25 x 35 cm (9⁷/8 x 13¾ in.).

contact: Vladimir Elvieri, A.D.A.F.A., via Palestro 32, (PO Box 19), 26-100, Cremona, Italy.
tel.: +39 (0)372 24679.
email: info@artetorchio.it
website: www.artetorchio.it

Le Locle Print Triennale
Open to artists of any nationality. All printmaking techniques admitted. Send a maximum of three unframed prints measuring no more than 120 x 80 cm (47¼ x 31½ in.). Next exhibition from Sept.-Nov. 2010, with submission in May of that year.

contact: Triennale de L'Estampe, Le Locle Prints, Musée des Beaux-Arts, 6 Rue Marie-Anne Calame CH-2400 Le Locle, Switzerland.
tel.: +41 32931 1333
email: info@mbal.ch
website: www.mbal.ch

L'Estampe de Saint-Maur Print Biennale
Themed exhibition of 'all traditional techniques of original engravings, except works produced on computer'. Up to five works. No fees chargeable. The next exhibition is in 2011.

contact: Bernadette Boustany,
Musée de Saint-Maur,
Carré Médicis-5,
rue St Hilaire,
94210 La Varenne St Hilaire,
France.
tel.: +33 (0)1 4886 3328
email: musee@marie-saint-maur.com
website: www.musee@marie-saint-maur.com

Lessedra World Art PrintAnnual - Mini-Print
Founded in 2001 'to gather and exhibit contemporary prints from all over the world'. Works in any print medium. Maximum dimensions 29 x 23 cm (11³/8 x 9 in.).

contact: Lessedra Gallery & Contemporary Art Projects,
25 Milin Kamak Street,
Lozenetz,
1164 Sofia,
Bulgaria.
email: georgi@lessedra.com
website: www.lessedra.co

Liège International Biennial of Engraving
Established in 1993. Traditional and experimental print techniques are allowed. Preliminary selection is based on photos. Send between 5 and 10 photos. Next exhibition in 2011, portfolio submission by July 2010, work submission by Oct. 2010.
contact: Regine Remon,Curator,
Liège International Biennial of Engraving,
Cabinet des Estampes et Dessins de la Ville de Liège,
Parc de la Boverie 3, B-4020 Liège, Belgium.
tel.: +32 (0) 4342 3923
email: cabinetdesestampes@skynet.be
website: www.cabinetdesestampes.be

Linocut Graphic Arts Prize of Bietigheim-Bissingen
Triennial inaugurated in 1989. Each artist can submit up to three works exclusively in lino. Initial selection is made through photographs. Next exhibition in 2012.

contact: Städtische Galerie,
Marktplatz 8,
Haupstr. 60-64,

D-74321 Bietigheim-Bissingen,
Germany.
tel.: +49 (0)7142 74 483
email: galerie@bietigheim-bissingen.de
website: www.bietigheim-bissingen.de

Lódź International Triennial of Small Graphic Forms
Exhibition established in 1969. Works no larger than 12 x 15 cm (4³/4 x 6 in.) made on paper no larger than 25 x 20 cm (10 x 8 in.) Next exhibition in June 2011, submissions by Dec. 2010.

contact: Elzbieta Fuchs,
Municipal Art Gallery in lódź,
31 Wolczanska St, 90-607 lódź,
Poland.
tel.: +48 (0)42 632 2416
email: mfg@miejskagaleria.lodz.pl
website: www.miejskagaleria.lodz.pl

Majdanek International Art Triennial
Established in 1992. Works on paper in any print technique, drawing and photography. Four works not exceeding 100 x 70 cm (39¹/2 x 27¹/2 in.) can be submitted. Next exhibition in 2010.

contact: Droga Mczennikow, Majdanka 67,
20-325 Lublin,
Poland.
tel: +48 (0)81 744 2647
email: zbiory@majdanek.pl
website: www.majdanek.pl

Miedzynardowe Biennale Miniatury
Set up in 1998 and organised by the Centre of Culture Promotion of Poland, any artists or student may apply. Each artist may send up to three images in any technique, with the exception of bookplates. Maximum format 10 x 10 cm (4 x 4 in.). Paper size may not exceed 20 x 20 cm (8 x 8 in.).

contact: Orodek Promocji Kultury,
42-200 Cz´stochowa – ul. Dàbrowskiego 1,
Poland.
tel.: +48 (0)34 324 3638; +48 (0)34 365 1760
email biuro@biennale.art.pl
website: www.biennale.art.pl

Miniprint Finland

All generally accepted print techniques welcome. Up to four works of maximum print size 17 x 20 cm (6¾ x 8 in.) and maximum paper size 30 x 35 cm (12 x 13¾ in.). Next exhibition in 2010, with work submitted in May of that year.

contact: Eija Piironen, International Miniprint Triennial,
The Graphic Artists Association of lahti,
Paijanteenkatu 11 15140 Lahti,
Finland.
tel.: +358 (0) 3783 2837
email: info@lahdentaidegraafikot.fi
website: www.lahdentaidegraafikot.fi

Mogososia International Experimental Engraving Biennial

There are no limitations regarding form, technique and means of expression. Works with experimental tendencies in any print media encouraged. Works remain the property of EuroCulturArt Association, Romania. No fees. Next event 2011, submissions by Nov. 2010

contact: Ciprian Ciuclea, Chair,
Centrul Cultural palatele Brancovenesti,
Strada valea parcului, nr 1,
Mogososia,
ILFOV 077135,
Romania.
email: experimentalproject@gmail.com
website: www.experimentalproject.home.ro

NBC Tokyo Screenprint Biennial

Established in 2007 and run by the Japanese Artists' Association, sponsored by NBC screen-mesh manufacturers. Send one work only. Artists must donate submission as no work will be returned. Maximum paper size 297 x 420 mm (11⅝ x 16½ in.). Grand prize of 200,000 yen plus other prizes. Next event in Dec. 2009, submissions received in Aug-Sept.

contact: NBC Inc. Biennial Dept,
2-50-3 Toyoda,
Hino,
Tokyo,
191-0053,
Japan.

email: biennale@nbc-jpn.com
website: www.nbc-jpn.com

Novosibirsk International Biennial of Contemporary Graphics

Established 1993. Works in three categories: printmaking, works on paper and new technologies. Maximum three works per artist. Next event in Sept 2011, submission in March by CD or photos.

contact: Vladimir Nazansky, Curator,
Novosibirsk International Biennial of Contemporary Graphics,
Novosibirsk State Art Museum,
Krasny,
Prospect 5,
630007,
Novosibirsk Russian Federation.
tel.: +7 (383) 223 4225
email: vladimir@gallery.nsc.ru
website: www.gallery.nsc.ru

Now Art Now Future, Lithuania

Major international print triennial, usually on a contemporary theme with accompanying conferences and masterclasses. Submissions of images by email or photograph in May of the previous year, whereupon selected artists from each country will be invited to submit. Next event in 2011. Submissions likely to be in May of that year
contact: Ignas Kasevicius, 5-10,
Kaunas,
Lithuania.
tel.: +370 699 92779.
email: info@nowart.eu
website: www.nowart.eu

Ottawa Miniature Prints Open

Established in 2006 and organised by the School of Art, this event is open to all professional artists in any generally accepted graphic technique. Each artist can submit a maximum of four prints. Maximum dimensions 10 x 15 cm (4 x 6 in.), maximum print matrix (paper, cloth, etc.) 20 x 25 cm (8 x 10 in.). Next event in April 2010, submissions in March of that year.

contact: Mini-Print Exhibition,
Ottawa School of Art,
35 George Street,

Ottawa,
Ontario,
K1N 8W5,
Canada.
tel.: +1 613 241 7471
email: gallery@artottawa.ca
website: www.artottawa.ca

Print Partners in Print Exchange

An Australian-based non-profit artist-run association for printmakers, photographers and all media artists who want to share their work and ideas. Open to all artists and varied media. 'We have been organising print exchange portfolios since 1992. Over 300 Australian and international artists have participated from around the world.' Exchanges are usually themed, with paper sizes stipulated.

Contact: Michael Florrimel/ Paul Somerset,
PO Box 974 Rozelle,
New South Wales,
2039 Australia.
tel.: +61 (0)419 362250
website: www.pnp.org.au

Prints Tokyo

Since its establishment in 1931 the Japan Print Association has hosted 74 exhibitions at the Tokyo Metropolitan Art Museum, Ueno.
contact: Prints Tokyo,
12-10 Naka-Machi,
Kodaira,
Tokyo.
187-0042,
Japan.
website: www.hangayoukai.com, (use google translate for English version)

Québec Internationale d'Art Miniature

Juried exhibition open to artists in crafts and visual arts who produce work that is original, unique or of a limited number. Exhibition categories are two-dimensional and three-dimensional work. 2-D work cannot exceed a total image area of 75 sq. cm (11⅝ in.), 3-D work must not exceed 560 cubic cm (34 cubic in.). Next event in 2011.

contact: Pauline Leboeuf,
Galerie d'Art des Deux-Ponts,

220 Route du Pont,
Saint Nicolas,
Québec,
Canada.
tel.: +1 418 835 4926
email: pleboeuf@ville.levis.qc.ca
website: www.ville.levis.qc.ca

Rosario Mini-Print Open, Argentina

Organised by the School of Fine Art, Rosario National University. Artists may submit two prints of the same image, and there will also be an exchange between participants. All techniques eligible except monorpints, photographs, photocopies and artists proofs. Maximum image size 100 x 100 mm (4 x 4 in.), maximum paper size 180 x 180 mm (7 x 7 in.). Next submission in early 2011.

contact: Prof. Liliana Lucia a Guston,
Muestra Internacionale de Miniprint en Rosario,
Rioja. 2173 pb 'B' 2000,
Rosario,
Argentina.
email: miniprintrosario@yahoo.com.ar

St Petersburg Independent International Biennial of Graphics

Established in 2000, this event includes categories that accommodate all kinds of printed graphics, easel graphics, watercolour, drawing, ex-libris illustration, artist's books, graphic objects and photography'. Next exhibition in 2010.

contact: Evgineya Fedina,
President of the Foundation for Contemporary Graphic Art,
199155,
St Petersburg,
Kapitanskaya Street, 5,
kw.242,
Russia.
tel.: +7 (812) 352 8357
email: BIN2010spb@rambler.ru

Sarcelles Biennale Internationale de la Gravure

Exhibition established in 1981. Only works using engraving techniques are accepted. Maximum size of paper 80 x 60 cm (31½ x

23½ in.). Next event Nov.-Dec. 2009, submissions accepted in July and August.

contact: Mairie de la Gravure,
Biennale de la Gravure,
4 Place de Navarre,
B.P. 101,
95203 Sarcelles,
France.
tel: +33 (0)139 905417

Seoul Space International Print Biennial
Established in 1982. Maximum two prints per entrant. Paper size not to exceed 110 x 80 cm (43¼ x 31½ in.). Next event in Sept.-Oct. 2010, submissions by March 2010.

contact: 219 Wansea Dang,
Jonagna-Gu,
Seoul,
110-280 Korea.
tel: +82 2 747 2892
email: master@spaceprintbiennial.org
website: www.spaceprintbiennial.org

Taiwan International Biennial Print and Drawing Exhibition
One original work to be submitted for initial assessment to qualify for finals. Paper not to exceed 120 x 120 cm (47¼ x 47¼ in.), and no smaller than 60 x 40 cm (23½ x 15¾ in.). Next event in August 2010, submissions by April of that year.

contact: Taiwan Museum of Art,
2 sec.1,
Wu-Chuan,
W.RD.,
403 Taichung Taiwan,
Republic of China.
tel.: +886 4 237 23552 (ext. 304)
email: prints@tmoa.gov.tw
website: www.tmoa.gov.tw

Tallin Print Triennial
Themed exhibition – in 2007 this was 'Political/Poetical' – coinciding with the IMPACT Print Conference, Estonia, held in Kumu Kunstimueseum. All print processes and approaches acceptable. Next exhibition Nov.-Dec. 2010, submissions in September.

contact: sekretär, Tallinna Graafikatriennaal,
c/o Kumu Kunstimuuseum,
Weizenbergi 34 / Valge 1, Tallinn 10127.
tel.: +372 602 6022
email: tallinn@triennial.ee
website: www.triennial.ee

Tetovo International Exhibition of Mini-Prints
Established in 2001. All traditional print techniques. Each artist may submit five mini-prints 15 x 15 cm (6 x 6 in.), maximum paper size 20 x 20 cm (8 x 8 in.). One print will remain with the museum. Next event in 2009-2010, deadline in Nov. 2009.
contact: Velimir Cvetanoski, Art Manager, Museum of Tetovo Area, Radovan Conic 92,

Tetovo, Republic of Macedonia.
tel.: +389 44 338902
email: tetovo_muzej@yahoo.com
website: www.mini-prints-biennial-tetovo.blogspot.com

Trois-Rivières International Print Biennial
Open to all printmakers. Accepted techniques: intaglio, relief prints, lithography, silkscreen. Artists should submit between three and seven prints, and works must not exceed 100 cm (39½ in.) per side. Next event in 2011, submission of slides by Oct. 2010, submission of artworks by Jan. 2011.

contact: International Print Biennial,
Trois-Rivières,
1425 Place de L'Hôtel-de-Ville,
C.P. 368 Trois-Rivières,
Québec,
G9A 5H3,
Canada.
tel.: +1 819 370 1117
email: biennale.trois-rivieres@cgocabl.ca
website: www.sites.rapidus.net/biennale.trois-rivieres

Uzice International Drypoint Biennale
Established in 1993. Each artist may submit two original prints. Only drypoint prints accepted. Works to be no larger than 112 x 80 cm (44 x 31½ in.). Next event in May 2011, submissions by April

contact: The City Gallery,
31000 Uzice,
Slanuska 10,
Serbia.
tel.: +381 31 512 505
email: office@drypoint.org.yu
website: www.drypoint.org.yu

Varna International Print Biennial
The next event is in 2011.

contact: Venteslav Antonov,
Varna Art Gallery,
1 Lyuben Karavelov St,
9002 Varna,
Bulgaria.
tel.: +359 52 612 269
email: graphic.gallery@telecoms.bg

Xativa International Biennial of Engraving
Open to artists of any nationality and to any
works except serigraphs, digital prints and
monotypes. A maximum of two works per
artist. Minimum size 30 x 42 cm (12 x 16½
in.), maximum size 100 x 70 cm (39½ x
27½ in.). No fees.

contact: Jusepe de Ribera,
Casa de Cultura de Xativa,
C/Moncada, – E 46800 Xativa, Valencia,
Spain.
tel.: +34 96 228 23 04
email: casacult@servidex.com
website: www.xativa.es

Xylon International
This is a unique society of artists that work
with different techniques of relief printing,
crossing truly international boundaries. It
was founded in 1953 at the Kunsthalle,
Zurich, with Belgian artist Frans Masareel
as both one of its founders and its first
president. International triennials are
accessible to non-members, 'not least in
order to keep in touch with trends and
developments, but also to win new
members'. 'Sections' exist in Argentina,
Austria, Belgium, Canada, France, Germany,
Italy, Poland, Sweden and Switzerland –
though not England (someone, please!).
Each organisation arranges their own
events and forums. Xylon exists to unite
artists from all over the world who employ
any type of relief printing, to facilitate
discussion, to exchange experiences and
information and to organise international
triennials.

website: www.xylon-international.org

USEFUL WEBSITES

www.worldprintmakers.com
An extensive site for printmaking around the
world with articles, printmakers' forum and
details of workshops around the world.

www.globalprintstudios.org
A major listing site run by London Print
Studio with countries by alphabetical search.

www.printmaker.co.uk
Site run by Printmaker Art Editioning in
Reading, with a very useful small ads and
listings page.

www.eastlondonprintmakers.co.uk
A very useful links page for suppliers, events
and print workshops.

www.printmakingtoday.com
The site for Printmaking Today magazine.

www.impact.uwe.ac.uk
Site of the international print conference
started in 1999 by The University of West of
England.

www.britishletterpress.co.uk
Excellent site for places where letterpress is
active, how-to-guides, suppliers etc. (see also
www.letterpressalive.co.uk)

www.fpba.com
Site of The Fine Press Book Association.
American site with good links to resources
and events across the USA.

www.printalliance.org
The site of The American Print Alliance linking
print councils across America.

www.billfisher.dreamhost.com
Extensive site for University Printmaking
Departments in the USA

NOTES

NOTES

NOTES

NOTES

NOTES

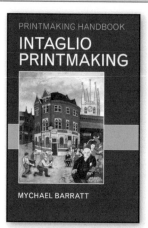
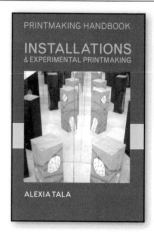

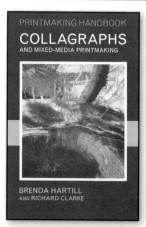

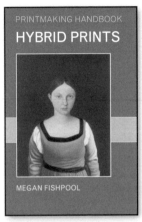

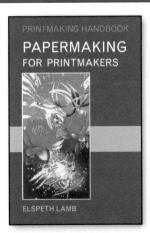

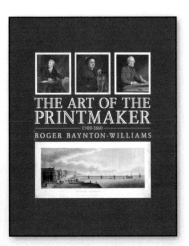